BETWEEN CONFLICT
AND COLLEGIALITY

BETWEEN CONFLICT AND COLLEGIALITY

Palestinian Arabs and Jews
in the Israeli Workplace

Asaf Darr

ILR PRESS

an imprint of

CORNELL UNIVERSITY PRESS

Ithaca and London

First published 2023 by Cornell University Press

Library of Congress Cataloging-in-Publication Data

Names: Darr, Asaf, author.
Title: Between conflict and collegiality : Palestinian Arabs and Jews in
    the Israeli workplace / Asaf Darr.
Description: Ithaca : ILR Press, an imprint of Cornell University Press,
    2023. | Includes bibliographical references and index.
Identifiers: LCCN 2022050732 (print) | LCCN 2022050733 (ebook) |
    ISBN 9781501770685 (hardcover) | ISBN 9781501770753 (paperback) |
    ISBN 9781501770692 (pdf) | ISBN 9781501770708 (epub)
Subjects: LCSH: Work environment—Political aspects—Israel. | Teams in the
    workplace—Political aspects—Israel. | Employees—Israel—Attitudes. |
    Palestinian Arabs—Employment—Israel. | Jewish-Arab relations. |
    Israel—Ethnic relations.
Classification: LCC HD6957.I75 D37 2023 (print) | LCC HD6957.I75 (ebook) |
    DDC 658.4/022095694—dc23/eng/20230208
LC record available at https://lccn.loc.gov/2022050732
LC ebook record available at https://lccn.loc.gov/2022050733

Contents

Acknowledgments

This book is the culmination of twelve years of academic work. It has benefited from the help and generosity of many people and organizations. My sincere thanks go to my colleagues at the University of Haifa, Yuval Yonay, Yuval Feinstein, and Vered Kraus, who have provided much valuable advice and criticism over the years. I am grateful to the Israel Science Foundation (agreement no. 667/10), which funded the first study on which this book is based, and to the Israel Democracy Institute for sponsoring and administrating the second study, and in particular to Nasreen Hadad Haj-Yahya, director of its Arab Society in Israel Program. Nasreen Hadad Haj-Yahya, together with her colleagues Eli Bahar and Dana Blander, engaged me in stimulating and critical discussions that contributed to deepening my thinking on the broader meaning of my findings. Nasreen and Eli also furnished important assistance in securing research sites in the health and high-tech sectors.

During the research for this book, I have benefited from the feedback and critical comments of many colleagues in various fora where I presented aspects of my work. My appreciation goes to the participants in the 2012 Jaffa Convention (Jaffa); the 2016 (Tel Aviv), 2019 (Haifa) and 2020 (Ramat Gan) conferences of the Israeli Sociological Society; a session of the 2016 International Labour Process Conference (Berlin); and the 2016 Annual Meeting of ESPnet Israel (Haifa). Their pertinent comments and questions helped me hone my analysis of the relations between Palestinian Arabs and Jews at work.

I am deeply grateful to Philippa Shimrat, who edited the text with great skill and patience. I am fortunate to have worked with her. Huge thanks are due to the editorial staff of Cornell University Press, especially Jim Lance, who guided me through the complex process of bringing the book to press.

I would like to express my warm thanks to my three very talented research assistants, Fadwa Aftima, Luda Garmash, and Mahmoud Kanaaneh, who not only helped me conduct and transcribe the interviews but also took part in data analysis. Their thoughtful feedback on early drafts of the findings provided important insights.

My informants and interviewees in the different work organizations I studied were very generous with their time and their willingness to trust me and share their work experiences with me and my research assistants. Especially for the Palestinian-Arab interviewees, the questions touched on sensitive topics and at times required them to recall unpleasant incidents. I am most grateful for everything that they contributed to this project. I would also like to thank the top and middle managers in the various work organizations who granted me access and provided me with administrative support such as suitable interview spaces.

Chapter 2 elaborates and places in a comparative framework some ideas that appeared in my 2018 article in "Work, Employment, and Society." I use material from this article with permission.

Finally, my deepest thanks are to my family. My wife Orna was the first to hear and criticize nascent ideas during the years of this study. She was part of many stimulating discussions, a perceptive commentator on my many drafts, and supported me emotionally during this long process. Her love is my main source of strength in our mutual journey through life. I also want to thank our beloved children, Rimon and Adam, simply for being there. They are the source of so much happiness and pride.

BETWEEN CONFLICT
AND COLLEGIALITY

Introduction

The fraught days and nights of the Second Intifada (Palestinian uprising, 2000–2005) were punctuated by frequent suicide bombings inside Israel and punitive military operations in the territories occupied by Israel in the 1967 war (the West Bank and Gaza). Many of the Palestinian-Arab militants targeted Jerusalem, the country's deeply divided capital city. An Israeli Palestinian-Arab nurse described her fear and discomfort while working in a public hospital in Jerusalem during these difficult times:

> You are on your night shift, and people start saying that there was a suicide bombing, and you hear the ambulances around the hospital and immediately people start to watch the news and they start looking at you as if you are to blame. It happened to me many times. . . . I remember that once there was a suicide bombing, and I was working on a shift together with another Arab and two Jews. And this Arab guy was very, very loyal to his Palestinian identity, you know, a young guy who takes part in every political argument. And I knew that when we're together and there's a political event, well, the shift won't end without confrontation [laughs]. And another time I remember that one Jewish nurse told him that they [the Israeli army] should enter his village, with a tank, and not leave anyone of the village [*sic*], and then he asked, "And if I was there?" and she replied, "You can defend yourself," exactly in those words.

This interview excerpt reveals the extent to which external violent events, underpinned by the ethnonational and interreligious conflict between Palestinian Arabs and Jews within Israel and the occupied territories, infiltrate the workplace and impact workplace relations. The nurse described how the news of a suicide bombing and the sounds of ambulances rushing the wounded to the hospital rapidly spread throughout the hospital and created tensions within the work team. Horrifying images from the site of the suicide bombing immediately appeared on the television screens in the waiting areas and contributed to the anxiety that was shared by all members of the medical team and patients, regardless of their ethnonational affiliation. Yet, the nurse also described how, on top of her natural anxiety, fear, and horror, she had to bear what she perceived as the accusatory gazes of her Jewish colleagues, as if, despite her Israeli citizenship, her ethnonational identity as a Palestinian Arab made her responsible for the violent events outside the workplace. The speaker's account also reveals that political discussion among the members of the medical teams was common and that violent external events sometimes prompted fierce exchanges. Although the Jewish nurse's aggressive words toward the Palestinian-Arab male nurse reported by the interviewee could be read in light of the violent times, they clearly shocked the speaker. The Palestinian-Arab nurse described the male nurse's attempt to remind the Jewish nurse that they were colleagues, not enemies, individual human beings and not just members of an opposing ethnic group. The speaker's shock was probably the result of the temporary yet abrupt suspension of collegiality and the intrusion into the workplace of antagonistic relations between Palestinian Arabs and Jews. As we shall see, this was hardly a unique occurrence. Following suicide bombings or other violent events stemming from the deep ethnonational cleavage, some Jewish and Palestinian-Arab workers stopped treating their colleagues as individuals and regarded them instead as part of a hostile collective.

Israel offers an excellent research setting for studying how an active and violent ethnonational and interreligious conflict is manifested in the workplace. The conflict between Jews and Palestinian Arabs spans more than a hundred years, with frequent eruptions of violence followed by calmer periods during which it takes on subtler forms. Israel is also a place where Jewish and Palestinian Arab citizens frequently meet in work organizations. They work side by side for long periods of time, learn to trust and depend on one another as part of the local divisions of labor, and get to know each other and develop personal ties across the ethnonational and religious cleavage. These workplace encounters provide an absorbing object for research into a neglected and dynamic aspect of the broader ethnonational and interreligious conflict. A study of interethnic relations in the workplace in war-torn countries also allows us to observe the complex relationship between economic praxis and occupational identity on the one hand, and social and political chasms, such as the national, ethnic, and religious identities of workers, on the other.

This book describes how the ongoing conflict between Jews and Palestinian Arabs inside and outside the Israeli borders strains workplace relations and constitutes a daily threat to the social fabric of ethnically mixed work teams. The book also explores how workers cope with the effects of the broader social and political conflict on the workplace. Nonetheless, it should be borne in mind that fierce ethnonational-religious tensions in the workplace are not unique to the Jewish–Palestinian conflict in Israel and can be found in other countries torn by war and political strife, such as Northern Ireland, Iraq, and Turkey. Ethnic-religious tensions also appear in Western countries like the United States, France, Germany, Spain, and Sweden, partly as a result of the recent mass immigration from Muslim countries such as Syria and Afghanistan, which is perceived by some people as threatening the basic fabric and identity of these traditionally Christian societies. This wave of immigrants has evoked at times violent resistance from ultranationalist groups that have mushroomed all around Europe and the United States. The wave of terror attacks in the United States and European capitals during the past twenty-five years, carried out mainly by Muslim extremists, has exacerbated these tensions and sometimes resulted in violence against innocent Muslim populations in Western countries. Considering this global need to better understand how an active ethnonational-religious conflict is manifested in the workplace, this book addresses the following broad questions: First, how is the wider ethnonational-religious conflict reflected inside ethnically and religiously mixed workplaces and what impact does it have on their daily life? And second, how do workers in conflict-ridden countries deal with external ethnonational-religious pressures?

This book seeks to shed light on these issues by focusing on the conflict between Palestinian Arabs and Jews, which is a fact of daily life in Israel, a deeply divided society with a large minority of Palestinian-Arab citizens (about 20 percent of the general population within its pre-1967 borders). Palestinian Arabs who reside in the occupied territories have no citizenship rights, and live either under Israeli, Palestinian Authority, or Hamas rule. In view of the centrality of the Jewish–Palestinian conflict in the political sphere, its ramified representation in specialist sociological fields is to be expected. It figures prominently, for instance, in studies of stratification and inequality (Semyonov 1988), political and historical sociological research (Bernstein 2000; Smooha 1978) and studies of split labor markets (Lewin-Epstein and Semyonov 1994; for Israel and the occupied territories, see Semyonov and Lewin-Epstein 1985). Surprisingly, little attention has been paid to the manifestations of this ethnonational-religious conflict inside the Israeli workplace, specifically from the perspective of the sociology of work and in organization studies. Although most Jewish and Palestinian-Arab citizens of Israel live in separate towns and villages, or separate neighborhoods of large cities such as Haifa and Jerusalem (Kraus and Yonay 2018), they do meet at work. Their encounters provide opportunities to examine the complex and dynamic manifestations of the ongoing, often violent, political struggle in the context of Israeli work organizations.

Other than a few recent studies of specific manifestations of ethnonational-religious conflict in the workplace in Northern Ireland and Israel, no study has compared these manifestations across sectors and occupations in war-torn countries or developed a comprehensive theoretical explanation for the daily management of ethnonational-religious tensions on the shop floor. This book wishes to close this gap in the literature by focusing on an array of workplace manifestations of the broader ethnonational conflict in three sectors of the Israeli economy: health, high tech, and production. Specifically, the book examines how external violent events impact interethnic workplace relations and workers' perceptions of their employing organization and identifies distinct grassroots strategies adopted by members of opposing ethnonational groups in order to cope with external pressures that penetrate the workplace.

To be sure, the issue of intergroup encounters at work is an important area of study that has produced vast amounts of research, dominated by diversity management theory (Ashkanasy, Härtel, and Daus 2002; Jackson, May and Whitney 1995) and contact theory (Allport 1954; Pettigrew 2008; Pettigrew and Tropp 2006). Yet, as I explain in chapter 2, neither of these theories specifically addresses workplace encounters in war-torn countries, as they focus rather on interethnic integration in stable economies and political regimes. Furthermore, both contact theory and diversity management leave external political friction, coupled with periodic violence, outside their purview. Contact theory and diversity management also embrace different research questions than are posed by this book, and they highlight the various obstacles faced by interacting social groups, mainly minorities, immigrants, and women in advanced economies, when striving to assimilate into the core economy and to obtain positions of authority in the workplace. Additionally, the top-down prescriptive nature embraced by many of the studies within diversity management (Ashkanasy, Härtel, and Daus 2002), and the emphasis typically placed by contact theory scholars on positive outcomes of intergroup encounters (Pettigrew 2008), render these approaches inadequate for the study of workplace manifestations during an active and violent political conflict and prevent them from identifying grassroots coping strategies of workers in light of external interethnic struggle. Since such coping strategies are at the heart of this book, a different theoretical framework is required for the empirical investigation of these research questions. In light of its particular research agenda, this book draws on a stream of research known as the sociology of work practice, which has proved the most adequate theoretical framework for the study of grassroots strategies of coping with intense ethnonational tensions that penetrate the workplace.

The sociology of work practice is particularly useful for the study of Jews and Palestinian Arabs at work, since it is geared toward the way work is actually carried out, as opposed to the way work should be organized, managed, and executed (Bechky 2006). The sociology of work practice also has a developed vocabulary for discussing workplace dynamics and social ties within occupational communities and work teams. Scholars within this school examine the types of skills workers employ, the weaving of their skills into local divisions of labor, the emergence of collective occupational identities, and the constitution of occupational communities (Van Maanen and Barley 1984). The sociology of work practice has also developed special sensitivity to grassroots strategies of action devised by workers to deal with the complexities of working life (e.g., Anteby [2008] for the case of grassroots strategies for managing organizational gray zones). This sensitivity makes the sociology of work practice particularly apt for the bottom-up study of coping strategies of workers dealing with profound external tensions grounded in ethnonational-religious struggles.

The sociology of work practice builds on a tradition of workplace studies of interethnic relations. A notable example is the Manchester School of mainly social anthropology that, during the 1950s, produced a wave of studies on work settings in colonial Africa and the United Kingdom (Gluckman 1964). The study by Lupton and Cunnison (1964; also see Lupton 1963) of the Dee Garment Company is of special importance here, since they explicitly explore how gender and religion stratify the workforce and clearly state that workplace relations and grouping cannot be decoupled from social systems and cultural settings outside the workplace, such as sociocultural and religious affiliations.

Labor historians have had a notable influence on the sociology of work practice, in particular those who address interracial relations at work. Arnesen (2017), for example, writing about New Orleans's biracial union of dock workers in the years 1860–1930, finds that, despite growing racial tensions and a strong racial hierarchy outside the workplace, shared work and union membership promoted "interracial collaboration and, indeed solidarity, but with limits. It did not promote interracial alliances outside the workplace, nor did it eliminate all racial inequalities" (40). A closely related research stream on contemporary workplaces offers grounded studies of social inequality at work, which is also related to the sociology of work practice, and describes how race, social class, and ethnicity play out on the shop floor (for the case of blue-collar work, see Halpern 1992; Lamont 2000). Employing case study methodology, these scholars demonstrate how broader social variables and hierarchies are reflected in the workplace, impact the local division of labor, the construction of occupational identity, and intergroup relations more generally. These insights are integrated into data analysis in the different chapters of this book.

By exposing employees' systems of meaning, case and ethnographic studies of work practice can prevent the imposition of theoretical concepts onto the empirical realm (Darr 2006). Case study methodology applied to grounded workplace studies also allows a detailed examination of work-related processes, and the way these processes are socially constructed and executed on the shop floor (see Bechky 2006, 1759; Darr 2009). Thus, the sociology of work practice can provide a theoretical framework for the study of the occupational identities of Israeli Palestinian-Arab and Jewish workers who are members of the same occupational community. For example, within this theoretical framework, we can examine whether or not Jewish and Palestinian-Arab physicians working within the same Israeli hospital develop distinct occupational identities based on their ethnonational-religious background, which shapes their work experience, or whether shared membership in a professional community mitigates the broader social cleavages between Jews and Palestinian Arabs in Israeli society.

In the context of work routine, Palestinian-Arab and Jewish workers who are citizens of Israel share class consciousness, career ambitions, and a desire for economic security. Although, as noted, most Palestinian-Arab citizens live in ethnically homogenous towns and villages or separate neighborhoods of the mixed cities (see also Yiftachel 1992), they do regularly meet Jewish citizens during their studies and professional training and at work. In professions such as medicine and engineering, Palestinian-Arab and Jewish citizens often study together for extended periods of time in Israeli institutions of higher education, where they are socialized together into their professional community. These variables, coupled with a shared occupational identity and social ties constituted at work, create an intricate picture of the conflict between Jewish and Palestinian Arab citizens of Israel. As this book demonstrates, this picture differs greatly from that emerging from the political literature and from studies in various specialist sociological fields, mostly on the macrolevel, which tend to stress the structural separation and basic antagonism of the Palestinian-Arab and Jewish sectors. The sociology of work practice can assist to empirically test questions that are currently neglected, such as the possible moderating effect of occupational identity and social networks in the workplace on the nature of social ties between Palestinian-Arab and Jewish workers. Another question is whether social relations created at work spill over into social life more generally.

Though the literature about workplace relations of opposing ethnonational-religious workers is scant, such studies, which partly apply concepts from the sociology of work practice, have begun to emerge in recent years, mainly with regard to Northern Ireland and Israel. A short review of this literature will clarify why is it important to study interethnic relations at work from the theoretical perspective of the sociology of work, and to ground such research in work organization, the career expectations of workers, and the occupational identities they develop as part of their affiliation to work teams and occupations.

Studies of Ethnically Mixed Workplaces in War-Torn Regions

War, interreligious tensions, and political strife are common around the globe, and so are workplace encounters between rival ethnonational, religious, and political factions. Yet, studies of workplace relations in war-torn regions tend to focus on a small set of countries such as Northern Ireland and Israel, and on caring and consulting occupations and professions such as social work (Hewstone et al. 2006; Ramon et al. 2006), psychology (Bar-On 2001), and organizational consultancy (Katz et al. 2005). This literature describes how the professional ethos of equal treatment of all patients and clients, regardless of their ethnonational-religious identity, becomes strained, when the conflict erupts into violence outside the workplace. A common thread running through these studies is that social workers, organizational consultants, and psychologists in war-torn areas, particularly during politically charged periods, adopt a technocratic and neutral approach to clients and peers, whether from their own or opposing social groups, and refrain from explicit political or moral discourse with colleagues and clients. For example, Ramon et al. (2006) note that, despite important regional variations, in the war-torn areas they study (Northern Ireland, Israel, and Palestine) "social workers generally appeared to accept the 'abnormal as normal' as a way of coping with fear and prejudice, avoiding in their silence the more sensitive issues which raised moral dilemmas for them" (447). These studies stress that during tense political times workers retreat into their religious-national identity to the detriment of existing workplace ties across the religious-national divide (Hargie, Dickson, and Nelson 2005). Dickson et al. (2009), who conducted a series of studies in Northern Irish workplaces employing Catholic and Protestant workers some years after the 1998 Good Friday agreement, document shop floor manifestations of the broader political tensions, such as forbidden but tolerated by management displays of national-religious identity (flags, emblems) that management generally sees as representing "tolerable sectarianism." These authors further conclude that, compared to the open war of the 1970s and 1980s, workplace sectarianism today is "much less prevalent than had once been the

case" (60). By contrast to the Northern Ireland case, the Jewish–Palestinian conflict is still far from resolution, and the mixed workforce in Israel copes with its
manifestations daily.

Another body of literature, mostly historical in nature, highlights the unique
qualities of encounters between Jewish and Palestinian-Arab workers in work
organizations, mainly in the period when Palestine was under British rule, from
the end of World War I and during the Mandate granted to Britain by the League
of Nations (1922–48). Historical accounts of workplace ties across the ethnonational divide in Mandate Palestine are particularly telling, since they expose not
only hostility among Palestinians and Jews, but also cooperation on workplace
and personal levels.

Historical Accounts of Workplace Encounters between Palestinian Arabs and Jews

Historical sociology is probably the most significant body of literature describing
and analyzing social encounters and social relations between Jews and Palestinian Arabs in work settings. One of the central questions it addresses is how the
structural separation between Jewish and Palestinian-Arab workers was created
on the shop floor and on an institutional level. A less central question considered by historians of work organization is whether certain patterns of cooperation between Palestinian and Jewish co-workers can be identified, despite the
structural separation. Historical studies on the Mandate period rely on archival
materials that provide a wealth of information on the relations between Jews and
Palestinian Arabs in the labor market level in general and, more specifically, in
the public sector, large private workplaces, and subcontracting networks in the
ethnically mixed city of Haifa in northern Israel, such as dock labor at the port,
the oil refineries, and the Nesher cement works (Bernstein 1995, 1998, 2000; De
Vries 1993, 1994, 2004, 2017; Shalev 1992).

Indeed, several studies that analyze encounters between Jewish and Palestinian-
Arab workers at work focus on the Nesher plant, which was established in 1923
and where Jewish and Palestinian-Arab workers engaged in identical jobs (Bernstein 1995, 2000; De Vries 1991). De Vries (2014) also offers a meticulous socio-
historical analysis of how the Jewish- Palestinian conflict impacted strike action
in the late Ottoman era, during the British Mandate, and up to the early years
of the state of Israel. While most studies of work organization during the British Mandate of Palestine point to the widening structural divide in the labor
market between the Jewish and the Arab sectors of the economy, some studies
of mixed work teams at the Nesher plant have revealed local cooperation and

shared class interests that transcended ethnonational divides. For example, Bernstein (1995) describes an interesting case of cooperation among local Jewish and Palestinian-Arab workers and another group of skilled Arab Egyptian workers. A Belgian company that manufactured the machines for the new cement works at the Nesher plant brought in a crew from Egypt to assemble the machinery. Although the Jewish workers at the plant at first strongly opposed this move, voicing the Zionist demand for "Jewish labor," shortly afterward class interests superseded ethnic and religious considerations, and even the national divisions, when in 1925 all three groups, Palestinian Arabs, Jews, and Egyptians, went on strike together. The skilled Egyptian workers, who were closely acquainted with the activity of the trade union in Egypt, had no less class consciousness and organizational ability than their Jewish co-workers with their socialist ideology. In a similar vein, Lockman (1993) describes some cooperation between the Jewish and Palestinian-Arab railway workers' unions under the British Mandate, which resulted from the unions' weakness in face of the powerful employer—the colonial British government. Lockman also gives examples of personal amicable relations both between Jewish and Palestinian-Arab co-workers and between the Palestinian-Arab and Jewish leaders of the unions, which were manifested in reciprocal attendance at funerals of their fellow workers and an instance of Jewish and Palestinian-Arab union leaders relaxing together on the Tel Aviv beach after a meeting with the Mandatory railway management (618). Historical sociology is at times inclined to highlight such examples of cooperation and solidarity between Jewish and Palestinian workers because these run counter to what is expected, given the bitter political conflict, although these researchers do not claim that cooperation was the main or only characteristic of these relations. They also address intergroup antagonism as well as the strong structural separation between the Jewish and Palestinian-Arab sectors in the labor market and in labor unions.

Recent Studies Focusing on Interethnic Relations at Work in Israel

In recent years new research has begun to emerge on Palestinians and Jews in work organizations from the theoretical viewpoint of the sociology of work practice. These studies reveal unknown layers of the conflict, which at times contradict prevailing beliefs. For example, Shoshana (2016) describes forms of everyday racism that exist among professionals in Israel who work in mixed work teams. Jewish professionals, even when speaking with Palestinian-Arab colleagues, sometimes inadvertently use derogatory terms that have entered the Hebrew language such as "Arab work," denoting poor-quality work. This is a term that some Jewish professionals in Shoshana's study used quite casually, without considering its racist meaning and the offense it might cause their Palestinian-Arab co-workers. Even though the Palestinian-Arab professionals are insulted by the use of such terms, they typically remain silent, which, as we will see, is also the usual behavior chosen by professionals in the health sector in response to racist comments by patients and even peers. Darr (2020), in a policy book, aims to provide organizational consultants, managers, and policymakers with a practical model that can ensure a work environment and a labor market that can better contain external political tensions and provide Palestinian-Arab workers with opportunities to express their voice.

Does globalization—or rather the global business culture imported into Israel by multinationals, with its emphasis on diversity management—have the potential to change the texture of the relations between Palestinians and Jews at work? Ailon and Kunda (2009) deal with the relations between the global business culture of a multinational company and a national culture, in this case the attitude of Western European managers to their Jewish workers in Israel and their Palestinian workers residing in the occupied territories. This study centers on a very large multinational European supplier of services in communications and computers, which employs engineers and technical support staff at a large service center in Tel Aviv, Israel, and also at a notably smaller branch in Ramallah, in the Palestinian Authority. While there is a significant geographical separation between the workplaces of the Jewish and the Palestinian workers, and they rarely meet in person, they have the same managers from Western Europe, stationed at the headquarters in Tel Aviv. The authors claim that despite the image promoted by the company that it is one entity, the pay of the Palestinian workers remains lower than that of their Israeli Jewish counterparts. In addition, during a formal reception to celebrate Christmas and Hanukkah at the Tel Aviv headquarters, the national identity of an attending Palestinian manager remained unacknowledged, unlike that of the Israeli Jewish workers, the Western European managers, and a group of managers from Turkey who were visiting at the time. Thus, the few studies that have recently begun to examine encounters between Jews and Palestinian Arabs in Israeli workplaces still leave many questions unanswered, and these neglected domains are what that this book seeks to explore.

Corpus and Method

This book is based on two waves of field studies conducted between 2008 and 2018. The first wave, in 2011–12, was sponsored by the Israel Science Foundation, and consisted of a field study of mixed medical teams composed of nurses, nursing assistants, and physicians in two Israeli health facilities: a private Palestinian-Arab hospital operating in a northern Israeli city with a Palestinian-Arab population; and a retirement home operated by a Jewish charity in a larger northern city with a mixed population made up of a Jewish majority and a Palestinian-Arab minority of about 10 percent. Most Israeli hospitals are public, owned and run by the government or by major health insurance institutions. Most of the few private hospitals, like the one studied here, are owned and managed by Christian orders or other charities (for the history of private hospitals in Palestine and Israel, see Levy 1998). The health sector was chosen for this study since its work-force is mixed along the entire professional hierarchy, including nursing assistants, nurses, and physicians. The Palestinian-Arab hospital was founded by three Christian nuns in the late nineteenth century and continues to be run by their order, which is based in Western Europe. The nuns in charge of the hospital today are Palestinian Arabs, one of whom functions as the hospital's CEO. Palestinian-Arab managers and nuns handle day-to-day administration. The study focused on the hospital's maternity ward, which includes a small neonatal intensive care department and employs mainly Palestinian-Arab but also a few Jewish nurses. The vast majority of patients are Palestinian Arabs, but Jewish women also give birth in this hospital.

The second site, the Jewish retirement home, offers a range of care from assisted living to full geriatric nursing. The workforce consisted of a majority of Jewish workers, some recent immigrants from the former Soviet Union (FSU), and a minority of Palestinian-Arab health workers. Interviews in the nursing home were conducted with nurses and also with nursing assistants, who have no formal medical training. Jewish administrators run the home, and the vast majority of residents and patients are also Jewish.

The first wave of the study was originally designed to explore workplace manifestations of Israel's ethnonational-religious conflict and to examine how Palestinian-Arab and Jewish Israeli citizens deal with the broader conflict in their daily work. It soon became clear, however, that informants at the two study facilities in the health sector distinguished three, rather than two, ethnic groups of workers: "Jews," "Arabs," and "Russians." The first group included native-born Israeli Jews; the second, native Palestinian Arabs who were Israeli citizens (i.e., not from the occupied territories); and the third, immigrants from the FSU, who began arriving in Israel in the early 1990s. The immigration experience of the Russians and their education in the Soviet Union influenced their images of their Palestinian-Arab and Jewish co-workers. The workers in each group differentiated themselves from those in the other two groups. While the Jews and the Russians constituted distinct groups in their workplace, they were closely aligned and shared Zionist beliefs and an ethnonational-religious identity vis-à-vis their Palestinian-Arab co-workers.

From an analytical viewpoint, however, the three groups were heterogeneous. For example, the Arab group included Muslims, Christians, and Druze, all Israeli citizens. Among the Jews were three nursing assistants who, though Israeli born, were of Ethiopian origin, while others originated from Europe and North Africa. Nevertheless, because informants consistently grouped workers according to three categories, Jews, Arabs, and Russians, this book will also use these terms, with one important modification. The terms used to denote Palestinians in Israel (Palestinians, Arabs, Palestinian Arabs) are politically charged and have distinct meanings in different political and academic discourses. In the following text, workers will be referred to as "Palestinian Arabs," "Jews" or "Russians." I use the label of "Palestinian Arab" consistently in the rest of the book to highlight their specific Palestinian identity, which lies at the core of the ethnonational conflict, while retaining their self-presentation as Arabs in the vast majority of interviews. In line with emic presentations in interviews, members of the two other groups of workers are simply called Jews and Russians, although a certain overlap exists among these categories. I view the Israeli–Palestinian conflict as fundamentally national in nature, but with strong religious overtones. As I explain in chapter 5, ethnonational and religious identity is sometimes entwined.

Data in the first wave of the study are derived from forty-four in-depth interviews with nurses, assistant nurses, and physicians in the two health institutions. In the Palestinian-Arab hospital, the work teams in the maternity ward were composed of nurses (nine of them midwives) and physicians. The work teams in the retirement home were composed of nurses and nursing assistants. While the Palestinian-Arab nurses were overrepresented in the retirement home compared to their 20 percent share of the Israeli population, the Jewish and Russian nurses in the hospital were underrepresented. The location of the hospital at the center of a Palestinian-Arab city might account for the small numbers of Jewish and Russian nurses, though hospital hiring policy might also explain this underrepresentation. To ensure clear communication, the research team conducted all in-depth interviews in respondents' native tongues. Thus, Israeli Jews were interviewed in Hebrew, Palestinian Arabs in Arabic, and Russian immigrants in Russian. Most interviews were tape recorded and later transcribed. In a few cases, extensive notes were taken during the interview and later expanded. Arabic and Russian interviews were translated into Hebrew by the two research assistants, one a Palestinian Arab and the other a Jew who immigrated to Israel from the FSU at a young age.

The sample of interviewees in the first wave of interviews reflects broader employment trends in Israeli nursing. In 1995, 78.1 percent of nurses were native-born Israeli Jews, 14.8 percent were immigrants from the FSU, and 7.1 percent were Palestinian Arabs. In 2009, only 52.9 percent of nurses were native-born Israeli Jews, 31.3 percent were immigrants from the FSU, and 15.8 percent were Palestinian Arabs (Central Bureau of Statistics 1995, 2012). Thus, the percentages of the latter two groups have more than doubled over fourteen years. More recent statistical data (Central Bureau of Statistics 2021) reveals that 27 percent of nurses in the Israeli labor force in 2021 were Palestinian Arab and 27 percent were from the FSU. These data indicate that native-born Israeli Jewish nurses have been leaving the occupation while Palestinian Arabs and Russian immigrants have been entering it.

The second wave of interviews was launched in late 2016 and ended in the spring of 2018. This wave, sponsored and administratively managed by the Israel Democracy Institute, included sixty-one interviews in three sectors of the Israeli economy: production, medical, and high tech. In each of these sectors the majority of interviewees were Palestinian Arabs, and the minority either Russian- or Israeli-born Jews. Thus, this book is based on a total of 105 interviews.

The production plant studied is owned partly by an Israeli kibbutz and partly by private investors. The plant operates in the chemical industry, and the production line is composed of a few workstations with filling machines, where different chemicals are mixed and then poured into special containers, which are organized in cardboard boxes for shipment in the final workstation. The plant employs more than one hundred people, the vast majority of whom are production workers. The workforce is composed mainly of Palestinian-Arab workers, most of whom are Muslims, with a large minority of Druze and a few Christians and Circassians. Jews make up a minority of the production workers, and most of them are very young, just after their compulsory army service.

Macrolevel statistical data reveals that since the 1990s there has been a steady decline in the percentage of the Palestinian-Arab workers in manufacturing industries in Israel. The 1960s, Gozansky (2014, 134) argues, saw a shift in the Palestinian-Arab workforce, from agriculture to industry. Between 1960 and 1990, she notes, the number of Palestinian Arabs in manufacturing industries rose by 50 percent. This trend changed from the 1990s on, since more Palestinian-Arab workers found employment in public services and in commerce. Citing the annual reports of the Israeli Bureau of Statistics (CBS) for the years 1961, 1991, and 2013, Gozansky (2014, 217) states that of the total 1960 Palestinian-Arab workforce in the Israel, 48.4 percent worked in manufacturing, in 1990 this number stood at 22.1 percent, and in 2012 this number fell to a 13.7 percent low. This downward trend continued, and according to the 2021 Labor Force Survey of the CBS, the percentage of Palestinian-Arab workers in manufacturing of the total Palestinian-Arab workforce in Israel stood at 10.3 percent.

In the Israeli health sector, a very large public hospital in the north of Israel was chosen for the study. This hospital employs thousands of employees, including hundreds of physicians and nurses. Two wards were the focus of this study, and each ward consisted of a large number of physicians and nurses, including Palestinian-Arab and Russian medical staff. The medical teams were truly diverse, and on each shift Jewish, Palestinian-Arab, and Russian nurses and physicians worked side by side. The patients were also ethnically mixed.

Finally, an effort was made to represent different facets of the rapidly growing Israeli high-tech sector. Two multinational companies, each employing thousands of engineers, technicians, and administrators in Israel were chosen for the study. One multinational is Israeli, which has headquarters in Tel Aviv and branches all over the globe; the other is American, with a few production and R&D plants in Israel, as well as many other branches all over the world. These two companies represent the main growth engines of the Israeli high-tech sector. In addition to local companies that grew into multinationals, the hopes engendered by the 1996 Oslo Accord between the Israelis and the Palestinians resulted in a huge wave of foreign investments in the Israeli high-tech sector and the launching of many R&D labs by multinational companies from the United States, Europe, and China.

In recent years rising numbers of Palestinian-Arab citizens of Israel have enrolled in engineering and related programs. In 2016 Arab students made up 9.5 percent of all the computer science and electrical engineering students in Israel while their average percentage in the years 1985–2014 stood at a mere 2.3 percent (Central Bureau of Statistics 2019). According to a report of the Department of the Chief Economist in the Israeli Ministry of Science (2017), the proportion of Palestinian-Arab engineers who are employed in the Israeli high-tech sector has increased, from 0.2 percent in 2008 to 2 percent in 2016. A recent report of the Israeli Innovation Authority (Gabbay et al. 2019) cites the figure of 3.4 percent of Palestinian Arabs in the high-tech sector, pointing to a clear growth trend, but also to their meager representation, way below their 20 percent share in the total Israeli population. Despite these advances, 2017 data indicate that while 76.5 percent of Jewish graduates of high-tech occupations find employment in the Israeli high-tech sector, the figure for Palestinian-Arab graduates is only 54.7 percent (Department of the Chief Economist 2017, 9), suggesting ethnonational barriers to employment opportunities. While the Israeli high-tech sector is a major economic growth engine, it reflects the deep cleavages in Israeli society, the Palestinian–Jewish one being a key example. For example, Preminger (2020) challenges the meritocratic discourse common in the Israeli high-tech sector, claiming that it is employed to camouflage deep ethnic hierarchies in the Israeli labor market that remain unchallenged. Viewing Israel as an ethnocratic state, Preminger points to the individuation of the workforce promoted by the ideology of meritocracy, which hampers collective action that might challenge the Israeli ethnocratic principles that also shape the local economy.

The prominent role played by the Israel Defense Forces (IDF) in the development of the Israeli high-tech sectors is also an important factor that hampers Palestinian-Arab employment opportunities. Since the early 1960s the IDF has sponsored in-house employment of engineers and technicians in the development of weapons and communication and surveillance equipment for its intelligence units. The IDF is a major client of the Israeli high-tech sector (Chaifetz 2002) and has developed a dense network of collaborations with small high-tech companies working together with the army on various development projects (Kellerman 2002). IDF technological units recruit talented high school students, and these students acquire technological skills and experience during their compulsory army service (Dashti, Schwartz, and Pines 2008). Army service also provides socialization into the local high-tech scene and builds social networks in the high-tech sector (Berry and Grayeff 2009). Since Palestinian Arabs are exempt from military service, they cannot benefit from these opportunities. Moreover, Israeli high-tech firms working for the IDF often refrain from hiring Palestinian-Arab engineers out of security concerns, which means that these engineers find themselves in an inferior position in the labor market. Indeed, the Israeli high-tech sector is very homogenous in its gender and ethnic composition. Swed and Butler (2015) found that 95 percent of this workforce is Jewish, 65 percent is male, and 75 percent is made up of young people under the age of forty. Noting that Israeli high-tech firms prefer hiring those who have served in military technological units, they further argue that the main explanatory variable for this homogeneity is the human and social capital acquired during army service.

All the 105 interviews on which this book is based were combined into one data set, and data analysis was directed by grounded theory (e.g. Corbin and Strauss 1998) and involved the application of interpretive skills and interpolation between theoretical concepts and empirical analysis. Data analysis was conducted first within and then between sites. Attention was given to intergroup processes in all the work organizations that were studied. The interviews provide many examples of the sources of interethnic tensions in the Israeli workplace and of strategies used by members of the different ethnonational-religious groups to cope with the external conflict that penetrates the workplace.

Key Attributes of the Palestinian–Jewish Conflict

Scholars diverge with respect to the periodization of the Palestinian–Jewish conflict, but there is no doubt it existed decades before the constitution of the state of

Israel (Kabha 2010; Kraus and Yonay 2018; Saar 2016). Although a comprehensive review of this long history is beyond the scope of this book, it is important to highlight a few key attributes of this conflict to better understand the wider context for the workplace dynamics described in the following chapters.

The national identity of Palestinian Arabs developed gradually from the early twentieth century through a dialectical process with Zionism and the Jewish claim to a national home in Palestine (Kabha 2010). Already during the British Mandate, there were violent clashes between Jews and Arabs in Palestine, particularly in 1921, 1929, during the Arab Revolt from 1936 to 1939, and in the late 1940s, which escalated following the 1947 UN decision on the partition of Palestine (Morris 1987, 2013). With the expiration of the British Mandate in May 1948 and Israel's immediate declaration of independence, the surrounding Arab states also intervened, leading to a full-scale war that resulted in the Palestinian Nakba, or "disaster," namely the defeat of the Arab forces and the flight and forced expulsions of hundreds of thousands of Palestinian Arabs who became either "internal refugees" within the borders of the emerging state of Israel (see Manna [2017] for accounts of their personal experiences) or refugees in neighboring Arab states such as Jordan and Lebanon. As Kraus and Yonay (2018, 15) describe: "Thirteen percent of the original Palestinian population of 1947, about 150,000 people, remained within the internationally recognized borders of the new state of Israel and became its citizens." In the formative years of the state of Israel, most Palestinian Arabs inside the 1949 borders lived under military rule, with many restrictions imposed on their basic freedoms and their access to the Israeli labor market. With time, these restrictions were relaxed, until the final abolition of military rule in 1968, at which point the Palestinian Arab citizens of Israel formally assumed full citizenship rights. Social, political, and economic discrimination, however, has lasted to the present, with the labor market being no exception.

The conflict continued after the constitution of the state of Israel, in the form of wars and armed clashes with the surrounding Arab countries. Most significant for the Palestinian context was the 1967 war between Israel and its Arab neighbors, as a result of which Israel took control of the West Bank and the Gaza Strip, with their Palestinian-Arab inhabitants. Unlike those residing within the Israeli borders, the Palestinian Arabs in the newly occupied territories were not granted citizenship. While those in the Gaza Strip live today under Hamas rule, their counterparts in the West Bank live partly under the civil rule of the Palestinian Authority and partly under Israeli military rule. The violent conflict with the Palestinian Arabs intensified during the first (1987–93) and second (2000–2005) Intifadas of the Palestinians against the Israeli occupation and, more recently, during repeated Israeli military operations in Gaza. Daily life in Israel continues to be punctuated by violent events perpetrated by Palestinian Arab militants against Israeli targets, as well as by the Israeli army in the occupied territories, and the ongoing Palestinian–Jewish conflict is omnipresent in the Israeli public sphere. As we shall see, the broader and often violent conflict has a strong presence also inside Israeli work organizations.

Palestinian Arabs who are citizens of Israel must deal with the continuing conflict between the state of Israel and the Palestinian people, many of whom live not only in the occupied territories, but also in Jordan, Lebanon, and Syria. The cleavage between Palestinians and Jews is today the deepest one in Israeli society, with the divisions between Ashkenazi and Sephardic Jews and between secular and religious Jews playing a less prominent role in shaping the Israeli economy and politics (Smooha 2001). Currently, Palestinian-Arab citizens comprise about one-fifth of the Israeli population, 84 percent of whom are Muslims, 9 percent Druze, while 7 percent define themselves as Christians (Feinstein and Switat 2019). Importantly, the Palestinians are a native minority group, while members of the majority group, the Jews, include immigrants coming from diverse parts of the globe. Since, in sociological terms, Israel remains a highly segregated country, the workplace is an important location where Palestinian Arabs and Jews meet and engage in meaningful interactions.

Israel was designated from its inception as a nation to absorb Jews from around the globe. In fact, the Israeli Declaration of Independence defines Israel as a Jewish state, which will respect the rights of the Arab minority within its borders. The Law of Return constituted in 1950 grants Jews from all over the world the right to become citizens once they immigrate to Israel. This right is not applied to Muslim or Christian immigrants. Additionally, being Jewish is not only a religious affiliation but also means ethnic belonging to the Jewish people, so that secular Jews are also formally considered Jewish by the Israeli state. These distinct features led Sammy Smooha (1978, 2012) to describe Israel as an "ethnic democracy," in which citizens from all ethnonational and religious backgrounds enjoy the individual rights common to Western democracies (such as equality before the law and the right to vote and be elected), yet some ethnic groups are more closely aligned with the state's goals and Zionist ideology and also enjoy certain privileges denied to members of other ethnic groups. Importantly, the Israeli economy is also stratified along ethnonational lines, leading scholars to define it as a dual labor market composed of an underdeveloped Palestinian-Arab economy, plagued by institutional discrimination and lack of infrastructural government investment, and a fast-growing Jewish economy (see Bernstein 2000; Sa'di and Lewin-Epstein 2001). Palestinian Arabs were included within the Israeli labor market, scholars argue, but never truly integrated (Sa'di 1995). While these macrolevel data provide a very broad framing for this book, the socioeconomic consequences highlighted in this literature are reflected in various ways in the interviews presented in the empirical chapters and in relation to diverse facets of the Israeli work organizations covered by this book.

Book Outline

Chapter 1 describes and explains when and how external tensions arising from the ethnonational-religious cleavage between Jews and Palestinian Arabs in Israeli society permeate the workplace. The chapter identifies two main triggers of increased tensions in the workplace. The first is the occurrence of violent events that are motivated by the ethnonational struggle, such as Palestinian-Arab suicide bombings or Israeli military operations in the Gaza Strip and the West Bank. The chapter compares the particular impact of such events on the daily work routine of ethnically mixed work teams in the three research settings studied—the production, health, and high-tech sectors in Israel. The second trigger, which is typical of the health sector and service work, is when patients or clients express offensive and racist views toward minority group staff members. Chapter 1 also demonstrates how the frequency and severity of such racist comments increase during periods of violence. While Palestinian-Arab physicians tend to brush off patients' insults by referring to their suffering and to the physician's ethical obligation to treat everyone, they do expect their Jewish colleagues and managers to react and confront the offending party.

Chapter 2 presents the main strategy employed by minority group members to cope with these tensions. I dub this strategy "split ascription," a term that denotes a clear separation made by minority group workers in ethnically mixed teams between the direct work environment and structural elements of their employing organization (Darr 2018). All production, high tech, and medical staff members tend to describe their immediate work environment as politically neutral, and their social ties with members of other ethnonational groups as either positive or neutral. At the same time, minority group members of ethnically mixed work teams tend to describe the formal procedures and structures of their employing organization as inherently prejudiced and even racist. This cognitive separation between the interactional and structural domains of their working life allows minority group members to manage fierce external tension that threatens to disrupt the fragile web of social ties within the work team. Chapter 2 also compares the ways in which split ascription is implemented in the three research contexts. The chapter locates the production, high tech, and medical workers along a continuum ranging from high to low levels of split ascription. Palestinian-Arab production workers expressed the highest level of separation between their immediate work environment and the structural elements of their employing organization, followed by the members of the medical teams, with the high-tech sectors expressing the lowest levels of split ascription. Importantly, the grassroots strategy of split ascription offers a putative critique of the two dominant theories of interethnic relations at work, contact theory and diversity management. The chapter engages with these literatures and concludes with a discussion of the theoretical contribution that emerges from tracking the ways workers actually cope with external ethnonational tensions.

The deep and often violent conflict between Jews and Palestinian Arabs in the political sphere is also ingrained in the ways in which workers perceive different aspects of their career trajectories. Chapter 3 explores the impact of the ongoing conflict on the career aspirations and expectations of minority workers, mainly Palestinian Arabs. The chapter discusses the mobility strategies of Jewish and Palestinian-Arab workers in mixed work teams, and how the ethnonational conflict might impact these strategies. The chapter finds that in all the research contexts, minority group members feel, to varying degrees, that their ethnonational and sometimes religious identity shapes their prospects of promotion.

In the production plant, Palestinian-Arab workers were adamant that they can expect only horizontal careers, either within the production plant by taking a different job along the production line, or outside the plant, by moving to a new production job at a different plant. They claimed that managerial positions beyond line managers were all but closed to them. While physicians in the health institutions studied considered that many career opportunities were open to them, they also felt that a glass ceiling existed, preventing their promotion into top management. For example, Palestinian-Arab physicians in the large public hospital could point to only a few ward managers who were Palestinian Arab and claimed that their representation among the top management of the hospital was meager. Further down the professional hierarchy, the Palestinian-Arab nurses in the health institutions were even less positive about their career chances, noting that very few of them could ever hope to reach the position of head nurse. Interestingly, the Jewish midwives and nurses in the Palestinian hospital also reported that they could expect no promotions to managerial positions, and that the nuns running the hospital almost exclusively promoted Palestinian-Arab nurses from a Christian background into management.

Palestinian-Arab engineers in the two multinational firms studied were the most positive regarding their promotion opportunities. Most Palestinian-Arab engineers did believe that top management was interested in their promotion, but felt that middle managers were sometimes an obstacle to the desired position of team manager. In the high-tech sector career opportunities are broadly divided into technical and managerial positions. When promoted on the technical career ladder, engineers can become experts, consult different teams in their area of expertise, and gain technical, rather than managerial, authority as well as increased pay as an expert in their field. By contrast, a managerial promotion means moving up the organizational hierarchy and obtaining increased administrative authority over other workers by becoming a team manager. It is significant that Palestinian-Arab engineers in the two firms preferred promotion on the technical ladder and were less likely than their Jewish counterparts to reach managerial positions such as team managers.

Language is an important symbolic arena in which individuals and ethnonational groups can express their distinct identity and culture (Le Page and Tabouret-Keller 1985). The spoken language serves as a repository of oral history and maintains a sense of continuity from one generation to the other (for the oral cultures of occupational communities, see Orr 1996). Language is also a public marker of ethnonational affiliation, since members of distinct ethnonational groups are often identified in the public sphere by the language that they use. In this sense, language constitutes and marks symbolic divisions between ethnonational groups and forms a barrier for outsiders who wish to study the cultural intricacies of other ethnic groups. As chapter 4 demonstrates, in wartorn countries the use of different languages at work sometimes becomes a point of contestation between rival ethnonational groups. Israel provides a vivid illustration of this situation, and this chapter portrays how the use of Arabic and Russian at work manifests the identity of the minority group and can become a source of tension, particularly during politically charged periods. Hebrew constitutes the hegemonic common ground for members of minority ethnonational groups, and both Palestinian Arabs and Russian immigrants typically have a good command of Hebrew and are expected to speak Hebrew in the presence of members of other ethnic groups. As chapter 4 illustrates, in each of the three research contexts local norms have emerged for managing language use within ethnically mixed work teams. The chapter also analyzes the daily management of these norms and the tension caused by their perceived violation.

Ethnicity, nationality, and religion are intertwined in shaping daily realities in the Israeli workplace. The workplace celebration of religious and national holidays and memorial days are also important markers of Palestinian-Arab and Jewish identity and provide a striking example of this intertwining. Chapter 5 explains how work organizations are immersed in the broader sociocultural context and how they choose which holidays to celebrate at work, and which holidays they tend to ignore. The chapter explains how holidays serve as an occasion for a public display of cultural, national, and religious identity, and how ignoring certain holidays affects minority group members' sense of belonging to their employing organization. For obvious reasons, the holidays and memorial days of the hegemonic group in Israeli society, the Jews, are most likely to be celebrated at work, but the question remains to what extent the holidays of other ethnonational-religious groups are marked. Chapter 5 also offers a comparative examination of how the broader ethnonational and interreligious conflict is reflected in the celebration of holidays and memorial days in the workplace.

Do personal ties constituted at work across the ethnonational cleavage spill over to nonwork activities? Chapter 6 tackles this question and presents instances where Palestinian-Arab and Jewish workers develop personal ties at work, share intimate information, and consult each other on personal issues. The chapter also examines the degree to which workplace encounters encourage deeper cultural understanding by members of opposing groups and how they influence the levels of prejudice and stereotypical images across the ethnonational and religious divide in each of the three research contexts. Surprisingly, the production workers, with the lowest levels of educational attainment and the least occupational socialization, reported the highest levels of personal ties with members of other ethnonational groups that spill over into the private sphere. While medical workers and high-tech engineers reported cases of personal friendships between Jewish and Arab colleagues, these ties rarely spilled over to the private sphere, other than participation in formal events such as weddings and funerals.

The book concludes with a discussion and overview of the main findings of this book and their theoretical implications. The following chapters thus provide a comprehensive and in-depth examination of the hidden and dynamic dimensions of the Palestinian–Jewish conflict and expose multiple aspects of the difficulties confronted by members of rival ethnonational and religious groups in the workplace in war-torn countries.

INTRODUCING TENSION INTO THE WORKPLACE

How does an active and sometimes violent ethnonational-religious conflict manifest itself in the workplace? How do workers in different work environments experience politically charged periods? Are these interethnic tensions manifested differently in the three research contexts studied? This chapter wishes to tackle these questions.

The chapter examines the two main aggravating factors that introduce ethnonational-religious conflict into the workplace and strain relations among members of different groups. The first, manifested to varying degrees in all three research contexts, is the occurrence of violent events outside the workplace such as Israeli military operations against the Palestinians or Palestinian suicide attacks on Israeli civilians. The second, which is distinctive to the health sector, is the expression of offensive and even racist remarks by patients toward caregivers, which reflect the deep ethnonational schism between Jews and Palestinian Arabs within Israeli society.

The Impact of External Violent Events

The Health Sector

The difficulty of maintaining collegial relations during periods of violence is particularly acute among members of mixed health teams, since patients' lives are sometimes at risk. This difficulty was illustrated in an interview with a young Palestinian-Arab physician, who a few years previously had completed his six-year internship in the Israeli public hospital that was studied. Responding to a question regarding political discussions at work, he said, like many of his Jewish and Palestinian-Arab colleagues, that political issues were indeed frequently raised in conversations among the workers, but argued that they injected tension into the workplace. He also felt very strongly that it would be better to refrain from discussing political events at work and described an incident that had occurred ten years earlier, during a large-scale Israeli military operation in Lebanon in 2006 (known in Israel as the Second Lebanon War), when he had just graduated from medical school and was starting his training in a different public hospital:

> PHYSICIAN: There was a brother of a nurse in the ward who was killed during one of the [military] incidents. I don't remember exactly.
> INTERVIEWER: Yes.
> PHYSICIAN: And then she simply took a drastic step and she stopped talking to all the Arabs.
> INTERVIEWER: Whoa!
> PHYSICIAN: In the ward.
> INTERVIEWER: So it was a big thing then.
> PHYSICIAN: No, it was [that she] simply stopped talking [to us] altogether. Not hello, not that. Nothing.
> INTERVIEWER: And did management react to that [pause]?
> PHYSICIAN: No.
> INTERVIEWER: No?
> PHYSICIAN: No, I don't know what [pause]. We didn't raise the issue. Simply, that's what she wants so that's how it'll be [pause].
> INTERVIEWER: Yes, so you respected her wish in the sense that . . . ?
> PHYSICIAN: Yes. There was obviously a lot of anger among us.
> INTERVIEWER: Yes.
> PHYSICIAN: But [pause] we spoke among ourselves [pause] but [pause] with her we didn't speak.

Later in the interview the speaker explained that what had angered him and his Palestinian-Arab colleagues was the fact that the nurse's behavior showed that she regarded them as bearing collective responsibility for her great loss. Nonetheless, the speaker understood and respected her suffering, and the Palestinian-Arab members of the medical team shared their anger with each other but did not report her behavior to the head of the ward.

Broader ethnonational tensions also strained interethnic work relations in the retirement home. Questioned about the social ties among the medical staff in her ward, a Palestinian-Arab nurse responded:

> I want to tell you one thing, that in working life, it doesn't matter where, relations between Arabs and Jews are good until something political happens. Then you can feel it really strongly. Other squabbles start, and if you try to defend yourself in such situations you are told, "You're a racist" and you are sent to the [disciplinary] committee. For this reason we prefer to remain silent. In many cases they humiliate you and you remain silent, but they [her Jewish co-workers] say whatever they want. I'm uncomfortable every time a political event comes on TV in the news, and they increase the volume so that everybody should hear. In these situations, I prefer being off shift. It's only natural, I don't blame them [the Jews], but we [Palestinians], we are always silent.

According to this nurse, the generally positive work relationships were persistently threatened by the broader ethnonational conflict. She emphasized that silence was a common response to the blame directed at the Palestinian-Arab nurses when what she calls "political events" took place, since any verbal reaction to humiliating remarks on the part of her Jewish co-workers, she argued, exacerbated the strife. The Palestinian-Arab nurse's reluctance to express her views was also grounded in her fear of formal disciplinary action, although such action by the retirement home management, according to other interviews, was rare. Moreover, she felt that while it was regarded as legitimate for her Jewish co-workers to express their political views regarding violent events outside the workplace, she had to remain silent. Indeed, the choice made by Palestinian-Arab workers to remain silent in politically charged situations and the difficulties they faced if they wished to display their distinct Palestinian-Arab identity in the workplace are themes that loom large in the scant existing literature (Ailon and Kunda 2009; Shoshana 2016), and they also featured to varying degrees in all three research contexts in this study.

The private Palestinian-Arab hospital presented a mirror image of the public hospital with regard to the composition of its medical teams, since Jewish nurses were in the minority. As most of the Palestinian-Arab nurses had previous work experience in public hospitals dominated by Jewish workers and managers, they could compare their past experience with their current employment. Recalling the atmosphere at the Jewish-dominated public hospital during one of the Israeli military operations in Gaza, a Palestinian-Arab nurse in the private Palestinian-Arab hospital pointed out an important difference between the behavior of

Jewish and Palestinian-Arab staff members as minorities in the workplace during politically charged periods:

> Once, not recently, when we had the war in Gaza, I remember that we expressed our views here in the ward, and I felt then that the Jews weren't afraid to express their racist views right in our face, despite the fact that we felt that these views weren't objective, and let's say wrong, for example, claiming that the war is fair despite the huge gap in the number of casualties on both sides.

As members of the majority group of workers in the private hospital, the Palestinian-Arab medical staff members did not hesitate to express their political views and did not retreat into silence, as they often did in public hospitals in these circumstances. Moreover, this nurse explicitly defined the views expressed by her Jewish colleagues as racist and as especially infuriating since they were aired in a Palestinian-Arab institution and within a team composed mainly of Palestinian-Arab nurses. She apparently expected the Jewish nurses to adapt to their Palestinian-Arab work organization and behave in the same way as Palestinian-Arab nurses in Jewish institutions. The fact that the Jewish medical workers did not refrain from expressing their opinions can perhaps be seen as reflecting their sense of entitlement as a result of belonging to the hegemonic Jewish majority in the state of Israel.

We live in the digital age, and colleagues sometimes communicate off working hours on social media. At times, external political events also infiltrated into the workplace through written communication, when staff members posted controversial views on social media and thereby elicited a managerial response. The daily communication between members of the medical staff took place with little administrative interference, but when outside events threatened work and staff relations, managerial involvement increased. Normally, the administrators and even the head of department had little knowledge of or control over private discussions among staff members on pressing political issues, but when opinions concerning the external ethnonational conflict were expressed on public media, management could be informed, and occasionally they intervened. The interviewees in the public hospital and the retirement home reported a few such instances when a staff member had expressed views, usually on Facebook, that engendered a heated political argument online and subsequently in the workplace, involving other members of the medical staff. In these cases, according to their account, it was always a Palestinian-Arab staff member who was asked by management to tone down the argument. One example was given by a young Palestinian-Arab physician who had recently finished his internship and who explicitly stated that he felt comfortable expressing his political views in the hospital and was not concerned about their impact on his future employment or promotion. However, when asked about external events that might affect relations among medical staff members, he recalled an incident when he had posted a status on Facebook relating to ongoing political events at that time:

> INTERVIEWER: Yes, this is an important place, an important platform [referring to Facebook].
>
> PHYSICIAN: Right. So [pause] there, I don't know what exactly happened, I wrote something, a status [pause]. A perfectly naive status, like not [pause]
>
> INTERVIEWER: This was also on the platform, it's yours? A personal account?
>
> PHYSICIAN: Mine, yes, mine. But sometimes someone [pause], sometimes people write statuses that are a bit challenging or a bit [pause]
>
> INTERVIEWER: Yes?
>
> PHYSICIAN: I personally [pause]
>
> INTERVIEWER: No, The Facebook [page] is yours, not the hospital's?
>
> PHYSICIAN: Right, it's mine, but I've got there on Facebook [pause]
>
> INTERVIEWER: Friends?
>
> PHYSICIAN: Friends who also work here.
>
> INTERVIEWER: OK, I understand.
>
> PHYSICIAN: Nurses, midwives, physicians and interns.
>
> INTERVIEWER: I see.
>
> PHYSICIAN: So one of the midwives wrote a kind of a comment, on the status, and then a kind of an argument broke out, an argument in which other people started to be involved, and they each started writing what they thought, and it started to get unpleasant. Even though I kept all the time... [pause]. Then things started rolling, and when I had a conversation with management—every six months we have a conversation with management of the whole wing—so they reminded me [of the Facebook argument] in some way. It's worth your while not to [pause], to reduce a little [activity on Facebook] [pause].
>
> INTERVIEWER: It [the reactions to the comment on Facebook] came up in the discussion?
>
> INTERVIEWEE: Right, in some way, [they told me] that "you should ease up in these matters."

This physician described himself in the interview as a person with very definite political views, who had been a member of one of the Arab political parties in

Israel since he was a teenager and had a strong Palestinian identity. As noted, he was not afraid of expressing his views in discussions with Jewish and Palestinian-Arab friends at work, and it is clear from this excerpt that he resented that in the periodic meeting with top management there had been an allusion to the status on Facebook that had ignited a heated debate among some members of the medical team. In effect, management had tried to restrict his freedom to express his views and to present his Palestinian-Arab identity during a tense political time, despite the fact that the discussion had taken place outside of working hours and on social media. In this case, management reacted long after the argument had terminated, which indicates that this intervention was not the result of a hasty decision but had a long-term goal. It was also done indirectly. The physician was asked, in passing, to "ease up in these matters" without any explicit threat of future sanctions. Yet, he clearly understood the implied message and the limitation on his freedom of expression on Facebook. Interestingly, in a different interview, a Jewish physician from the same ward mentioned this incident and was aware of the managerial involvement that came afterward, which he supported, out of a desire to keep work and politics separate. However, Facebook and other social media accounts that include colleagues from work as friends constitute an arena that belongs neither to the professional nor to the private sphere. This example demonstrates how social media can exacerbate political tensions precisely because workers feel more comfortable displaying their ethnonational identity and political views on these platforms than at work. As the next section shows, external violent events also impacted workplace relations among the production workers, but these tensions were manifested in a different way.

The Production Sector

Like their counterparts in the health sector, the Palestinian-Arab production workers described their day-to-day relations with their Jewish co-workers as generally pleasant or neutral. It should be borne in mind that on the production line Jewish workers were in the minority. Although some of them were older, Russian-speaking Jews, most of them were young workers participating in the Israeli government's "preferential work" program, under section 174 of the Social Security Law. This program encourages young army veterans to work in certain kinds of jobs by means of a sizable subsidy to their salary, which is transferred by the government into their bank account following six months of employment. Many of these young workers leave their production or service jobs after receiving the funds. Since the vast majority of Palestinian-Arab citizens are exempt from serving in the Israeli army, they are ineligible to participate in this program. The Palestinian Arab workers, according to their own accounts, were also divided into groups, the largest one being Muslim workers, followed by Druze, then Christians. A few workers belonged to the Circassian minority. Both Muslim and Christian workers expressed a clear Palestinian-Arab identity.

Relations among the production workers were undermined when ethnonational violence erupted outside the workplace. In these periods, the conversations that took place on the production line and during coffee, smoking, and lunch breaks were far more candid than the conversations among medical staff members, and ethnonational tensions often manifested themselves in discussions related to religious beliefs, a topic that hardly came up in such circumstances among workers in the health sector.

Like their counterparts in the health sector, Palestinian-Arab production workers claimed that the attitude of their Jewish co-workers changed drastically during military operations or after suicide bombings. According to some accounts, after suicide bombings the Jewish workers tended to ignore their Palestinian-Arab colleagues and gave them suspicious and accusatory looks. The tension usually diminished after a few days, when there was a return to the more positive attitudes characteristic of most working days. One of the Palestinian-Arab production workers gave an example of his Jewish co-workers' reactions to a suicide bombing carried out by Palestinian-Arab militants a few years before the interview, when he worked for a different production plant:

> They [the Jewish co-workers] change when suicide bombings take place, and this you would feel. The looks they give you change, and they treat you differently for a week or two, [and then] they come back, slowly. For example, [the Jewish co-worker] would stop saying good morning to you. He wouldn't stop and talk to you, wouldn't speak to you. Among the Jews, all is normal, "my brother, my brother." But he doesn't approach you [the Palestinian-Arab co-worker] any more. You feel there is [pause], that he is angry. But what am I guilty of? I'm just like you.

The speaker clearly found this sudden change of attitude in his Jewish co-workers to be offensive, since it exposed the fragile nature of the personal ties between them. As the last rhetorical question shows, he rejected such behavior, which treated Palestinian Arabs not as individuals but as members of a hostile ethnonational group.

When political conversations became offensive, with racist overtones, Palestinian-Arab workers did not hesitate to complain to management, which indicates that they felt confident that they would gain managerial support for their claims. This is demonstrated in the following account of a veteran

Palestinian-Arab worker, who held a low-level managerial position in the plant, describing an exchange with a Jewish co-worker that had clear racist content:

> He [the Jewish worker] started saying to me that Arabs shouldn't be allowed in this plant. There were other Arabs around, nobody responded to that. I approached him, I told him: "Even if you are joking, don't ever say such a thing! Don't bring these matters inside the plant." He answered: "No. I'm not joking, it should be forbidden for Arabs to enter here." I didn't remain silent, and I confronted him. I went to the manager here. He reprimanded him and shouted at him. Management backs us because here they trust the Arabs and not the Jews. All the workers here are Arabs. If the Arabs stop working, there is no one else to replace them.

In this example when a Jewish worker expressed racist views, even though the other Palestinian-Arab workers who were present remained silent, the speaker confronted him and even complained to top management, all of whom except two were Jewish. Nonetheless, he explained management support for the Palestinian-Arab workers in economic rather than moral terms, and in another part of the interview he noted that the Palestinian-Arab workers were more willing than their Jewish counterparts to come to work on short notice and to work overtime when large orders arrived at the plant.

Another veteran Palestinian-Arab production worker recounted his reaction when a Jewish co-worker asked for his view on an incident that had taken place long before, in 1997, and had left a deep mark on Israeli society. In this incident, the so-called Commando Disaster, thirteen Israeli commando soldiers on a secret mission were killed in an explosion deep inside Lebanese territory:

> He [the Jewish co-worker] asked me for my opinion about the soldiers, the thirteen who all died. I told him: "The same way that you defend your land, you say it's your land, [and you] want to defend it, and you have an army and soldiers defending it, he [the Lebanese soldier] also wants to defend his land. Where are your soldiers? They are in Shabaa [a contested piece of land on the Israeli-Lebanese border]. Take them out of there, [and] there wouldn't be anything [tension or quarrel] between you." He [the Jewish co-worker] remained silent since he knew [pause] that sometimes I would start arguing with them [the Jewish co-workers]—over the land of Palestine. They start laughing when I tell them that it's not theirs. This was a regular argument [pause]. They would call me a racist, but I was nothing of the kind! But [pause] I would say it jokingly, but I meant to get the message across.

Thus, even a military event that had occurred many years before could elicit passionate reactions among the production workers. This worker did not hesitate to clearly present his view that the land of Palestine, which he did not define in geographical terms, is not the land of the Jewish people, but rather of its native Palestinian population.

According to the Palestinian-Arab production workers, not only were they not afraid to confront their Jewish co-workers in political discussions, but they also took pride in these verbal confrontations and felt they had the upper hand in such arguments. It is interesting that many of the political discussions took a religious turn, which was a unique attribute of workplace encounters in the production plant. Thus, for example, a Palestinian-Arab production worker described how, following a deadly suicide bombing, a female Jewish worker who operated the same filling machine as himself placed the blame on all the Muslims:

> The last time when they [Palestinian suicide bombers] murdered [pause] I don't remember who, a Jewish woman came and started lecturing us, so we jumped in the air [meaning got very angry]. She said: "Arabs, may they be taken [to hell], the Muslims all of them, the people who are doing that." I told her: "Okay, they are doing that, but why? You know that the person who did that, maybe they [the Jews] killed his brother or his sister or someone. It's the same thing. What is painful for you is painful for us." She didn't respond.

Significantly, in this as well as in the previous example, it was the Jewish workers who initiated the verbal exchange, possibly representing a broader trend resulting from their majority status in wider society. The offensive comment by the Jewish worker was directed not only at Palestinian Arabs, but specifically at Muslims, once again framing the conflict in religious rather than national terms. The Jewish view of Muslim rather than Christian Palestinians as the main perceived threat to the Jewish state has deep historical roots. Thus, as Manna (2017) argues, during the 1948 war, the Israeli army was more likely to expel Muslim Palestinians from their villages in the Galilee to Lebanon than the Christian inhabitants of the region. Unlike the reactions of some Palestinian-Arab medical workers in similar situations, who try to remind their Jewish co-workers that they are colleagues, not enemies, and are not to blame, this production worker tried to vindicate the actions of the suicide bomber by suggesting that he might have been avenging the killing of a relative by Jews. This attempt to create a symmetry between the violent actions of both sides and to highlight their victims demonstrates that Palestinian-Arab production workers feel more comfortable displaying their identity than their counterparts in the medical sector. As I suggest in chapter 5, the articulation of the ongoing conflict in religious terms might have also contributed to the Palestinian-Arab attempt to create an egalitarian discourse in the production plant, within the broader power asymmetry between Jews and Palestinian Arabs. As we shall see, in the high-tech sector top management was more active than management in the hospitals and the production plant in trying to prevent external pressures from interfering with workplace relations, but these attempts were not always successful.

The High-Tech Sector

Of the three research contexts, engineers and technicians in the high-tech sector reported the fewest incidents involving offensive or racist comments at work. All these incidents were directly related to the occurrence of violent events outside the workplace. In addition, management in the two high-tech plants under study mandated a clear policy of zero tolerance for any form of prejudice or racism, which was also implemented with disciplinary action when required. Partly as a result of their confidence in top management, only a minority of Palestinian-Arab engineers chose to ignore a racist incident or remain silent in the face of such occurrences. They reported that most of their complaints to management yielded formal action, in the form of a reprimand to the offending party. These complaints were made directly to the Human Resources (HR) department or top management, thus bypassing their immediate supervisor, the team manager. As we shall see in chapter 4, Palestinian-Arab engineers often had more trust in the top managers than in their direct supervisor, whom they sometimes perceived as an obstacle to their promotion. The examples presented below correspond to the different coping strategies used by high-tech workers to contend with offensive or even racist comments on the part of their colleagues.

External violent events naturally became a topic of conversation between Palestinian-Arab and Jewish engineers, but unlike in the medical or production sectors, they very rarely caused overt tensions. The interviewees in the two multinational companies studied reported only a few instances in which offensive comments were directed toward Jews or Palestinian Arabs as a collective. One unusual event occurred against the background of the 2006 war, which involved Israeli military operations in Lebanon and Gaza and the launching of thousands of missiles from Lebanon and the Gaza Strip into Israel. During the war, a Jewish engineer mailed a PowerPoint presentation to all his team members that included photographs of what seemed to be phosphorus bombs attacking Gaza during the night and lighting up the skies. One of the Palestinian-Arab interviewees, an engineer by education, expressed her objection to the presentation in a direct reply to the mail:

> ENGINEER: Yes, I had an incident. I started working in 2006 during the war . . . there was this case [pause].
>
> INTERVIEWER: It was an unpleasant time. What do you remember from that time?
>
> ENGINEER: I remember that someone sent a message. Once again, this was my first year [at work]. In practice, it was difficult because of the war, and you don't know the people.
>
> INTERVIEWER: So, just a second. There was this period, and you don't remember anything specific?
>
> ENGINEER: It wasn't specific, it was a mail I remember [pause] that someone at work sent, he sent it to the team in the company, with a picture of the phosphorus bombs [pause].
>
> INTERVIEWER: In Gaza? Did he write anything?
>
> ENGINEER: In Gaza [pause] he didn't write, but there was [attached] a PowerPoint presentation of things, and then [pause].
>
> INTERVIEWER: Unpleasant.
>
> ENGINEER: Yes.
>
> INTERVIEWER: So what was the reaction? Was there a formal reaction? Did the organization react to that?
>
> ENGINEER: No, no one reacted [pause]. But I sent him a reply saying [pause].
>
> INTERVIEWER: What did you write?
>
> ENGINEER: Take me off your mailing list. These are not pictures of fireworks [said in English], and take me off the list!

The engineer's reluctance to describe this incident is typical of other interviews with high-tech workers, in which engineers and technicians were ill at ease when describing offending events, as if they threatened to shatter the image of their employing organization as a safe haven for members of minority groups, one that scrupulously implemented an ideology of diversity management. This reluctance might also be the reason for the scant examples of racist incidents provided by informants in this sector. However, in this case the speaker did not remain silent, as many of the physicians in the public hospital did. Instead, she reacted by expressing her explicit resentment of the photographs, which she perceived as celebrating the bombing of Palestinians in Gaza and thereby demonstrating little compassion or empathy not only toward the residents of Gaza but also toward the Palestinian-Arab members of the team. Her act was symbolic, but public and clear.

In the second incident, an R&D engineer recounted how during a different Israeli operation, a Jewish co-worker sent what the speaker perceived as an offensive email to all the other team members:

> ENGINEER: There wasn't anything personally directed at me, or that I felt was personally directed at me. But it happened once or twice that during military operations or wars, in the middle, people sent things by e-mail . . ., things like that.
>
> INTERVIEWER: Yes.
>
> ENGINEER: But the truth is, that also in this case I sent a complaint [to management] and the matter was dealt with.
>
> INTERVIEWER: You reacted? You didn't stay silent? You didn't let it go?
>
> ENGINEER: Right.
>
> INTERVIEWER: And the way it was handled was to your satisfaction? You felt that [pause]?
>
> ENGINEER: Yes.

While the speaker did not describe the content of the offending emails, he did say that on both occasions he had responded, though apparently not directly to the authors of the emails, as in our previous example, but to management. His acknowledgment following the interviewer's question that the matter was dealt with to his satisfaction suggests a formal rather than an interpersonal response.

Both Jewish and Palestinian-Arab engineers agreed that top management strove to create a politics-free environment in both high-tech companies that were studied. They also expressed confidence that management was ready to back its policy with swift action against offensive comments and racist workers. In fact, in the example below, a Palestinian-Arab engineer explains how his Palestinian-Arab friend threatened a Jewish co-worker with a complaint to the HR department, following repeated offensive comments about Palestinian Arabs, and particularly Muslims, being terrorists:

> ENGINEER: A friend of mine . . . the guy who sat opposite to him [in the office they shared] was a bad person, who all the time makes [offensive] comments.
>
> INTERVIEWER: This was here in the company?
>
> ENGINEER: Yes, here in the company. So [my friend] told him, "If you want to continue this way, I'll go the HR department, just like that!

Don't even think this is a laughing matter. [If] you make a joke about it once or twice, I can ignore the first time or respond to you another time, and then [I can] pretend I didn't hear you. But don't think I'm stupid. Because the things you are saying are unhealthy, and they were not said like that [jokingly]. If you want us to sit down and talk, argue about things, like a normal argument, that's okay. But when you just utter words [saying] "because of the Arabs and the Muslims," and I don't know what, "terrorists," that's not okay. We all came here to work!"

This example is telling in a number of ways. The speaker was clearly proud of his Palestinian-Arab colleague who became tired of the offensive comments made by a Jewish co-worker, whom he described as a "bad person," which implied that there had been previous unpleasant encounters. The speaker's friend acknowledged that while he was willing to put up with occasional remarks of this nature when they were made in a joking fashion, when these remarks recurred, he could no longer ignore them. His threat to report his Jewish co-worker to the HR department reinforces the impression that the Palestinian-Arab engineers trusted the HR department, and top management more generally, to discipline Jewish offenders and prevent such occurrences. This finding stands in sharp contrast to the situation of Palestinian-Arab members of the medical team, who believed that they could not always rely on the Jewish management of the public hospital or the retirement home, perceiving it as biased in favor of their Jewish co-workers.

Indeed, workers in the health sector were particularly vulnerable to the effects of political tensions because, unlike the workers in the production plant and the high-tech companies, who did not come into direct contact with clients, they had close daily interactions with patients and their families. The following section therefore focuses on the particular problems faced by workers in the two hospitals and the retirement home.

Patients as Bearers of Ethnonational Tensions

One example of how interactions with patients and their families sometimes reflected the broader cleavages in Israeli society and attitudes to the Arab-Israeli conflict was related by a Palestinian-Arab physician in the maternity ward of the private Palestinian-Arab hospital. She had previously been employed at a public hospital in southern Israel where she had felt that she "had to work double to prove to others that I'm a physician." She recalled a case of a child who came in for a lumbar puncture (spinal tap), accompanied by his mother, who did not want a Palestinian-Arab physician to treat her son:

> [The] mother told me, "You are not touching my son," and she was a pediatrician herself [at a different health care facility]. I told her that there were no other physicians that could treat her son, but since she was a physician and knew that there is always another physician on call, she asked to speak to him, and he told her that there was no one else other than Fatima and if that didn't suit her she could go to a different hospital. And that's how I came to treat her son. Before she spoke with the [Jewish] physician . . . I called him up myself and told him that only I would treat this boy, and he backed me up.

In this case, not even collegiality and shared membership in a professional community mitigated the patient's mother's expression of racism toward the Palestinian-Arab physician. This indicates that some Jewish patients, even educated ones, were not embarrassed to express racist views directly to Palestinian-Arab medical workers. While the speaker was able to enlist the support of her Jewish colleague on call, who rejected the mother's racist demand outright, a Jewish physician would not have been faced with such a situation and the need to seek such support.

When exposed to blatant racism on the part of patients, many Palestinian-Arab nurses and physicians in the public hospital studied simply ignored the comments or responded with humor and irony, as in the following incident related by a Palestinian-Arab nurse:

> Once I admitted someone religious, a religious Jew, and I started interviewing her, taking her anamnesis, in Hebrew of course, and naturally you need to show her the room. After you interview her and all that, you [show] her the restrooms and so on. And then she and I went to the room together, and I told her "I now want to show you the room, where it is." And then she tells me "I'm ready for everything, but I don't want to have Arabs next to me." And I told her "meanwhile there's no Arab in the ward other than myself." And she got scared, and the next day she came to me and apologized, she and her husband.

The Jewish patient expressed her racist request only because she thought that the nurse she was speaking with was also Jewish. The nurse's choice to respond with irony, rather than confront the patient, was a strategy that was also used by other Palestinian-Arab staff members when faced with such comments. Although this strategy can be understood as a way of moderating their reaction, possibly to avoid direct conflict, the offense they suffered was real, and many of them bore the scars of instances such as this one. The Palestinian-Arab nurse may also have doubted that she would be backed up by management if she decided to respond more aggressively.

Most of the Palestinian-Arab nurses and midwives in the hospital had been trained in public hospitals, which some referred to as "Jewish places." Many of their encounters with patients' racism occurred during the formative stages of their careers, when they were inexperienced and therefore more sensitive and vulnerable. A nurse in the private Palestinian-Arab hospital described one such incident:

> When we were doing our practical training during our studies, we were in Jewish places, and I encountered in not a few cases very unpleasant reactions from Jewish patients or Jewish families [of patients], such as "I don't want an Arab to treat me." There were such reactions during my practical training and it did affect us, us Arabs, adversely and we always felt we were less than the Jewish students. But here [the private hospital], since this place is Arab, I don't feel that.

This exposure to patients' racist comments was symptomatic of the institutional context in which Palestinian-Arab nurses often found themselves in an inferior position relative to their Jewish colleagues. The interviewee quoted above noted that the Palestinian-Arab institution where she was now employed was free of the institutional discrimination she and others had encountered in the Israeli health sector. Other Palestinian-Arab nurses said that even though the private Palestinian-Arab hospital paid less and offered fewer career opportunities than government hospitals, they preferred to work in an institution where they felt welcome.

It was, however, not only patients in Jewish health institutions who expressed racist views. Jewish and Russian nurses at the Palestinian-Arab hospital also reported derogatory remarks on ethnic or national grounds that were made by Palestinian-Arab patients or their relatives, even if these were somewhat less blatant. For example, a Russian nurse in the maternity ward testified to the discomfort she sometimes felt in her dealings with the patients and their families:

> We [the nurses] are used to working together but sometimes I feel about myself, sometimes when, for example, the fathers of newborn babies . . . address me in Arabic and they hear that I answer them in Hebrew, this is a little annoying for them, and there are those that don't want to talk to me. Not mothers, but there are others who say, "I wanted my child to be born in an Arab hospital, and all of a sudden Hebrew is spoken to me!"

Despite the positive atmosphere within the work team and between the nurses and the women they assisted through labor and childbirth, the speaker resented the expectation on the part of the women's spouses that staff speak to them in Arabic instead of Hebrew. The disappointment explicitly expressed by these men when she addressed them in Hebrew indicates how language provides a stage for the performance of national and ethnic identity and a tool for drawing ethnic boundaries (see Shoshana 2016), a topic that will be discussed in chapter 4. This excerpt also conveys the Palestinian-Arab father's pride in his identity, which made him choose to have his child born in this particular hospital. The very identity attributed to the health institution is yet another factor in the nature of workplace encounters in such divided societies.

In the retirement home, many patients were elderly and required extensive assistance with basic functions. A Palestinian-Arab nurse described an instance when a patient's racist comment was followed by what she perceived as an even more offensive reaction from the Jewish head nurse:

> NURSE: I was distributing medicines and the head nurse was with me, she is in charge of the entire old age home. I was handing out the drugs in a ward full of patients' families. A patient of ours—it's very difficult to feed him—arrives and with him his Arab carer [privately hired by the patient's family]. And the Arab carer was feeding him, and the patient starts screaming, "You Arab, you're disgusting." So, at the time, I wanted the earth to open up and swallow me, and the head nurse started laughing.
>
> INTERVIEWER: Laughing?
>
> NURSE: Laughing, like I didn't know what she was thinking.

In similar cases, nurses tended to brush off comments from elderly patients, many of whom were in poor mental condition. The nurse in this example was surprised and offended not only by the patient's words but also by the laughter of the head nurse, which she felt was directed at her. She also felt that this reaction from a high-ranking staff member expressed approval of the patient's comments. While this interpretation could be contested, the example does underscore the importance of Jewish colleagues' reactions to racist comments directed toward the Palestinian-Arab staff. Indeed, while Palestinian-Arab medical workers played down racist comments on the part of patients, they expected their Jewish co-workers to show solidarity and come out in their defense. Failure of their Jewish colleagues to support them often added insult to injury.

A senior Palestinian-Arab physician in the public hospital recalled events that had occurred when he was still a medical student and worked on weekends for a private medical center owned by religious Jews and located in an ultra-Orthodox Jewish neighborhood in Jerusalem. Since Orthodox Jews are not allowed to work on Saturday or to hire other Jews to replace them, the entire medical and administrative staff during the weekend was Palestinian Arab:

> PHYSICIAN: I worked there for a couple of years during my studies, in this medical center [called] Health, if you know it.
> INTERVIEWER: Oh yes, sure, yes.
> PHYSICIAN: And there [pause] it was more apparent, these things [racist remarks by patients].
> INTERVIEWER: And what, for example, what do you remember?
> PHYSICIAN: They don't want Arabs to treat them, and [they say] "You [Arabs] have taken over the whole place" and all kind of comments like that.

When asked how he had reacted to such comments, the physician said that he used to say: "You have the right, if you don't want to be here, so okay go home." This speaker described numerous incidents when patients expressed racist views. He seemed to accept this racism as a fact of nature and reacted merely by reminding the patients that they had the right to seek treatment elsewhere. Here, again, we see Palestinian-Arab workers' tendency to find ways to avoid direct conflict while still retaining their professional and personal dignity. Another Palestinian-Arab physician described with evident pain an incident experienced by a Palestinian-Arab colleague from the maternity ward in the public hospital while working on a shift in the emergency room:

> PHYSICIAN: This happened to a colleague of mine, [pause] it is just that someone, the [maternity] emergency unit was very crowded, and, well sometimes women are admitted according to their medical condition and not according to their place in line. And when she [a patient] was admitted she started yelling at her [the speaker's colleague]: "It's because you give priority to your Arab friends, and it's because of this and that, but I don't [pause] I don't want you to examine me," and so on [pause].
> INTERVIEWER: So what do you do in a case like that? Let's say; how did your colleague react?
> PHYSICIAN: She didn't [pause] she, well [pause].
> INTERVIEWER: Didn't respond?
> PHYSICIAN: She didn't answer her. She said that if you don't want me to examine you, I won't examine you. This is because we control ourselves, [pause] we come [pause] to do our job.
> INTERVIEWER: But nonetheless [pause].

PHYSICIAN: True, it hurts.

INTERVIEWER: It hurts but [pause].

PHYSICIAN: And she reported it to management, and management took care of it for sure.

As this excerpt illustrates, it is not easy for the Palestinian-Arab physicians and nurses to bring up painful events such as patients' racist comments. Sometime I had to return to the issue of racism and racist comments at work a number of times before the interviewees opened up and told me about such instances. When reporting racist events, the interviewees often paused between sentences. They also often distanced themselves from the situation by reminding themselves that they were physicians and, as professionals, should not be offended by patients, who are in a stressful situation and often in pain. This Palestinian-Arab physician said later in the interview that while her colleague had wished to avoid confrontation, it was important to react to such comments and to inform management, as her friend had. Although she did not know how the complaint had been dealt with, she expressed confidence that management had reacted by sending a letter to the patient. Nevertheless, racist comments do hurt the Palestinian-Arab medical workers, and sometimes Jewish and Russian members of the medical staff as well. For example, one Russian nurse reported in an interview that she had been accused by a Palestinian-Arab patient of hurting her on purpose because of the patient's ethnonational origin. While racist comments by patients are a direct insult to those who are targeted by them, co-workers from the same or the other ethnic group may also be offended by this manifestation of racism, and some of them react to protect their colleagues.

The interviews with Palestinian-Arab members of medical teams clearly show that when patients express racist views, they expect their Jewish colleagues to support them. A nurse in the public hospital described an instance when the silence of her Jewish colleagues following a racist comment by a patient caused her more pain than the comment itself:

NURSE: I received a patient with a fracture, and, of course, she was in pain and [pause] we used a stretcher to move her into bed, me and another religious Jewish nurse. And it was painful for her so she said that I'm hurting her because I'm an Arab [pause].

INTERVIEWER: And how did she know you were Arab?

NURSE: What?

INTERVIEWER: How [pause].

NURSE: I don't know, don't know. Maybe I was wearing a cross, could be.

INTERVIEWER: So she accused you of that, and how did you react? What did you actually do?

NURSE: I was very upset.

INTERVIEWER: Sure, it's upsetting.

NURSE: Yes [pause].

INTERVIEWER: Did you say anything to her?

NURSE: I think I answered her. I don't remember.

INTERVIEWER: You don't remember.

NURSE: I answered her, something like [pause] "It's not nice what you are saying," this is what I told her, that it's not right and not nice.

INTERVIEWER: Yes, and your colleague supported you? The religious Jewish [nurse].

NURSE: She didn't say anything.

INTERVIEWER: She was silent?

NURSE: Silent, yes.

A Palestinian-Arab physician in the public hospital stated that when he was confronted by racist comments from patients or patient families, such as "I don't want an Arab physician to treat me," he felt angry because his attempt to help the patient had been met with an insult. Usually, he did not confront these patients but rather walked away and reacted directly only in the minority of cases:

INTERVIEWER: And what happens then? [pause] Let's say from your [Jewish] colleagues, do you feel that you receive support in situations like this, when you're [pause] being attacked in some way?

PHYSICIAN: In most cases yes. Sometimes you feel that it's not enough [the reaction]. Let's say, in my opinion, a patient who feels this way [doesn't want an Arab physician to treat him] and utters such a remark, he shouldn't have a place, let him go elsewhere.

INTERVIEWER: Yes?

PHYSICIAN: But it doesn't always happen. In my opinion that's how it should be.

INTERVIEWER: Sometimes they just let it go?

PHYSICIAN: Yes.

INTERVIEWER: And say it's okay?

PHYSICIAN: Yes, Yes.

INTERVIEWER: And you feel that? [pause].

PHYSICIAN: No, in most cases I receive backing, they [Jewish colleagues] don't accept such comments. But I think it [the reaction] should be more radical.

Even though this physician acknowledged that in most cases he received support from his Jewish colleagues, he clearly would have preferred an unequivocal hospital policy that left no room for racist comments and even refused to admit patients who refused to be treated by Palestinian-Arab members of staff.

Identifying the Main Sources of Interethnic Tensions

As these interviews reveal, workplaces in war-torn countries are not immune to the social tensions arising from fierce and violent ethnonational-religious conflict. These tensions permeate the workplace and play an important role in the daily management of interethnic relations at work. In all the research settings, work ties are exacerbated by violent events outside the workplace caused by the ethnonational struggle. However, in the health sector these tensions permeate the workplace more frequently as the result of racist remarks made by patients or clients and their families toward minority group staff members. The field data also showed that the frequency and severity of such racist comments in the large public hospital increased in times of violent events outside the workplace.

The cross-sectoral design of the research project helped to identify the variables that determined workers' experiences in the three sectors. The first is workforce composition—whether the Palestinian-Arab workers constitute the minority or the majority group in a particular workplace. Palestinian-Arab workers felt more secure when they were in the majority in the Palestinian-Arab hospital, where Palestinian-Arab nuns also held top managerial positions, or in the production plant, despite its Jewish management, and were therefore more willing to expose their political views and interpretations of political events in discussions with their Jewish co-workers.

Another variable is managerial policy, which proved very important for regulating interethnic workplace ties during troubled times. Thus, since the Palestinian-Arab engineers strongly believed that management was committed to their ideology of diversity management and to preventing racist comments by Jewish co-workers during periods of heightened tension, they felt free to submit a formal complaint in the few cases cited in the interviews. The managerial policy in the two high-tech firms also encouraged workers to refrain from political discussion at work and to cease such discussion when it did occur if requested to do so by a participant or listener. By contrast, in the public hospital, where, as the literature implies (Kraus and Yonay 2018, 34), it would be expected to find the clearest and most formal managerial policy against prejudice and racism, many gray zones existed, and Palestinian-Arab physicians sometimes preferred to ignore racist comments by patients and their families and even to accommodate racist requests, simply to avoid conflict. Their tendency to ignore such incidents might indicate their lack of trust in management support. They did, however, expect their Jewish co-workers to come to their aid when they encountered such behavior and were disappointed when such support was not forthcoming.

Paradoxically, it was in the production sector that Palestinian-Arab workers felt most at ease in expressing their distinct Palestinian identity and political views in general, and radical interpretations of violent events outside the workplace in particular, despite their strong dependency on their employer, their relatively lower skills compared to physician and engineers, and the lack of a professional community or union that could support them during difficult times. The fact that they had hardly any expectations of promotion, combined with their majority status among the workers, may explain their relative freedom to engage in political discussions with their Jewish co-workers. The role of religion in these political discussions is another factor that may have contributed to their willingness to present their views, which will be discussed in chapter 5.

This chapter documented and explained the main sources of tension among members of rival ethnonational groups in the workplace, in light of the fierce conflict between Palestinian Arabs and Jews in Israel. The following chapter will explore the strategies used by workers to deal with these tensions and to maintain social ties across the ethnonational and religious cleavage.

THE GRASSROOTS COPING STRATEGY OF SPLIT ASCRIPTION

This chapter describes the main coping strategy employed by members of minority groups for dealing with the tensions that the broader Palestinian-Israeli conflict introduces into the workplace. In a previous study (Darr 2018), I have termed this strategy "split ascription," which refers to the conceptual separation that members of minority groups create between their direct work environment, composed of personal social ties with team members, and the structural elements of the employing organization, including hiring and promotion procedures and decisions. As we shall see, members of both minority and majority groups depict their direct work environment as politically neutral and generally describe personal work ties between Jewish and Palestinian-Arab workers as positive, collegial, or neutral. By contrast, minority group members often regard structural elements of the employing organization as prejudiced and even racist. The recourse of minority group members to split ascription demonstrates the importance of examining the intersubjective views of workers in diverse work teams, along with their perceptions of structural and interactional elements, in order to fully comprehend interethnic workplace relations in war-torn regions. Understanding the grassroots strategy of split ascription in terms of a unified coping strategy also points to a possible critique of existing theoretical approaches to the study of interethnic workplace relations.

The Palestinian-Arab workers' weaving together of interactional and structural elements of the employing organization into a unified coping strategy potentially challenges the two theoretical approaches that currently dominate analysis of intergroup encounters at work: diversity management (Ashkanasy,

Härtel, and Daus 2002; Jackson, May, and Whitney 1995) and contact theory (Allport 1954; Pettigrew 2008). In presenting the theoretical concept of split ascription, I propose in this chapter a novel way of comprehending how workers in mixed teams cope with workplace manifestations of broader ethnonational cleavages.

A close examination of the ways in which Jewish and Palestinian-Arab workers try to manage the fierce ethnonational tension that threatens daily work in ethnically mixed work teams points to the lacunae in both contact theory and the diversity management approach. The top-down prescriptive nature of diversity management (Ashkanasy, Härtel, and Daus 2002) and the emphasis within contact theory on positive outcomes of intergroup encounters (Pettigrew 2008) make it difficult for these approaches to discern grassroots coping strategies. The concept of split ascription further suggests that each approach provides only a partial understanding of the daily management of workplace relationships among members of diverse ethnonational backgrounds. Nonetheless, the two approaches do provide important theoretical tools for achieving that goal, as highlighted in the following section.

Diversity Management and Workplace Intergroup Encounters

The roots of the extensive diversity management literature lie in the US civil rights movements of the 1960s. It emerged in response to occupational segregation during that era (Ivancevich and Gilbert 2000), and its growth was accelerated by a shift in the US workforce toward teamwork, a division of labor that required intense interaction among workers from diverse backgrounds (Ashkanasy, Härtel, and Daus 2002). This literature is activist—its explicit mandate is to create a diverse workforce, to promote tolerance and acceptance of ethnic and racial minorities in the workplace, and to establish equal treatment of all workers regardless of color, ethnic origin, or gender (for critiques, see Kelly and Dobbin 1996; Sanchez and Brock 1996). Furthermore, diversity management is often presented by its proponents as an efficient managerial tool for achieving practical and financial gains. It has had important practical implications, offering models and methods to improve the management of mixed work teams and to reduce ethnic tensions in workplaces, mainly in immigrant societies and under stable political circumstances such as the United States (Ashkanasy, Härtel, and Daus 2002).

While diversity management literature tends to focus on immigrants seeking to assimilate, rather than on political partisans, it offers a structural analysis examining organizational rules, career ladders, and managerial decision making. Diversity management theorists are particularly interested in how prejudice and discrimination can be inscribed in organizational structures and procedures, and they highlight the role of structural discrimination and prejudice in shaping career trajectories of members of different social groups, typically women and minorities (Mor Barak 2005). Scholars advancing this approach argue that better integration of minority groups into work organizations hinges on structural and institutional-level changes. This emphasis on structural elements as carriers of prejudice and discrimination also informs the current study.

Intergroup contact theory claims that encounters among members of different social groups may reduce prejudice, given certain framing conditions, including support by authoritative figures, equal status of the participating groups, basic cooperation among the groups, and common goals (Allport 1954). Although it has experienced exponential growth over the past sixty years, contact theory has also been the target of various kinds of criticism, mainly from within. Scholars have pointed to its tendency to focus on variables that promote positive, rather than negative, outcomes of intergroup encounters, and also on the perspective of majority groups when measuring prejudice reduction (Pettigrew 2008), which can be partly explained by contact theory's focus on stable Western democracies that need to integrate immigrants into their economy. Pettigrew and Tropp (2006) also criticize researchers' tendency to rely on retrospective accounts of participants in intergroup contacts, while Pettigrew (2008) points to a neglect of situational elements in social encounters as well as a lack of longitudinal data. Yet another critique targets the lack of a middle-range theory that can explain whether and how microlevel accounts of intergroup prejudice reduction are translated into reduced macrolevel conflicts among opposing groups (see Pettigrew 2008, 195). This line of critique is prominent in studies of conflict zones such as Northern Ireland, Israel, and Palestine (e.g., Dickson et al. 2009; Hewstone et al. 2006). In war-torn regions, however, the careful integration of middle-range theory in order to establish micro-macro links is of paramount importance for social scientists who wish to understand the structuration of violent political conflicts. Although the concept of split ascription does not constitute a complete middle-range theory that could clearly explain how microlevel occurrences are translated into macrolevel changes, it is useful for demonstrating how interactional elements and structural reflections of broader political divisions are combined in workers' mechanisms for coping with such conflicts.

Contact theory posits that social engagement across ethnic cleavages, when managed correctly, lowers levels of intergroup prejudice (Pettigrew and Tropp 2006). Originating in social psychology, this approach measures individual actors' subjective perceptions of members of other ethnic groups, typically before and after meaningful interaction. This chapter describes how most members of mixed work teams, who interact daily on the shop floor, seek to establish politically neutral interethnic relations at work. On the face of it, the constitution of a neutral work environment by members of ethnically mixed work teams, which is presented here as an outcome of split ascription, can be seen as a case of subjective prejudice reduction through workplace encounters, exactly as contact theory would predict. This depiction, however, is only partial, since it ignores structural factors, which figure prominently in split ascription. This chapter challenges contact theory by presenting field data systematically demonstrating that subjective perceptions of prejudice are not necessarily reduced through workplace encounters but, rather, are diverted from the interactional level to the structural and procedural levels of the employing organization. As will be shown, minority group members consistently describe structural elements of their employing organization as discriminating against them and even as reflecting the broader prejudice and racism against the Palestinian-Arab minority in Israeli society.

Unlike contact theory, diversity management targets objective organizational attributes rather than the subjective perceptions of individual actors, focusing more on structural elements than on interactional aspects of the workplace (Ewon 2013; Mor Barak 2005). As noted, the explicit goals of diversity management are to create a workplace that reflects the diversity of the larger society, to promote workplace tolerance and acceptance of ethnic and racial minorities, and to establish equal treatment of all workers in all aspects of organizational life. The coping strategy of split ascription described in this chapter challenges diversity management by highlighting workers' grassroots tools for managing interethnic relations rather than structural models designed to reduce workplace discrimination. It demonstrates that workers are active human subjects who react to various managerial policies and incorporate both structural and interactional aspects into a unified grassroots coping strategy.

The first part of this chapter offers empirical examples of how the direct work environment is constituted as apolitical in the Israeli production, medical, and high-tech sectors. The second part presents evidence of split ascription, that is, the attribution of prejudice and racism to structural elements of the employing organization. Empirical evidence of split ascription appears in various degrees in all the three research contexts and can be placed along a continuum representing the degree of separation between the apolitical direct work environment, on the one hand, and prejudiced structures and procedures, on the other. The manufacturing sector manifests the highest levels of split ascription, followed by the health sector, while the high-tech sector displays the lowest levels. I will also discuss the reasons for these variations. Before I present empirical evidence of split ascription, I demonstrate how, despite the fierce ethnonational struggle and the frequent penetration of the broader conflict into the workplace, members of the three groups of workers deliberately attempted to create a neutral work environment. While the ethnonational cleavage remained deeply entrenched, the efforts made and the means used to protect the direct work environment from outside tensions deserve attention.

The Ideal of the Apolitical Work Environment

The efforts to create an apolitical work environment are found in all the health institutions studied, and particularly in the private Palestinian-Arab hospital. Palestinian Arabs, Israeli-born Jews, and Russian immigrants in the two hospitals and the retirement home all agreed that cultural, not political, divides in Israeli society were represented in their workplaces, but they asserted that cultural affiliations played only an auxiliary role in shaping their daily experiences and social ties within the work team. Workers in ethnically diverse work teams repeatedly argued that they tended to treat their colleagues as individuals and to judge them by their personal traits, rather than conceiving them as part of an ethnonational or religious collective. As we have seen in the previous chapter, some Palestinian-Arab members of the mixed work teams felt that when extreme violent events erupted outside the workplace, Jewish workers tended to consider them as collectively responsible. Yet, this was the exception and during day-to-day work, when tension was low, both Jewish and Palestinian-Arab workers usually treated their colleagues as individuals and portrayed their personal ties as positive or neutral. For example, when asked about relations between the nurses in the hospital maternity ward, a Palestinian-Arab nurse in the private Palestinian-Arab hospital confirmed that "we have very good relations among all team members . . . we share a lot of things with each other. We're one team really, nurses, physicians, and assistant nurses. We're together in times of joy and sorrow." She portrayed the work team as cohesive and supportive, and the ties among all members of the medical staff, including physicians, as positive. While it could be argued that the ideal work environment described by this nurse is probably exaggerated, the tendency to depict work relations in such positive terms is important and indicates a desire or need that warrants further investigation.

A Russian nurse in the same hospital echoed this sentiment when asked about the degree to which she shared personal issues with her colleagues: "Background has no significance. What's important is the degree to which I'm a friend of someone or not a friend of hers. There are some people that I'm ready to share things with and others I'm less ready to share with, and still others I'm reluctant to speak to." She rejected the idea that what she dubbed "background" affected her choice of workplace friends, focusing instead on the personality traits of her colleagues. The use of the term *background* is itself a euphemism, which attests to the efforts to neutralize the discussion of ethnic or religious differences within the work team. A Jewish midwife on the maternity ward presented a similarly positive picture of relationships in the ward:

> I feel that between the nurses, nurses and midwives, I include both, there are very good relations, so much so that it's a pleasure for me to work with the team. You can have a quarrel, not a quarrel but more of an argument with a physician or something like that, but when it comes to the nurses I feel it's fun to work with them.

This midwife implied that any tensions that arose among the nurses were related to work, not to politics, and involved disagreements with physicians, who held formal authority over the nursing staff.

The Palestinian-Arab members of the hospital staff also reported sharing intimate personal information with their Jewish co-workers. As one Palestinian-Arab nurse in the maternity ward put it, "Yes, we all do, I'm not the only one." In response to the question whether there was a specific team member that she preferred to confide in, she stated,

> Sure, with Dana [a Jewish nurse], because we have a good mutual understanding. We talk, we also talk with the others, but me and Dana share more with one another. She tells me more, I tell her about my children, but very little about myself. The nurses here are very young, they're like my daughters, and they tell me things sometimes, but Dana tells more.

As this example demonstrates, personal traits and mutual understanding could override the ethnonational-religious divide and were sometimes sufficient to allow for a degree of intimacy between nurses from the two groups. Claims of workplace intimacy should be treated with caution, however, since the wider social and political context always loomed large in the background. Yet this and other interview excerpts reflect a deliberate attempt to exclude politics from the direct work environment. Thus, the head nurse of the neonatal unit in the private hospital, a Jordanian-born Christian Palestinian Arab, emphasized the harmonious relations among the nurses in her ward, which she attributed to their shared work experience: "Many nurses care [about the premature babies], they worry about those who are at risk, and they call from home and ask how he's doing now. . . . All the team is the same, no difference between an Arab and a non-Arab."

Depictions of a politics-free work environment were not restricted to the private hospital. When asked if ethnicity played a role in her decision regarding which co-workers she chose to share private issues with, a Russian nurse in the retirement home replied, "Here, again, I think that it's more a matter of relationship. For example, there's an assistant nurse [a Palestinian Arab] I'm on very good terms with, so I share lots of things with her." A Jewish head nurse at the retirement home, commenting on the work relations among team members in her ward, described them as "okay, like other places. I won't start telling you that they all love each other, but we've all worked together for many years. . . . Everything's normal, like any other place, you spend more time with the team in the workplace than at home." Like her counterparts in the Palestinian-Arab hospital, this nurse explicitly described the work environment in the retirement home as neutral or "normal." Her reference to the long shifts suggested that the need to create a politics-free work environment was partly grounded in the amount of time the nurses spent together and to interdependencies created by the local division of labor. Political tensions, she seemed to imply, might cause strife and make the long working hours hard to bear. It is also plausible that when she mentioned that not all team members loved each other, she may have also been referring to some ethnonational tensions. Nevertheless, she tried to downplay these potential points of contention.

A related explanation for the deliberate portrayal of the work environment as free of politics was linked more explicitly to work practice, as indicated by a Russian nurse in the retirement home who described relations among the nurses in her ward as "very relaxed," adding that "it's very important in this type of work that reciprocity exists, mutual support, and if this is not the case then you start, how to put it, you start calculating: how much work you did and maybe I did less and this might lead to conflicts." She thus suggested that what governed relationships among team members was not the ethnonational origin of members, but the local division of labor and work-related interdependency. The constant need of medical staff members to rely on one another and reciprocate encouraged the maintenance of a calm work environment. In medical work, patients' lives are at stake, and nurses repeatedly cited the daily dependence on one another's skills and goodwill as fostering cooperation among them.

Production workers, despite their radically different work environment and their distinct ethnonational composition, exhibited striking similarities to medical staff regarding the depiction of the direct work environment during regular workdays as apolitical, neutral, or even friendly. Thus, a young Palestinian-Arab production worker emphasized the good relations with Jewish co-workers:

> PRODUCTION WORKER: In every place where Arabs and Jews are together, you find that they get along and connect to one another, especially in the workplace.
> INTERVIEWER: So you see workplace relations as particularly good when compared with [Jewish-Arab] relations elsewhere?

WORKER: Yes, I feel that out on the streets and in the media they say things that are different than what actually occurs between Jews and Arabs at work.

Here the production worker distinguished between the broader political discourse that emphasized the ethnonational cleavage and antagonistic relations between Palestinians and Jews, and the actual, day-to-day situation in the workplace. He claimed that daily ties on the shop floor were generally good, and that Jewish and Palestinian-Arab workers tended to establish workplace ties across the ethnonational cleavage. When asked about the types of social ties he had with his Jewish co-workers, another Palestinian-Arab production worker recounted his experience in both his previous and his current employment: "I'll tell you, the ties are excellent. That is, [in my previous workplace] I used to go out with Jews, we would sit [pause], night outs and events and everything. All of them were Jews, I'd go with two Arabs, and all the rest were Jews, who were our friends." This worker reported how positive workplace ties spilled over to leisure activities (a topic that will be explored in chapter 6) and even described the relations between them in terms of friendship.

Jewish production workers also emphasized positive aspects of workplace relations with Palestinian-Arab co-workers. For example, a twenty-two-year-old Jewish production worker, who was participating in the "preferential work" program in the plant, compared his experience in the plant with that in the previous job he had held shortly after his army service and also mentioned a closer relationship he had developed with an older Palestinian-Arab worker who had acted as a kind of mentor to him when he had started working in the plant:

PRODUCTION WORKER: So here people are good, more pleasant people [than in his previous employment], people who like to work...that's it, I just don't see beyond that. I go outside [of the production floor] and smoke a cigarette with them [referring to Palestinian-Arab co-workers]. I've become friendly with [pause] one Arab [worker].
INTERVIEWER: Yes?
WORKER: Ahmad, Yes.
INTERVIEWER: So you go out together to have a smoke?
WORKER: He also comes with me [to the plant from the nearby city]. Let's say, when I get up in the morning, I send him a WhatsApp message...smoke a cigarette with him...despite the fact that he's married and that, yes, but from the beginning when I first came here to work, he told me various things, he was my teacher.

The deliberate attempt to exclude ethnonational divides from the direct work environment was most clearly expressed by a Russian production worker in his mid-thirties, who had immigrated to Israel from Ukraine at the age of sixteen and worked in various production plants in the north of Israel ever since. When asked about his relations with Palestinian-Arab co-workers, he stressed that "here at work I don't label a Christian or a Druze, these are first of all human beings . . . these are human beings. There are those who help me at work despite the fact that they are Muslims or Druze, it doesn't matter what they are, they help . . . and all is fine."

This exemplifies the conscious efforts made by production workers to treat one another as people, rather than as members of an ethnonational or religious collective. The speaker implies that ethnonational-religious divides still apply in the wider society but are simply suspended in the workplace. Moreover, as in the health sector, he reveals that he divides people in his immediate work environment into those who help him and on whom he can depend and those who are less likely to provide support when needed. These attitudes demonstrate once again the close connection between local division of labor, task interdependency, and workplace relations. Thus, the constitution of an apolitical work environment emerges as a rational strategy that is deeply embedded in work practice, particularly in sequential division of labor, with high interdependency and responsibility.

As noted in the previous chapter, the high-tech sector exhibited the lowest levels of ethnonational or religious tensions when compared with the health and production sectors. The lack of direct client contact, coupled with clear and decisive managerial action against racist remarks, can partly explain this finding. Nonetheless, we also saw that some tensions did permeate the multinational companies and disrupt social ties in socially diverse work teams. In the following excerpt, a veteran hardware engineer in one of the multinational companies described how Facebook introduced tensions into the work team, and what is important here, how she made a deliberate effort to insulate her direct work environment from these tensions in order to maintain her view of workplace relations across the Jewish–Palestinian cleavage as positive and supportive:

> ENGINEER: . . . but once again it's also during wartime [pause] it's [heightened tension] always during wars, and during the Lebanon war [2006] Facebook didn't exist, so you don't really [pause] just the things they speak about in front of you, so you know what they think [pause] and no one speaks [their mind at work]. And then, during the war three years ago, there was the war [pause].

INTERVIEWER: Three years ago we had Operation Protective Edge [launched by the IDF in 2014 against Gaza].

ENGINEER: Yes, and then we had Facebook, and my [work] friends are in it, and I'm their friend on Facebook, and then you see what they really think. This was also a kind of a change. At the time I'd been working with them for about five years, without seeing anything, and then all of a sudden, there is Facebook and I see, [pause] and that was also the period when I deleted a lot, it got to a place that I couldn't see, I didn't want to see [what her Jewish colleagues wrote on Facebook]. There were periods when I took them off from my Facebook, I prefer that we stay friends [laughs].

INTERVIEWER: So you don't want to see that side of them? Their views, so that it wouldn't affect your relationships with them?

ENGINEER: I don't want to see their Facebook [page]. You see, one of them was my manager, and he was really great, but oops, you see his Facebook [pause], you don't want to see it!

This interview, like the example cited in the previous chapter, shows how Facebook can undermine the relations between Palestinian-Arab and Jewish engineers, especially at times of heightened tensions, by revealing team members' political views that they had refrained from expressing at work. The speaker describes Facebook as a hybrid space, one that is both exterritorial to the work organization yet brings together co-workers who become Facebook friends and are thus exposed to each other's political views. As this interview indicates, once political views become known, it is much harder to maintain positive working relations or an apolitical work environment. It is noteworthy that, rather than relinquishing the image of an apolitical work environment, this engineer took deliberate steps to limit her exposure to what she saw as offensive views expressed on Facebook by some Jewish team members and simply deleted them from her Facebook page. This is yet another example of the attempts by co-workers to actively limit the impact of the broader conflict on day-to-day work relations among members of ethnically mixed work teams. In other words, the speaker seemed to be willing to avoid a deeper acquaintance with her Jewish co-workers in order to maintain the image of an apolitical work environment.

A Palestinian-Arab engineer who had worked for fifteen years in the Israeli high-tech sector, the last five of them with the multinational company, also emphasized the apolitical nature of relations with his Jewish team members: "There are those [team members] who you tend to avoid and those [pause]. But today, it's not an Arab or a Jew, it's just [pause], for me it doesn't matter, let's say as a parameter, people are people, there are good and bad people." It is significant that Jewish engineers also promoted the image of their work environment as untainted by ethnic or political tensions. For example, a Jewish engineer who worked as a project integrator, coordinating a few work teams, described her immediate work environment as egalitarian, based on meritocracy, in which social variables such as ethnicity and gender did not play a role. She explicitly attributed this situation to the policy of the company's management:

> ENGINEER: They [management] created a very, very equal kind of feeling for everyone, there is no [pause].
> INTERVIEWER: You mean that who you are doesn't matter?
> ENGINEER: Yes, neither your origin nor your gender, nor even the way you dress.

It is clear that most workers in the three research contexts engaged in deliberate attempts to constitute a neutral work environment. However, the tensions caused by the ongoing, violent political struggle, which often permeated the workplace, necessitated the particular kind of coping strategy that I term "split ascription." The following section explores the various ways in which this strategy is applied in the three sectors studied.

The Application of Split Ascription

In all the research sites, Palestinian-Arab workers deployed split ascription to cope with broader tensions and to maintain social ties across ethnic groups. Split ascription enabled minority group workers to draw a clear distinction between their immediate work environment, which, as we have seen, they depicted as relatively apolitical and neutral, and structural elements of the employing organization, which they perceived as riddled with discrimination and even what they called racism, manifested in skewed promotion procedures and their unjust treatment by organizational decision-making processes. By ascribing discrimination and racism to an abstract institutional entity or to structural elements of the employing organization rather than to their co-workers, Palestinian-Arab workers could vent their dissatisfaction or anger toward what they regarded as their inferior workplace position while distancing their daily work encounters from the ethnonational conflict and striving to insulate their personal ties from events in wider society.

The clearest example of split ascription appeared in the production plant, even though most of the Palestinian-Arab production workers considered that they were treated better by the management of the factory that they currently worked for than by their previous employers. They specifically mentioned the improved safety and health procedures, which were crucial when dealing with dangerous chemicals. Yet, most of these workers also believed that they did not enjoy equal promotion opportunities and that the pay structures at the production plant were not the same for them and their Jewish co-workers. For example, after acknowledging that a few Palestinian-Arab workers had been promoted to low-level managerial positions, one of them added:

> Yes, you know, you sometimes feel [pause]. Okay, I know that this Jewish guy that was hired didn't really come to work with us on the machine. They [management] brought him to learn the system we work with. They put him to work with us for only one week, and then they transferred him to the offices. And they gave him something different than they gave us. They gave him [pause]. I'm here already for three years, they gave me [pause] pay and everything, but they didn't give me that Advanced Training Fund. If I'd been given the fund from my first year here, I could have withdrawn it after six years.... If I'd got the fund from my first year here like him, I would have felt something else. So you feel, one can say, this is an Arab and this is a Jew, no one can argue with that.

This Palestinian-Arab production worker describes how management of the plant, to which he refers by the impersonal term "they," systematically favors Jewish workers in terms of promotion and pay structure. The Advanced Training Fund he mentions is a widely used optional benefit that employers can grant their workers. Both employers and employees deposit money in the fund on a monthly basis, and the sums accumulated can be withdrawn once every six years, free of tax. Here, the speaker, like other Palestinian-Arab workers in the plant, claims that they are discriminated against because this benefit is offered to them only a few years after they are hired, while Jewish employees receive it immediately. He describes this unjust situation as a fact of life, a daily reality, something Palestinian-Arab workers must accept. A few other Palestinian-Arab workers also mentioned the Advanced Training Fund when describing their work experience. As one noted: "And there is also pay discrimination. It differs. I approached management [about] the Advanced Training Fund, and they denied it, but I know that he [the Jewish co-worker] was given it and I told them [management], You can deny it, but I know that he got it."

When another Palestinian-Arab production worker was asked if Jewish and Palestinian-Arab workers had equal chances of finding employment, he said that it was harder for the latter to find a job, and then referred to the differential career ladders for members of each ethnonational group:

> PRODUCTION WORKER: Here in the plant we have workers who have a certificate in quality assurance [pause], they've had it for a long

time, and they asked [management] to work in that department. For example, a [Palestinian-Arab] worker who's worked here for two to three years and has a [quality assurance] certificate, which means he can work in this job. What is better? To admit [to the quality assurance department] someone with [production line] experience, or to bring someone from the outside who doesn't have any experience of that kind?

INTERVIEWER: So you feel that they? [pause].

WORKER: They [management] prefer to bring their own.

INTERVIEWER: From among the Jews you mean?

WORKER: The Jews, and not let you [the Palestinian-Arab workers] in.

He was very clear about the preference given to Jewish workers in promotion decisions. Production workers regarded working in the quality assurance department as a type of promotion, and this speaker, while lamenting the fact that qualified Palestinian-Arab workers were not appointed to such positions, indicated that ethnonational considerations, rather than skill or production line experience, underpinned promotion decisions by plant management.

While split ascription was most evident in the production sector, Palestinian-Arab health workers also drew a clear distinction between their direct work environment and structural elements of the health institutions they worked for. Nurses and midwives who belonged (or had belonged) to an ethnic minority within their employing institution (whether Jewish or Palestinian Arab) explicitly acknowledged this strategy. Thus, Palestinian-Arab nurses in both the private hospital and the retirement home shared a conviction that public sector health institutions in Israel routinely discriminated against them and that Palestinian-Arab physicians and nurses who worked in those facilities could very rarely become heads of departments or head nurses. For some Palestinian-Arab nurses in the Jewish retirement home, institutional-level discrimination was a daily reality, manifested, for example, in preferential employment of Jewish nurses. Some of the Palestinian-Arab nurses also felt that they were more likely than their Jewish co-workers to be summoned before the facility's disciplinary committee, which they saw as another indication of institutional-level discrimination.

The application of split ascription by minority group members was not restricted to Palestinian-Arab health workers working in predominantly Jewish institutions. The few Jewish and Russian nurses working in the Palestinian-Arab hospital were also convinced that they were discriminated against, claiming that they were excluded from managerial positions and from decision-making processes. A Jewish midwife at the hospital described her experience after she accepted a temporary managerial position (head nurse) within the maternity ward when the manager went on maternity leave. Even though her position was defined as temporary, she encountered some discriminatory attitudes held by top management, composed of Palestinian-Arab nuns and senior administrators:

> At the time, when I was replacing the head nurse, I participated in management meetings with all the administrators, the purchasing manager, the hospital manager, and . . . also the nun. The nun here is a type of a CEO and she knows everything, she is involved, she visits every shift two or three times, she is also a general nurse, she comes and checks who's working, how everything is functioning. But this story is about another nun, and I was at a management meeting, I don't remember what I said, and she [the other nun] replied: "You should know that this is ours, not yours." First of all, the whole hospital belongs to European states since the nuns run all the financial side and there are donations from European countries and things. What she said [was], "This is ours, not yours."

Later in the interview, she stressed that "every time I tried to do something I was blocked. Now, a few of the things I understand now are maybe connected to Arab-Jewish relationships, a type of discrimination, so I told myself maybe they don't want me to be visible or something like that." Her temporary role as head nurse exposed the Jewish midwife to what she described as a discriminatory attitude on the part of top management, which she attributed to the fact that she was Jewish. In her eyes, the nun in the executive meeting had explicitly referred to her ethnic affiliation when she reacted negatively to one of her suggestions, saying, "This is ours, not yours." The nurse understood the nun's use of "ours" to mean that her employing institution was European, Christian, and Palestinian-Arab but definitely not Jewish, and her repetition of this phrase suggests that she took it as a personal offense. Whereas this midwife depicted the social relationships in her day-to-day work environment as transcending ethnic cleavages, she saw the antagonistic attitude directed at her in the management meeting as structural in nature. Her perception of structural discrimination against the Jewish nurses was amplified by the complete lack of Jewish managers in the private Palestinian-Arab hospital. As diversity management suggests (Ewon 2013; Mor Barak 2005), the nurse perceived discriminatory attitudes as inscribed in formal procedures and structures. In her view, the formal organization excluded her and all other Jewish nurses from the decision-making process. She also made a clear connection between structural discrimination and the broader ethnonational conflict. Later in the interview, she also expressed her skepticism, reflected in her choice to refrain from future initiatives.

Most of the Palestinian-Arab nurses in the private hospital had extensive experience working in Israeli government hospitals, which they perceived as institutionally discriminatory. For example, when asked to comment on differences in professional identities between Jewish and Palestinian-Arab nurses, the head nurse of the maternity ward made it very clear that, in her view, Israeli government hospitals discriminated against Palestinian Arabs while also noting that Palestinian-Arab institutions, including her own employer, were similarly discriminatory toward Jews: "The thing is, well, it has to do with the government hospitals, I think that there, ethnic identity has a meaning. Government hospitals prefer the Jews, and the private hospitals in my city prefer Arab workers." Like her Palestinian-Arab counterparts in the production plant, she referred to these forms of structural discrimination as a fact of life, a natural ingredient of Israeli society that had to be accepted. Moreover, having earlier portrayed relations among members of her mixed team as positive, this nurse was pessimistic about rectifying structural-level discrimination. Whereas contact theory could explain her positive depiction of interpersonal relations as an outcome of intense interactions between the two groups (Pettigrew 2008), and diversity management could account for her view that employing institutions were structurally discriminatory (Mor Barak 2005), split ascription enables the nurses' divergent views to be analyzed within a single sense-making explanatory scheme.

Another Palestinian-Arab nurse in the private hospital presented a similar picture of the government hospitals where she had received her basic professional training:

> Racism exists in this country [Israel], no doubt about it, and the selection of workers is based on ethnicity. If there is a job opening in a [public] hospital, for example, and there are two candidates, a Jew and an Arab, the hospital prefers the Jew. If you are an Arab, so you are worth less and you are less desirable. And this message is communicated in different ways, mostly indirect, like the requirement of military experience [to qualify for a job] or suchlike. In short, this is the way most workplaces are run, in the health sector and in other sectors as well, I assume.

This nurse described the public hospital as racist and discriminatory on an institutional level, part of what she saw as a wider, state-based pattern of discrimination against Palestinian-Arab citizens. Labor laws in Israel provide protection to and promote equality for all citizens. Section 2 of the Law of Equal Opportunities at Work, 1988 forbids discrimination in employment or hiring on the basis of gender, sexual orientation, personal status, pregnancy, age, race, religion, ethnicity, political affiliation, and other grounds. Completion of military service is not included in the list, although reserve duty in the army (which necessitates absence from work) is. Some social and economic benefits in Israel are contingent on completion of military service, which is compulsory for most

Jewish citizens and Druze to which only a small number of other Palestinian-Arab citizens volunteer (for a discussion, see Orgad 2007). The nurse pointed to a gray zone, open to judicial interpretation, where job requirements included the completion of military service. Here, again, the speaker perceived discrimination as structural and embedded in formal rules and procedures on the institutional level. Unlike the buffered work environment, the organizational structure in the Israeli health care sector, she argued, reflected broader ethnonational tensions and was designed to favor Jewish health workers over their Palestinian-Arab team members.

As we saw in the previous chapter, Palestinian-Arab nurses were not alone in depicting discrimination on an institutional level. A Jewish nurse in the Palestinian-Arab hospital, owned and managed by a Christian order, talked about the discrimination, based on religious affiliation, that both she and Muslim nurses experienced:

> When I started working here, about three or four years after that they started to train Arab midwives, five midwives every year, young girls who'd just graduated from nursing programs, and there was a feeling that they want to build here an infrastructure for midwives like in the X Hospital [a Palestinian-Arab hospital in the same city run by a different Christian order] where only Arab midwives work. But they have this issue, that's how I feel, well, there are things that are never discussed but which you feel, that working with the [Israeli] Ministry of Health, it is important for them to also have Jewish midwives, they are very clear about that. But to be the nurse in charge of the maternity ward or someone in charge of something, all the supervisors are Christians at the top. They apply this rule strictly.

This Jewish nurse attributed the private hospital's employment of Jewish nurses and midwives to the institutional logic of the Israeli health sector. The hospital received funds from the Israeli Ministry of Health for each birth it registered, and she hinted that it maintained a good rapport with the Israeli authorities by employing a few Jewish midwives. Despite the employment of a heterogeneous team, she asserted, the hospital, run by nuns, applied a discriminatory "rule" that prevented non-Christians from obtaining top managerial positions. Her use of the term *rule*, when no formal code actually existed, revealed that she attributed discrimination to the organization's norms, that it was part of the informal organization. Only a minority of the Palestinian-Arab nurses and one physician in the private hospital described its policy as fair toward all employees, and thus explicitly presented it as the polar opposite of government hospitals. The claim that the private hospital was fairer toward the Jewish minority within it made the structural discrimination of the public hospital even greater in the eyes of some of the Palestinian-Arab medical staff. After all, public hospitals would be expected to be more committed to equality and transparency than private hospitals, whereas in this case it was the private hospitals that were portrayed as less discriminatory.

The Israeli high-tech sector exhibited a different version of split ascription. As has been shown, engineers and technicians reported a low level of interethnic tensions at work, even during politically charged periods. In a similar vein, interviewees in the two multinational companies expressed confidence that top management was indeed committed to its meritocratic ideology and more specifically to the absorption, integration, and promotion of Palestinian-Arab engineers into managerial positions, according to their talent rather than their ethnonational affiliation. This confidence was partly grounded in the formal and transparent process of promotion applications. All internal job openings in the two companies were published online and candidates could submit their documents electronically. Here is how a Palestinian-Arab engineer, who had worked for many years in the Israeli high-tech sector, described this process:

> With my current employer, I think, and I have been working here for the past two years, there is no one person who makes all the [promotion] decisions. Here you have a system, and I have seen it, even with HR, we don't see them at all. Everything is part of the [computer] system, and this is something unique. And this is the difference between company X [his current employer], and company Y [his previous employer], where people were sitting down and making decisions and so on, and they can be prejudiced. Some people can be open and accept people regardless of their origin, but there are other people who will relate to the [candidate's] origin. What I have noticed here is that this doesn't exist, and everything works by systems and positions and by instructions that are part of the system, and everything is computerized.

This engineer perceived the bureaucratic rules, transparency, and computerization of the application process in his company as favoring minority group members, as they countered the ability of individual managers to prevent the promotion of Palestinian-Arab engineers. It is interesting that he used the term *origin*, rather than the more general *background* used by other interviewees, which masks the deep ethnonational cleavage in Israeli society.

Nonetheless, many other interviewees remained skeptical about Palestinian-Arab engineers' real chances of reaching high managerial positions, pointing to statistical discrimination, that is, the low number of Palestinian-Arab engineers in mid-level and top managerial positions. For example, when asked how she perceived the promotion procedures in her firm, one Palestinian-Arab engineer expressed her frustration:

> ENGINEER: There's still a lack of [Palestinian Arabs] in the managerial echelons. I don't see that [pause] that we are moving into managerial positions, despite the fact that, let's say [pause] I personally would like that [to become a manager].
>
> INTERVIEWER: You would like to?
>
> ENGINEER: I would like to, yes, yes. I believe that my experience and my knowledge and my tenure here should have allowed me to move in this direction [pause]. Now, I don't know what the reasons are, but I don't see [Palestinian Arabs in] managerial positions, not high level, and let's say not even in first level [management].
>
> INTERVIEWER: You mean team managers?
>
> ENGINEER: Yes.

So how did the engineers explain the discrepancy between their general belief in top management's desire to promote Palestinian-Arab engineers and the meager number who actually held mid- or top-level managerial positions? The answer to this question is twofold. Some Palestinian-Arab engineers claimed that their proportion in the Israeli high-tech sector had been steadily increasing in the past few years and that it would take more time before these growing numbers would translate into more Palestinian Arabs in managerial positions. Most of them, however, attributed their difficulty in reaching managerial positions to the Jewish team managers, who had a central role in deciding which team members would be promoted. Thus, one Palestinian-Arab engineer who had worked for many years in her multinational company drew a clear distinction between top and mid-level management. While describing top management as keen supporters of ethnonational diversity and the promotion of minorities, she perceived some team managers as more discriminatory and even racist and reluctant to promote Palestinian-Arab engineers to the position of team managers:

> The problem is that it [promotion to a managerial position] depends a great deal on your direct manager. A manager [pause] who is not a racist, and you see that [pause] that you receive really equal treatment and you [pause], you give everything that you've got, but you see results. And there is a manager, it doesn't really matter what you do, it's so clear, so transparent, and so brutal.

She also reported that when she had encountered a team manager whom she perceived as discriminating against her, she had chosen to move to a different team, only to discover that her promotion was still stalled. In the end she decided to accept technical, rather than managerial promotion and to become a consultant to different teams in her area of expertise. As we shall see in the next chapter, which examines career trajectories in the three sectors, this was a choice that was made by many of her Palestinian-Arab colleagues.

The distinction drawn by Palestinian-Arab engineers between top management, whom they perceived as committed to fair treatment of all workers, and some of the middle managers, whom they regarded as discriminating or racist, can perhaps be explained by the fact that they simply did not meet top managers on a daily basis and could not really judge if they indeed behaved according to their declared belief in meritocracy. This could, however, also be explained by the notion of globalization and ideology of diversity management propagated by top managers in the two multinationals, as an outcome of their global scope and their frequent encounters with non-Israeli managers.

Split Ascription in a Comparative Framework

The sociology of work practice that guided the analysis of the field interviews, with its sensitivity to grassroots activities and to sense-making mechanisms of workers in different sectors (e.g., Orr 1996), reveals split ascription to be an effective means of coping with fierce ethnonational tensions in the workplace. On the one hand, informants in the three research contexts employed interpersonal criteria to constitute the work team as bound together by neutral, collegial, and even friendly ties, regardless of members' ethnonational or religious affiliation. Many of the underlying explanations for the constitution of an apolitical work environment were related to the local division of labor and forms of interdependency that required workers to choose which co-workers they could trust to teach and support them during the workday. This choice was often based on personality traits rather than ethnonational identity. On the other hand, minority group members, whether Palestinian Arabs or Jews, often depicted institutional structures in their employing organizations as plagued by discrimination and even racism.

The empirical manifestation of split ascription points to certain inadequacies in the two approaches that currently dominate the analysis of interethnic workplace relations: contact theory and diversity management. By failing to pay heed to the grassroots strategies workers deploy to manage interethnic relations, these approaches do not yield a complete picture of worker responses to interethnic tensions during politically charged periods and in war-torn regions. Consistent with contact theory, the application of split ascription in the three research contexts illustrates that the intense social engagement and interdependency created by local divisions of labor function to maintain a neutral work environment (Pettigrew and Tropp 2006). The interviewees in the production, health, and high-tech sectors cited these factors as contributing to low levels of workplace prejudice and to the constitution of neutral and even friendly workplace relations across the ethnonational cleavage. Split ascription diverges from contact theory, however, in suggesting that interaction, even when managed correctly, does not necessarily reduce prejudice and racism at work but rather shifts them to the organizational level. Minority group nurses in this study, as well as production workers and to a lesser degree high-tech employees, saw discrimination as embedded in the structures and procedures of their employing institutions. While this finding is consistent with diversity management's assertion that discrimination can be inscribed into formal organization, split ascription theory has the advantage of drawing attention to grassroots coping strategies and is therefore better able than diversity management to incorporate interactional elements into interethnic workplace models.

The theoretical foundations of split ascription as an analytic tool for understanding interethnic workplace relations lie in the dramaturgical tradition within the social sciences, specifically Goffman's (1974) notion of "frame analysis." This theoretical approach is also applied in other chapters of this book, since it allows social engagement and broader structural attributes that frame the interactions between workers to be placed within a unified theoretical framework. In his interpretation of frame analysis, Gonos (1977) argues that intersubjectivity is shaped through interactions but that actors make constant and often explicit reference to structural elements that enable and disable certain lines of action. Frame analysis grants actors agency in shaping their viewpoints, which are based on social engagement but also take structural constraints into account. This theoretical grounding allows us to understand how workers in mixed work teams actively constitute an intersubjective view of interethnic work relations that incorporates both their social interactions with team members and their perceptions of structural elements of their organizations and the ongoing conflict between Palestinians and Jews.

It is significant that workers in the health, production, and high-tech sectors use a single coping strategy to address the interactional and structural dimensions of their employment. Nonetheless, they draw a sharp distinction between these dimensions, which also fail to inform one another. Whereas their depictions of interethnic relations within the work team are neutral or even positive, members of minority groups often have a negative view of their employing organizations—and of broader institutional contexts in general. They tend to take structural racism for granted and, indeed, express little hope that structural discrimination can be remedied. This cynical view is most strongly reflected in the accounts of the production workers, who see no prospect for a meaningful career, and is also seen in nurses' tendency to attribute ethnonational identities to health institutions. That some Palestinian-Arab nurses dubbed public hospitals in Israel "Jewish places" indicates their belief that the discriminatory treatment they have experienced there is deeply ingrained in broader Israeli society with its ongoing conflict between Palestinian Arabs and Jews, and unlikely to change. The Jewish nurse who was told by the nun-manager of the private hospital, "This is ours, not yours" and who understood the comment to mean that the facility was a Palestinian-Arab and Christian, but not a Jewish, institution, believed that discrimination was a defining feature of the hospital. She also expressed little hope for change.

Particularly in the high-tech sector, the views expressed by Palestinian-Arab engineers often oscillated between a discourse of meritocracy and a political belief that in reality their career trajectories are determined by their ethnonational identity. As Preminger (2020) points out, this inherent tension between the clear economic benefits of integration of the Palestinian-Arab minority and the political desire to exclude Palestinian Arabs from this sector with its economic benefits and high status, is common also in the Israeli political and public spheres.

This chapter has demonstrated the empirical manifestation of split ascription in the three research settings, and most markedly in the production and health sectors. The high-tech sectors exhibited reduced levels of split ascription, and racism was assigned not to top but rather to mid-level managerial practices. The next chapter will focus specifically on the impact of the external ethnonational conflict on career expectations and trajectories of minority group members, and the pivotal role of middle management in shaping the experiences of Palestinian-Arab workers in ethnically mixed work environments.

ETHNONATIONAL BACKGROUND AND CAREER TRAJECTORIES

For many of us, career expectations are part and parcel of our working life. From an early age middle-class children are socialized to aspire to move up the organizational and occupational ladder. The ambition to achieve better jobs, greater skills, better pay, and increased authority is regarded as entirely natural for the educated worker. Yet, our career aspirations need to be woven into the economic fabric of our society and must be screened and then harnessed by organizations in accordance with managerial goals. Indeed, as Edgar Schine and John Van Maanen (2013) teach us, formal career ladders are instituted by work organizations to connect personal ambitions with organizational needs and goals. Within the field of organization studies, and even before this lucid definition of career ladders, Max Weber already created a link between personal career ambitions and formal organizational goals in his model of the rational-legal bureaucracy over a hundred years ago.

According to the ideal typical model of rational-legal bureaucracies (Weber 1946), career should be based on the meritocratic principal. Employees should be promoted on the basis of their talent, skill, and experience, rather than their class background, ethnic origin, or family ties. This ideal typical depiction is, however, far removed from the daily realities of the workplace, where workers often feel that talent and skill alone do not explain many promotion decisions. In the workplace, groups of workers who are most familiar with prejudice and discrimination include minorities and women. These two groups continuously encounter obstacles that stand between them and their desire to further their careers. As many studies indicate, ethnic affiliations and gender often impact managerial decisions regarding promotion (Pudney and Shields 2000). The literature on careers of members of ethnic minorities in Europe and the United States repeatedly demonstrates that they are often absent from decision-making positions (Saxenian 2002), and their chances for promotion into managerial positions is lower than that of majority group members (Hultin 2003). It can also be argued that the career aspirations and expectations of women and minority group members are often shaped during early socialization and already reflect gender and ethnonational prejudice. This means that women and minorities internalize the obstacles that prevent them from pursuing managerial careers and that they sometimes adjust their organizational and occupational aspirations accordingly. The barriers to the promotion of women in work organizations are most vividly expressed in the "glass ceiling" metaphor coined by Marilyn Loden in 1978 to depict the invisible upper limit to the advancement of women into top managerial positions. While its existence and inner mechanism are often implicit, and denied by top management, a glass ceiling allows women to look up and to persist in their efforts to move into the managerial echelons, only to hit their heads against this transparent yet hard obstacle. Glass ceilings, however, are not restricted to women employees and can also exist for minority group members.

The Palestinian-Arab workers in the three sectors studied all felt, to various degrees, that their ethnonational identity within a war-torn society had an impact on their career trajectories. At the lowest end of the scale were the production workers, who perceived their career opportunities to be nonexistent. In the middle were the high-tech engineers, who were more positive about their chances for promotion but still perceived difficulties arising from their ethnonational background. Highest on the scale were the health workers, who perceived the least difficulties in managing their careers, with nurses expressing greater reservations regarding their chances for promotion than physicians, who were more optimistic. This chapter describes the perceived impact of ethnonational origin in each of the three sectors, and starts with the production workers who represent the harshest impact.

Perceived Career Opportunities in the Israeli Production Sector

For the Palestinian-Arab workers in the production plant, the metaphor that best depicts their career expectations is one of a concrete, rather than a glass, ceiling, which had all but eliminated their aspirations to move into the managerial ranks. For my informants, their inability to further their vertical careers was deeply rooted in their ethnonational-religious background, and many of them had to relinquish their desire for promotion. Their claims of discrimination in promotion were borne out by the meager number of Palestinian-Arab workers in middle and top management, even though they constituted a majority on the production floor.

To be sure, in some sectors of the economy, such as the production and service sectors, career opportunities are often limited, and workers can expect to hold a frontline position or a shop floor job for most of their working life. Instead of vertical careers, most production and service workers pursue horizontal careers, namely, they move every few years to a similar job in a different organization. But, for the Palestinian-Arab production workers, being a minority group member, particularly in a country torn by ethnonational conflict, exacerbated the more general lack of career opportunities in production and service jobs.

The previous chapter demonstrated the tendency of the Palestinian-Arab production workers to establish a complete separation between their immediate work environment, generally described in positive terms, and the organizational structure, depicted as prejudiced against them and even racist. Indeed, the majority of Palestinian-Arab production workers abandoned any career ambitions they may have had and settled for the dream of a secure and stable job that paid the minimum wage or slightly higher, and a safe working environment. Instead of aspiring to move into what they called "the offices," the production workers typically had career trajectories that included frequent moves between production plants in the Galilee, from one production line job to another.

When asked if they were aware of any Palestinian-Arab workers who served in managerial positions in the plant, the Palestinian-Arab production workers mentioned only one person, namely, the chief chemist in the plant. One of the interviewees, who had worked for ten years in the plant, even tried to explain what he perceived as the anomaly of a Palestinian-Arab chemist holding a top management position:

> If they [management] could have found a Jew who was willing to work for the same salary, he [the Palestinian-Arab chemist] wouldn't have been here. I tell you once again, maybe, if they call him in the middle of the night and tell him that they've got a problem in the plant, he [the Arab chemist] will get up and come to the plant. A Jewish worker wouldn't come. The Arab worker is all the time more available [than his Jewish counterpart]. We used to say, sorry for what I'm about to say . . . that the manual laborers are always Arab. All the work here is menial. You've got to use your hands to fill and to organize the containers in the boxes, I mean hard physical work. All the management [of the plant] is Jewish. But in the filling post [pause] there aren't many Jews. The Jews

are in the offices. Think about the procurement department, in procurement you don't find any Arabs! Just Jews. The same in the orders department.

According to this worker, the complete absence of a Palestinian Arab in the plant's top management was the normal situation that required no explanation. Rather, it was the exception that needed to be explained. He claimed not only that the Palestinian-Arab chemist was willing to work for lower pay than a Jewish one but also that he was available for management at all times of the day and night, which was not the case for Jewish workers who tended, according to this account, to be less cooperative and less easily exploited.

Even the one Palestinian-Arab worker who had been promoted to a low managerial position (as shift line manager) felt exploited and discriminated against when compared to the few Jewish workers on the production line, explaining his promotion in similar terms to the previous interviewee:

> They promoted me to being in charge because they know that Arabs work. Not only work but are also available at all times. For example, he [the Jewish head of the production department] can call me any time if a problem arises, he can tell me, for example, if there's a problem in the plant, "Come to the plant." The Jew can't come, I'm sure he wouldn't come and they [top management] know that.

As these interviews show, Palestinian-Arab production workers tended to ascribe these rare promotions to rational economic considerations, such as lower pay or greater availability than the Jewish co-workers, rather than to better skills.

The Palestinian-Arab workers stressed that Jewish workers were not interested in production jobs involving hard physical labor, lifting heavy weights, standing for long hours in one location along the production line, and being constantly on the alert to prevent chemical leaks. They also felt that management was more attuned to requests made by Israeli-born Jewish workers to be promoted into management, which left the Palestinian Arabs and the very few Russians behind. A Palestinian-Arab worker clearly expressed these views when asked about the career opportunities available to Palestinian-Arab employees:

> PALESTINIAN-ARAB PRODUCTION WORKER: At work, you see when a Jew arrives, they [management] promote him faster than an Arab, no doubt about that. I know that there were two or three [Jewish] workers who were working inside, on the "plate," they worked on the plate and then, slowly, they stopped working there.
> INTERVIEWER: What exactly is this "plate"?

PRODUCTION WORKER: It's where you lift all the containers [of chemicals] and put them into the cardboard boxes.

INTERVIEWER: Yes.

PRODUCTION WORKER: Suddenly they give them a piece of paper [meaning a promotion] and, see, they weren't performing even 25 percent of what we [Palestinian-Arab workers] were doing, 25 percent! Suddenly, they promote them!

INTERVIEWER: So first they promote the Jewish worker, and what about the Arab workers?

PRODUCTION WORKER: It's always, "Jews first."

This worker explicitly pointed to management's preference for promoting Jews over Palestinian Arabs, even though the latter often had longer tenure and higher productivity. When asked whether there were equal promotion opportunities for Palestinian Arabs and Jews, another Palestinian Arab responded:

WORKER: Listen, in my opinion, I repeat what I said [pause]. There's a certain limit.

INTERVIEWER: There's a limit?

WORKER: Yes. . . . it's impossible that one day you'll come visit here, in a few years, and find, for example [pause], a [Palestinian-Arab] head of department.

INTERVIEWER: Yes.

WORKER: Maybe you'll find a deputy this or deputy that.

INTERVIEWER: Yes, so you are saying that a ceiling exists?

WORKER: But [pause] a really high-ranking manager or a general manager, you won't find.

While this worker was less pessimistic than the previous interviewees and believed that Palestinian-Arab production workers could be promoted to a certain level, he also acknowledged the existence of a ceiling that prevented them from being promoted beyond the position of deputy head of department. This relatively optimistic voice was, however, rare, and most Palestinian-Arab workers pointed to blatant structural discrimination against them, for example, in terms of pay and benefits.

The Jewish production workers, mostly young people who had recently completed their military service, expressed a strikingly different image of their interactions with top management and their perceived career opportunities. When asked if his Jewish origin had any impact on his chances of promotion, a twenty-two-year-old Jewish production worker, who had worked only a few months in the plant, replied that his ethnonational affiliation never worked against him:

> JEWISH PRODUCTION WORKER: I receive positive treatment yes, very good treatment from managers.
>
> INTERVIEWER: Yes?
>
> PRODUCTION WORKER: Yes, and every time we meet he [the production manager] asks me to come to him personally if I run into any type of problem, even a personal one. And yesterday we even had a personal conversation.
>
> INTERVIEWER: So what did you speak about? About the way you feel here? Things like that?
>
> PRODUCTION WORKER: Yes, about how I feel and how I'd like to advance [my career here].
>
> INTERVIEWER: Really? They've already talked to you about that?
>
> PRODUCTION WORKER: Yes.

This account is supported by other interviews with Jewish workers who claimed that management expressed a desire to retain them in the plant since so few Jewish workers stayed for longer than a year. While rejecting any claim of prejudice in hiring or promotion, the CEO of the plant, in an introductory interview prior to the study, also asserted that he wished to see more Jewish workers on the production floor simply because there were so few of them. It is not surprising, then, that Palestinian-Arab production workers felt that they had hardly any prospect of moving up the managerial hierarchy. Compared to the production plant studied, the situation in the high-tech sector was very different, with Palestinian-Arab engineers portraying a generally positive image of their career opportunities, despite some perceived difficulties.

Perceived Career Opportunities in the Israeli High-Tech Sector

In the introduction I pointed to the rapid growth in the percentage of Palestinian-Arab engineers in the Israeli high-tech sector. I also noted that this percentage is still far from the 20 percent share of the Palestinian-Arab population in the state of Israel. Additionally, a Jewish engineering graduate has a 1.3 higher chance of finding a job in the Israeli high-tech sector than a Palestinian-Arab counterpart (Department of the Chief Economist 2017). The tension resulting from this rise in the number of Palestinian-Arab engineers in the Israeli high-tech sector, coupled with their still very low level of representation and their inferior position in the labor market, is well reflected in many of the interview excerpts presented and analyzed below.

The numerous foreign multinational high-tech companies that came to Israel in the wake of the 1996 Oslo Accord mostly opened research and development facilities but also a few very large production plants, such as in the case of Intel-Israel. An important engine of this influx was the mass immigration from the FSU into Israel, since many of these immigrants were technically savvy and willing to work for low pay.

The majority of the Palestinian-Arab engineers who were interviewed mentioned this period, the second half of the 1990s, as a turning point for their career aspirations. While an enormous segment of the Israeli high-tech sector is closely allied with the Israeli military and has therefore been all but blocked to Palestinian-Arab engineers for many decades, the foreign multinational companies opened their doors to all talented engineers. Some of the Palestinian-Arab interviewees thought that this policy arose from purely economic reasons, while others also attributed some weight to the diversity management ideology of those companies and to the emotional detachment of their top managers from the Jewish–Palestinian cleavage in Israeli society. One Palestinian-Arab HR manager emphasized the more rational and economic reasons for the current increase in the number of Palestinian-Arab engineers working for multinational firms in Israel. She also offered a potent critique of the diversity management ideology identified in Israel with multinational high-tech firms:

> PALESTINIAN-ARAB HR MANAGER: I believe that the entrance of the multinational firms into Israel increased the competition over the small pool of job candidates.
>
> INTERVIEWER: I see.
>
> HR MANAGER: And then this pool kept getting smaller and smaller, and companies that can't compete for the elite of the technical workforce, people that previously worked in the Israeli intelligence, so they apparently need, and I emphasize "apparently," to identify and build their next pool [of candidates]. And this pool is composed of [technical workers from] India or Arab Israelis.
>
> INTERVIEWER: So what you're saying is that economic reasons underpin all of this? A matter of supply and demand?
>
> HR MANAGER: Yes.
>
> INTERVIEWER: And you don't think that the multinational firms came into Israel with their ideology and said, "We simply recruit without any discrimination," and then Arab engineers were drawn to these companies?

HR MANAGER: Listen, I personally heard: "Diversity, diversity, diversity," but in reality what did all the diversity talk really do? All the HR spoke about diversity and . . . I asked them what do you do to translate this term into something real? "Yes," they say, "we interview Arab job candidates but they don't get the job." But, did you build a pool of [Arab] candidates? Did you develop specialized tools of how to interview an Arab candidate? Did you interview in their language [Arabic]? Did you post the job opening in places that Arab candidates search in? Did you specify that the job is open to candidates who speak a different language [than Hebrew]?

This HR manager had launched her career in a high-tech firm in the Galilee, which had been established by three Jewish entrepreneurs with the explicit goal of recruiting talented Palestinian-Arab engineers to help them integrate into the Israeli high-tech sector. She was later recruited by a very large Israeli multinational company in order to assist it in recruiting more Palestinian-Arab engineers. In this excerpt she emphasized the gap between the diversity management ideology of Israeli HR managers and the actual practices employed to recruit talented Palestinian-Arab engineers, expressing her frustration in a series of rhetorical questions about the actual recruitment policies applied by Jewish HR managers. She argued that HR managers in high-tech fail to adapt the candidate search and job interviews to the ethnonational identity of the recruits. One of her questions alluded to the fact that English, rather than Hebrew, is widely used in Israeli high-tech companies as a common language, which might work in favor of those Palestinian-Arab candidates who have a better command of English than Hebrew. Indeed, in the following examples the Palestinian-Arab engineers described how they perceived their career opportunities in the two multinational companies studied, and what strategies they devised to deal with the obstacles they encountered when trying to move into the higher managerial echelons.

Broadly stated, the Palestinian-Arab interviewees felt that the relative lack of Arab managers in their high-tech firms was the result of both extrinsic and intrinsic factors, as clearly expressed by a veteran Palestinian-Arab engineer who offered a nuanced account of what she perceived as the Arab engineers' apprehension about becoming team managers, and tried to explain why she herself had chosen not to pursue a managerial career:

PALESTINIAN-ARAB ENGINEER: It [choosing technical promotion] is also a matter of choice, but it involved fear, I think.
INTERVIEWER: Yes, I agree, it's also fear, but how do you deal with it? [pause]

ENGINEER: Listen, leaving aside ethnic origin and all that, everyone has this fear of being in charge of oneself and one's work, and here, you're put in charge of a team!

INTERVIEWER: Right, right.

ENGINEER: And dealing with [pause].

INTERVIEWER: People's problems and personal matters?

ENGINEER: Personal and also professional problems and [pause] there is fear, or concern.

INTERVIEWER: I see.

ENGINEER: Maybe in our ethnic group it's more strongly felt, and because of that you don't see them [in managerial positions].

INTERVIEWER: So they are less inclined to hold managerial positions?

ENGINEER: Yes, and I think that [pause] I don't see anyone pushing them there.

This engineer drew a distinction between two forces that might hamper the career trajectories of Palestinian-Arab engineers. The first force accords with what the literature dubs push factors (Kirkwood 2009), composed of an individual's motivation and desire to become a manager. According to this and other accounts of the intrinsic elements inhibiting promotion, Palestinian-Arab engineers experience a deeper fear of holding managerial positions than their Jewish team members. Being a minority group and with relatively little experience in managerial work, and specifically in managing Jewish workers, some Palestinian engineers felt that they lacked the necessary skills for a team manager position. But the speaker also referred to pull factors (Schjoedt and Shaver 2007), namely, the organizational encouragement of Palestinian-Arab engineers to move into management. She suggested that it was the lack of sufficient pull and push factors that explained the meager number of Palestinian-Arab engineers in management and their preference for technical rather than managerial promotion. The following discussion of Palestinian-Arab engineers' career expectations considers both the extrinsic and intrinsic barriers that they perceive as inhibiting their promotion into managerial positions.

Perceived Extrinsic Barriers to the Promotion of Palestinian-Arab Engineers

The Palestinian-Arab engineers as well as their Jewish co-workers expressed a high degree of trust in top management's sincere intention to implement the declared diversity management policy, according to which engineers should be evaluated by their skill and effort at work, and not by their ethnonational or

religious affiliation. The interviewees regarded the two multinational companies studied, one Israeli and the other American, as particularly good employers within the Israeli high-tech sector in respect to their diversity management
policy. Indeed, other Palestinian-Arab engineers clearly categorized companies
in the Israeli high-tech industry according to their perceived equal treatment of
all engineers, regardless of their ethnonational background. This is yet another
indication of the major role they ascribe to their ethnonational identity in shaping their career expectations. In the case of the American multinational, all HR
policies were imported and implemented worldwide, with local adjustments to
Israeli labor laws. The local HR managers were obliged to adhere to the global
policies of merit-based promotion. Similarly, the Israeli multinational company
was one of the first to adopt diversity management policies in the Israeli high-
tech sector. Since these companies are part of the private sector, these policies are
not imposed externally by the Israeli government, unlike in the public hospital,
where as we shall see below, both the career ladders and promotion procedures
are much more formal and transparent, a fact that contributes to the administrative and legal protection of the Palestinian-Arab members of the medical staff.

Some of the Palestinian-Arab engineers cited the published tenders for each
opening within the companies as a sign of the merit-based promotion policies.
Others highlighted the formal procedure of applying to a tender, and the public
presentation of guidelines and rules regarding the equal treatment of women and
minority group members in making promotion decisions. At the research site
of the American multinational the electronic billboards displayed an invitation
(written in Hebrew and English but not in Arabic) to an internal meeting of a
women-engineer support group. In one of the interviews one of the Palestinian-
Arab engineers told us about a company-based initiative to create an internal
support group for Palestinian-Arab engineers as a way of retaining these employees and devising ways to increase the numbers of recruits. This was seen by the
speaker as another sign of top management commitment to the recruitment and
equal treatment of Palestinian-Arab engineers.

But even with the trust in top management intentions, the interviewees
could not ignore the fact that very few Palestinian-Arab engineers were actually promoted into team manager positions. Unlike the production workers,
however, who also cited the low number of Palestinian Arabs in the "offices,"
the Palestinian-Arab engineers did not attribute this fact to top management
policy or practice. Instead, they mentioned an institutional distrust in the professionalism of Palestinian-Arab engineers, the short period of time that had
elapsed since Palestinian-Arab engineers entered the Israeli high-tech sector,
and primarily the difficulty of passing the initial screening of candidates by
the predominantly Jewish team managers, whose support was crucial for any

career move. The Palestinian-Arab engineers were skeptical about the willingness of these team managers to recommend them for managerial positions. Team managers were also required to perform periodic evaluations of their team members, and their reports were filed and stored, to be consulted when making future promotion decisions. A few of the Palestinian-Arab interviewees cited instances when Jewish team managers had actively thwarted their promotion into the managerial ranks. Yet, only a few interviewees accused the team managers of being racist or even consciously prejudiced. Instead, the majority of them felt that the Jewish team managers were simply more inclined to recommend the promotion of Jewish candidates with a similar background to theirs, which included military service in one of the elite intelligence units and studies in leading universities and technological institutes. This tendency of managers to promote people similar to themselves is well documented in studies of gender-based discrimination in the United States and Europe (for an excellent discussion, see Ibarra 1992).

An engineer who had worked for ten years in the Israeli high-tech industry spoke about her desire to advance into managerial positions and her belief that she was being blocked as a member of two underprivileged minority groups in the high-tech world: women and Palestinian-Arab engineers. She described how she had had to earn what she dubbed "fair treatment" by her teammates, rather than receiving it as a matter of course:

> PALESTINIAN-ARAB ENGINEER: One reason for the fair treatment I receive in my team, I'm not talking about top management and things like that, [but] among the people [team members], is because they know that I'm strong. I'm very professional [pause] . . .
>
> INTERVIEWER: They? [pause]
>
> ENGINEER: Yes, I'd have liked to have worked less hard to earn their respect. But I did receive it, yes?
>
> INTERVIEWER: Yes.
>
> ENGINEER: But I worked hard to receive it!
>
> INTERVIEWER: You feel that? [pause]
>
> ENGINEER: It didn't come naturally [pause].
>
> INTERVIEWER: As a minority you need to invest more?
>
> ENGINEER: Yes, more, and not only socially, also professionally. But I need to invest more [pause] to prove myself to them [as a strong person].
>
> INTERVIEWER: Socially?
>
> ENGINEER: Socially, personality wise, to be strong, I'm not a mosquito that you can simply tread on and keep on walking.

The metaphor of the mosquito vividly captured the speaker's sense of vulnerability as a member of the two minority groups within the high-tech sector, and she emphasized her need to project not only professionalism but also personal strength in order to gain the respect of her other team members.

A Palestinian-Arab engineer who had worked for one year in the American multinational firm, but for many years in the Israeli high-tech sector, expressed high satisfaction with the promotion policy of his current employer when compared with his previous employers. When asked if he felt that he was obliged to be better than his Jewish counterparts in order to be promoted, he replied: "It's possible that the answer is yes, like, we [Palestinian-Arab engineers] once again, why do I say yes [pause] because the feeling is that we need to work harder in order to [pause] you've got to be really exceptional in order to be promoted." A clear sense of ambivalence can be detected in this account. Alongside his appreciation for the generally fair promotion process, he still felt that Palestinian-Arab engineers needed to be much better than their Jewish counterparts in order to be considered by their team managers for promotion.

Thus, although the rapidly increasing number of multinational companies operating in Israel, particularly in R&D labs, provided new employment opportunities for the most talented Palestinian-Arab engineers who had previously been blocked from entering vast segments of the Israeli high-tech sector, some Palestinian-Arab engineers still felt discriminated against when it came to promotion into managerial positions. An experienced engineer who had been working for the American multinational for over ten years offered an original explanation for the fact that very few Palestinian-Arab engineers could be found in the managerial echelons:

> PALESTINIAN-ARAB ENGINEER: The percentage is [pause] close to zero, really marginal.
>
> INTERVIEWER: There aren't many Arab managers?
>
> ENGINEER: Yes. Now this [discrimination] isn't the only reason. Many Arab [engineers] have left the country. They've relocated [inside the multinational] in order to advance into management. And they [those who left Israel] explicitly told me: Here [in Israel] we weren't able to advance our career since we are constantly blocked. They wouldn't let us advance, to reach positions of authority, I mean managerial positions. And people who were relocated [outside of Israel] they [pause] ...
>
> INTERVIEWER: Is it really easier for them? Let's say that you work for [the name of the current employer] and you say "relocation," so this means I simply move within the company to a different country?

> ENGINEER: Yes, that's the path they took. I mean they moved abroad within the same company, and [pause] while abroad moved to other companies.

According to this account, some talented high-tech engineers devised a strategy for overcoming the ethnonational barriers that impeded their managerial career by relocating to a different country, where, they believed, their chances of promotion would improve. The speaker implied that Jewish managers, or maybe the broader impact of the Israeli–Palestinian conflict, were the factors that obstructed their chances for promotion in Israel. For the Palestinian-Arab engineers who decide to leave Israel, working for a multinational company serves as a stepping-stone for managerial careers abroad, opening the door into the global high-tech sector and dramatically expanding their range of options. As this speaker explained, some of the relocating Arab engineers subsequently moved on to other companies in the receiving country. It can be assumed that this strategy is also partly infused by a desire to emigrate from Israel, and to leave the conflict at least partly behind.

Another Palestinian-Arab engineer who had only recently started to work in the American multinational but with a previous tenure of fifteen years in the Israeli high-tech sector, elaborated on the practice of leaving Israel in order to improve the chances for a managerial career:

> I see that, at least in Israel, I'm discriminated against in terms of [career] opportunities. But when I search, and look at the whole world, I see that I'm not at all discriminated against there, and I've got a lot of opportunities in this world. Even in the Muslim world, you can go to Turkey, a place that has been developing very quickly today in the world.

In this case he suggested the possibility of combining a religious-cultural desire to live in a Muslim country with his ambition to improve his professional status.

These two examples exemplify how Palestinian-Arab engineers who experienced limited career opportunities based on what they perceived as discrimination sometimes chose to use their foreign multinational company as a platform for emigration by asking for relocation, on the assumption that team managers in countries other than Israel were likely to be less prejudiced against them. What is clear is that the massive entrance of multinational companies into Israel broadened the horizons of Palestinian-Arab engineers and strengthened their self-confidence and belief that new options existed for them within the global high-tech sector. Nonetheless, while the Palestinian-Arab interviewees felt that middle managers represented an extrinsic factor inhibiting their career chances, most of them referred also to intrinsic elements that hampered their pursuit of a managerial career.

Perceived Intrinsic Barriers to the Promotion of Palestinian-Arab Engineers

A middle-aged Palestinian-Arab engineer in the Israeli multinational company, with extensive experience in the Israeli high-tech sector, offered a psychological explanation, or what he called the "mental problems" that made Palestinian-Arab engineers feel that they had to work much harder than their Jewish colleagues in order to prove their worth:

> It might be that we have our "subconscious" [said in English] that tells us that in order to prove myself I need to be better [than the Jewish engineer]. So you'll work much harder than the others, so most of my [Palestinian-Arab] friends, you see that they work much longer hours and you see that they do much more work. If someone does ten "tasks" [said in English] a day, then you will do forty-five. This tendency might be because you're a foreigner in your workplace or because you're new, or because all the other workers come from one environment and I come from a different one, and I need to prove myself.

His choice of the word *foreigner* is particularly striking, since it conveys his sense of the enormous social distance that lies between his Palestinian-Arab colleagues and their predominantly Jewish environment, even in companies that adhere to diversity management policies.

A few other Palestinian-Arab engineers cited their own insecurity when trying to explain the small number of Palestinian-Arab engineers in managerial positions. They referred to what one of them called an "inferiority complex" vis-à-vis their Jewish co-workers, which made them apprehensive about managing a team composed mainly of Jews. Some of the interviewees consequently refrained from competing for managerial job openings. One of them, who had previously worked for another high-tech company before being recruited to the American multinational a few years prior to the interview, commented on this lack of self-confidence on the part of the Palestinian-Arab employees, which led them to downplay their managerial skills. When asked where she saw herself in five years' time, she answered in the plural, and asserted that Palestinian-Arab engineers tended to set low targets for themselves and for their periodic evaluations, which reduced their chances for a managerial career:

> The mentality as well as personality [of the Palestinian-Arab engineer] are less suited [compared to their Jewish co-workers] for positions with greater power or managerial authority. So we are less likely to step forward and say outright: "I want to manage!" So, you have what is called a "Review" [said in English] each year, when you come and present everything you've done in the previous year, and your manager evaluates

everything you've done. So you tend to set a low target. I mean, this is something that's typical of most Arab [engineers].

Another Palestinian-Arab engineer in the American multinational also invoked personality traits and culture in order to explain why Palestinian Arabs were less likely to be promoted:

> This is true in many areas, in promotion decisions and in salary increases, in all of that. I mean if you don't demand, but instead simply leave it to your manager to decide, so, let's say the manager has a cake that he [*sic*] wishes to divide among the team members, so, he plays with it, and when someone demands [more] he considers that. And we [Palestinian-Arab engineers] are less likely to demand.

According to this account, Palestinian-Arab engineers tended to respect the authority and judgment of their team manager and to refrain from initiating demands for promotion or salary increases. He also recognized that team managers usually tended to be influenced by such demands when making their allocation decisions. In this instance, he did not accuse the team managers of being prejudiced or racist, but rather viewed them as reacting to the pressure of the mostly Jewish team members who wished to be promoted.

A senior Palestinian-Arab engineer who was promoted on the technical career ladder and now consults with a few development teams in his areas of expertise attributed his apprehensions about holding managerial positions to the need to perform periodic evaluations of team members:

> People with whom I discuss careers, and even personal discussions, for me anyhow, it was more challenging to start talking to Jews than to Arabs. When I've got to ask him [*sic*, referring to a hypothetical Jewish team member] about family, about what he's doing, about his plans for the future, do you want to develop yourself etc., of course, talking about such issues with Arabs is more natural for me since, once again, I'm not a person that finds it easy to relate [to people].

Later in the interview, he drew a link between these apprehensions and his decision to choose the technical rather than the managerial promotion ladder:

> This might be one of the things, I'll say it without thinking, what helps me to exercise my authority is that from a technological perspective, I have technical authority. . . . And my technical authority is acknowledged and I'm leading [my area of expertise]. This might be part of the reason I chose the technical ladder.

These interview excerpts reveal various concerns that some Palestinian-Arab engineers had with regard to managing Jewish team members. When it came to technical expertise, this speaker felt confident about his ability to consult other engineers, whether Jews or Palestinian Arabs, but was deterred by the prospect of having to conduct periodic evaluations of Jewish team members, which was one of the managerial responsibilities of team heads. It remained unclear whether this anxiety arose from a lack of social acquaintance with Jewish co-workers, their distinct cultural background and forms of communication, or the fear of exercising formal authority over Jewish subordinates. However, the above excerpt indeed suggests that the latter consideration certainly played a role in some Palestinian-Arab engineers' choice of the technical rather than the managerial track to promotion.

Freidson (1970, 1984) draws an important distinction in the sociology of work practice between administrative and occupational careers. The former is associated with a move up the organizational ladder, the desire for power and the acquisition of formal administrative authority over subordinates. An occupational career, by contrast, is conceived as a move from the periphery of a given occupational community toward the center. Rather than formal authority vested in a higher administrative position, it is the principle of imputed expertise— the ascription of various levels of expertise by community members to other members—that operates as the source of occupational authority. The notion of imputed expertise is based on social interactions among members of an occupational community and allows members to identify experts and to draw boundaries between center and periphery. Put in these terms, it can therefore be said that Palestinian-Arab engineers often chose an occupational career, with its corresponding form of technical authority, rather than an administrative career, with its formal authority over other team members.

The distinction between managerial and technical promotion has a long history in the high-tech sector. The relatively small number of managerial positions in high-tech companies, combined with the companies' desire to retain talented engineers who are in high demand, has given rise to two parallel career ladders. The managerial ladder leads to the position of team manager, then to that of area manager, who is administratively in charge of a few teams operating in the same specialty area, and finally to top management, as heads of engineering divisions. All the career moves in the managerial ladder entail increased formal authority over other employees, a higher salary, and other benefit packages. By contrast, a move up the technical ladder means greater professional authority. Technical experts become consultants to various development teams, as part of matrix management, and their advice is sought by team managers or team members.

The interviews show that Palestinian-Arab engineers developed a unique strategy for coping with their perceived difficulties, both intrinsic and extrinsic, in being promoted into managerial positions. Five of the six Palestinian-Arab interviewees who had been promoted since they had started work in the two multinationals had chosen the technical rather than the managerial ladder. As a result, they became recognized technical experts in their field rather than team managers, leaving key managerial positions in the hands of their Jewish colleagues.

Perceived Career Opportunities in the Israeli Health Sector

Two structural factors work in favor of the promotion opportunities of Palestinian-Arab physicians when compared with the production and high-tech sectors. First, the profession of medicine has clear career trajectories and formal milestones that each and every medical student must pass before becoming a senior physician. These include two major exams during the six-year internships, one after three years and the other at graduation. Further promotion is contingent on one or two years of residency in hospitals outside of Israel, in countries such as the United States, the United Kingdom, and Australia. Second, the Israeli health sector is predominantly public, and organizational career ladders are structured and transparent when compared with career ladders in the private sector. A review of studies comparing pay and promotion structure in the private and the public sector led Kraus and Yonay (2018, 34) to conclude: "Racism, prejudice and intergroup tension do not stop at the threshold of the public sector, but public accountability, political pressures by minorities, and greater emphasis on formal procedures have turned the public sector, especially in democratic countries, more egalitarian in employing and promoting minority workers." These findings are partly true for the Israeli labor market, but many barriers and obstacles still stand in the way of Palestinian-Arab nurses and physicians, wishing to fulfill their career aspirations (Yonay and Kraus 2001).

Nursing is considered a semiprofession, which requires an academic degree and a high level of specialization. Yet, unlike the profession of medicine, nurses have very few promotion opportunities, since their occupational hierarchy is limited and includes, in addition to the basic role of ward nurse with various areas of expertise, the position of deputy head nurse and head nurse. A handful of nurses move up the administrative ladder in the hospital and assume positions in the chief administration of the whole nursing workforce, as part of top management. Most nurses try to specialize within their areas of expertise and to gain occupational authority rather than the formal authority that accompanies managerial roles.

The interviews revealed that Palestinian-Arab nurses were more likely than physicians to describe prejudice and to bemoan the ways in which their ethnonational background impaired their promotion into managerial positions. When asked about her career opportunities in the public hospital, a veteran Palestinian-Arab nurse replied:

> NURSE: They [management] won't let you [advance your career]. I, for example, I always have this thought that Arab [nurses] are given less [pause].
>
> INTERVIEWER: Yes?
>
> NURSE: Important jobs, I mean.
>
> INTERVIEWER: Managerial?
>
> NURSE: Let's do a survey. If you conduct a survey in [names two other hospital wards], well, who else is Arab? Almost no one. Deputy [head nurse] you have one Arab nurse. But head nurse? Take a tour of the wards. I think that we [Palestinian-Arab nurses] are blocked, they [management] won't promote us.

This nurse referred to what can be called statistical discrimination, by counting the small number of Palestinian-Arab nurses in managerial positions, which she translated into a sense of frustration, a belief that there was little hope for them to assume managerial roles.

Some of the Palestinian-Arab physicians also believed that Palestinian-Arab nurses were being discriminated against. When asked about instances when ethnic background impacted promotion opportunities, a senior Palestinian-Arab physician working in the public hospital recounted a case involving a Palestinian-Arab male nurse:

> PHYSICIAN: Once they had one [a Palestinian-Arab male nurse] who wanted, they had a tender in one of the wards for a head nurse, and there was an Arab candidate who had better credentials [than the other candidates], and a better CV.
>
> INTERVIEWER: Yes?
>
> PHYSICIAN: And he didn't get the job.
>
> INTERVIEWER: And did he? [pause] ...
>
> PHYSICIAN: He sued [the hospital] and, if I remember correctly, they canceled the tender and had a new one.
>
> INTERVIEWER: Really?

PHYSICIAN: But he [the Arab nurse] was fed up with all of it and went somewhere else.

A few important issues emerge from this interview excerpt. First, the senior physician was not directly involved in the screening of candidates for the position of head nurse but learned about this story through hospital gossip. He claimed that the Palestinian-Arab nurse was not given the position of head nurse, despite his better credentials, because of his ethnonational identity. It is significant that the Palestinian-Arab male nurse did not remain silent in face of what he perceived as outright prejudice, and instead sued the hospital. The hiring process in public hospitals requires the publication of formal tenders, which made it easier to sue on account of discrimination. This account also demonstrated the greater protection enjoyed by women and minorities in the public sector, where job applications and promotions are regulated by tenders and formal guidelines that guarantee due process. In this case, the legal process eventually yielded a positive outcome for the plaintiff, but by that time he had already decided to leave the hospital. The relative protection that the public sector affords minorities and women is particularly striking when compared with the case of the production workers in the private sector, who are at the mercy of their employers, with no formal career ladders and no notion of due process other than the very limited rights regarding promotion stipulated by Israeli labor laws.

The head nurse of each hospital ward decides on new hires, sometimes consulting her deputy. The head nurse also recommends to the hospital's HR department which nurses should be dismissed from their jobs. In the following example a veteran Palestinian-Arab nurse reported an incident in which her deputy head nurse in the public hospital, whom she dubbed "a bit of a racist," had caused two Palestinian-Arab male nurses to be fired, according to this account, simply out of prejudice:

PALESTINIAN-ARAB NURSE: About three or four years ago we had two Arab brothers who were nurses, and in the end they fired them.

INTERVIEWER: Why?

NURSE: They [the head nurse and her deputy] made their life miserable, since the deputy head nurse didn't want them.

INTERVIEWER: She didn't want them?

NURSE: She didn't want them because they were Arab, that is what we felt, there was this tension, really.

INTERVIEWER: A certain tension?

NURSE: She [the deputy head nurse] had influence over the head nurse, who recently left, and now she [the deputy head nurse] is in charge.

Later in the interview she added that she had known the deputy head nurse for many years and had always felt that she was prejudiced against Palestinian-Arab nurses. She lamented the fact that this person had now assumed the role of head nurse.

While the Palestinian-Arab nurses agreed that some level of prejudice against them existed in the hospital, the Jewish nurses were divided on this issue. Thus, a Jewish deputy head nurse denied any prejudice toward Palestinian-Arab job candidates, basing her argument on economic factors of supply and demand: the short supply of nurses in the Israeli labor market, and the relatively large number of Palestinian-Arab nurses among the nursing students:

> DEPUTY HEAD NURSE: I don't think that it [ethnic origin] matters, since, once again, in our occupation [nursing] there are many Arabs and Russians, let's say. They go to study nursing [laughs].
> INTERVIEWER: So they have to hire them?
> NURSE: Yes.

One can argue that she implicitly admitted that prejudice against Palestinian-Arab nurses might exist but that the shortage of nurses in the Israeli health sector and the large numbers of Palestinian-Arab (and Russian) candidates made such prejudice impractical.

A Jewish nurse, who had worked for more than twenty years in the profession, in various capacities, most of them in her current place of employment in the public hospital, albeit in three different wards, also denied the possibility that ethnically grounded prejudice influenced decisions regarding promotions of medical staff members:

> INTERVIEWER: Do you think that an Arab nurse has to work harder than a Jewish nurse in order to be promoted?
> JEWISH NURSE: No, you've simply got to be a decent human being, perform your work, show that you're a good nurse, or a good physician, and that's it, nothing else.
> INTERVIEWER: And what about being accepted for a job here?
> NURSE: It's the same thing. In my opinion there's no problem.
> INTERVIEWER: No problem?
> NURSE: No problem. My boss, if you go and tell her, "I have a new candidate nurse," she won't ask you for her ethnic background. Maybe she'll ask you what [nursing] school she graduated from, and if she has experience.
> INTERVIEWER: So, your boss you say [pause]

> NURSE [INTERRUPTS]: All of them, you see? It works also all the way up
> the ladder, I mean even in [names a different ward] there's an [Arab
> physician] who is the head of ward, there are many Arab physicians
> [serving as heads of wards] and this is good, this is how the hospi-
> tal should be managed, without consideration of a person's ethnic
> background.

This Jewish nurse, who worked in a different ward than the Palestinian-Arab
nurse quoted above, depicted a very different picture with regard to ethnic prejudice. According to this account, her head nurse was blind to ethnic origin and
was concerned only with formal credentials. Nonetheless, in order to support her
claim about the equal treatment of all hospital workers she cited the promotion
of a Palestinian-Arab physician to head of ward, rather than the promotion of
nurses, thereby possibly reflecting the greater equality enjoyed by the physicians
in the hospital.

The case of the private Palestinian-Arab hospital allows us to ask what happens when Jewish nurses are in the minority and how they perceive their career
opportunities within a Palestinian-Arab institution. When asked if there were
any differences between the treatment of Jewish and Palestinian-Arab nurses in
her previous and current employment, the Palestinian-Arab head nurse of the
maternity ward responded:

> Definitely not, at least as far as I'm concerned. My promotion at work
> and the degree to which I feel confident in myself as a nurse and a mid-
> wife has nothing to do with being Jewish or Arab. But it's possible that in
> a different workplace I wouldn't have reached a position like I reached
> here, for example, if I'd been working in a Jewish place. In hospital X
> [names the large public hospital that is also part of this study] it's clear
> that there I wouldn't have reached the position of head nurse at my
> young age. Here I have greater promotion opportunities since this hos-
> pital is Arab, Christian, and all the nuns, you know, I mean to say that
> I've got good promotion opportunities here.

There is, however, an internal contradiction in her portrayal of the situation in
the hospital. On the one hand, she denied that there was any prejudice in the
private hospital but, on the other hand, she hinted that her Christian background
had assisted her in being promoted to head nurse, and also claimed that she
would not have gained this position in the public hospital, at least not so quickly.
Indeed, the Jewish nurses and midwives in the private Palestinian-Arab hospital felt that there was a very real glass ceiling preventing them from reaching
managerial positions. In this sense they experienced difficulties similar to those

experienced by the Palestinian-Arab nurses in the public hospital. Yet the two cases are not really symmetrical. One expects a public hospital to implement much stricter formal procedures to ensure due process and equality in promotion than a private hospital run by nuns. While nurses who were members of ethnonational minorities expressed reservations about their career prospects, Palestinian-Arab physicians were much more optimistic about their chances of advancing into managerial positions. A comparison between the career perceptions and expectations of nurses and physicians can benefit from considering another concept from the sociology of work practice: the strength of professional and semiprofessional communities.

Physicians' Perceptions of Ethnonational Affiliation and Career Trajectories

Palestinian-Arab physicians expressed the highest degree of satisfaction with their career opportunities. As noted above, working in a public hospital granted the physicians a high degree of protection against prejudice and racism, since all tenders were public and promotion procedures were subject to due-process principles that are applied to public sector workers (Kraus and Yonay 2018). Moreover, medicine is a well-established profession, with clear occupational career ladders, based mainly on long-term training and scholastic achievement, and is a field that has a strong professional body with influence in the political sphere. Probably as a result of these important factors, Palestinian-Arab physicians cited the relatively large number of Palestinian-Arab physicians in the public hospital who did hold managerial positions such as head and deputy head of department. This situation stands in sharp contrast not only to the experience of the production workers but also to that of the Palestinian-Arab high-tech engineers, who, while believing that top management was committed to diversity management principles, needed to grapple with the low number of Palestinian-Arab engineers among management. In the following excerpt a senior Palestinian-Arab physician described his generally positive view of the promotion of Palestinian Arabs into management in the public hospital:

> PALESTINIAN-ARAB PHYSICIAN: I think that specifically in X hospital [the public hospital] the two populations [Palestinian Arabs and Jews] are together, so they understand one another better.
> INTERVIEWER: Yes?
> PHYSICIAN: I think that the interaction itself already eliminates much of the [pause]. The more interactions [between Palestinian-Arab and

Jewish physicians], coupled with a higher percentage of Palestinian-Arab physicians, and Palestinian-Arab members of the medical staff more generally, the more acceptance [of Palestinian-Arab nurses and physicians] you find, and also better treatment.

INTERVIEWER: So does this mean that management needs to do something specific?

PHYSICIAN: Maybe, let's say this, when they increase the percentage [of Palestinian-Arab physicians] . . . but, really, the percentage is high as it is . . . . The percentage of Arabs here is high, and we also have heads of department.

INTERVIEWER: Are there many [Arab] managers?

PHYSICIAN: Yes.

It is clear from this interview excerpt that the relatively large number of Palestinian-Arab physicians in the public hospital, and, more important, the existence of Palestinian-Arab heads of departments, made other Arab members of the medical staff more confident about their own career chances. Rather than direct criticism at the hospital management, a few young Palestinian-Arab physicians mentioned other factors, related to their particular labor market, that worked against them in developing their careers, particularly at the important stage of finding a residency abroad. After finishing the long internship and passing the final exams, the young physicians are expected to receive what they call "fellowships" that can pay for their residency period in other hospitals, predominantly outside of Israel. A fellowship includes funding for this period, a hosting hospital, and a physician in the hosting hospital who agrees to train the young physicians in his/her area of expertise. A young Palestinian-Arab physician described her own experience on completing her six years of internship at the public hospital as follows:

INTERVIEWER: Do you feel that you've got to be better than Jewish physicians in order to be promoted?

PHYSICIAN: Yes.

INTERVIEWER: Yes, you feel like that?

PHYSICIAN: Yes . . . as a minority you . . . you feel that you need to be super, super, super for promotion. Let's say now, when I was looking for a residency [pause].

INTERVIEWER: Yes?

PHYSICIAN: I'll give you an example: so there are places that they [more senior physicians in her ward, with whom she consulted] told me that I wouldn't be accepted to. That they have connections with these

places, and they told me that I can't send [my application] because
they only want Jews there.

INTERVIEWER: You mean that there are hospitals in New York City that
give priority to Jews?

PHYSICIAN: Yes.

INTERVIEWER: And their money is also from American Jews and the
host is Jewish?

PHYSICIAN: Not necessarily. I'm talking about someone who acts as a
mentor [implying it's a Jew], not the one who pays the money.

INTERVIEWER: Well [pause] this is interesting, I wonder if it's legal at all,
since the United States is a country that [pause].

PHYSICIAN: No, it's not legal, but he won't tell you well, I'm not [accept-
ing you since you are a Palestinian Arab].

INTERVIEWER: I understand, he'll take a look and say no [pause].

PHYSICIAN: I don't want you based on your CV.

This young physician pointed to what she saw as camouflaged informal discrimination that occurred outside of her ward or hospital, and even outside of Israel.
According to this account, some Jewish host physicians in New York prefer to
award the fellowship to a Jewish physician rather than a Palestinian Arab. It is
interesting that she learned about this informal discrimination from the senior
physicians in her wards who wanted to help her find a fellowship. Moreover, she
seemed to accept this situation as natural. Another Palestinian-Arab physician
also mentioned that there were Jewish organizations in the United States and
Canada that designate funds to helping Jewish physicians finance their internship. It seems that other sources of funding, dedicated to the needs of Palestinian-
Arab physicians, are rare, which makes the task of securing a residency harder
for them.

Ethnonational Dimensions of Careers in a War-Torn Country

Despite the existence of perceived discrimination, mainly by nurses and to a
lesser extent by physicians, the relatively large numbers of Palestinian-Arab physicians and nurses in the Israel health sector, and the managerial roles some of
them occupy, are striking. Palestinian-Arab physicians, for example, constitute
about 13 percent of Israeli physicians. This high percentage relative to the production and high-tech sectors reflects the fact that the medical sector is a predominantly public sector, whose formal promotion procedures, which are open

to judicial scrutiny, make it more accessible to minority group members than the private sector. It is also important to bear in mind that the Israeli medical sector has been open to Palestinian Arabs for much longer than the high-tech sector. In addition, medicine offers an attractive path into a respected profession that may not be available to Palestinian-Arab employees in other sectors of the Israeli economy. Finally, unlike the engineers, Palestinian-Arab physicians do not shy away from management positions that give them authority over Jews. The reason for that requires additional empirical investigation. I can only speculate that this may be due to the sense of shared belonging to the profession of medicine. A well-established profession such as medicine provides all physicians with a strong occupational identity that can partly blur interethnic divisions and provide the most talented Palestinian-Arab physicians with a common normative basis and confidence in their ability to manage their Jewish colleagues. The production workers seem to suffer the most from a lack of career prospects, which could be attributed to the fact that they are employed in the private sector and lack an organized occupational community that could improve their chances of promotion.

LANGUAGE USE AS A SYMBOLIC ARENA FOR ETHNONATIONAL DISPLAY

Ethnonational tension caused by language use is well illustrated, in all its complexity, by the following incident, which was related by a Palestinian-Arab nurse in the retirement home. A Jewish nurse, whose family had originally immigrated to Israel from Morocco in the 1950s, complained to management that the Palestinian-Arab nurse had spoken Arabic with a fellow Palestinian-Arab nurse during her work shift and in the presence of patients' families:

> So she [the Jewish co-worker] went and complained about me and said, "Fadwa speaks Arabic all the time in front of the families." And the supervisor called us to a meeting and she [the complainant] told the supervisor, "We have an Arab mafia here because they talk only in Arabic, and it's terrible because no one understands." But she could speak Arabic herself! And she understands everything! But it upsets her, it upsets her terribly to hear Arabic.

The Jewish nurse was probably basing her complaint on management's instruction to speak Hebrew at work, in particular in the presence of patients and their families. The mafia metaphor employed by the Jewish nurse is clearly exclusionary and derogatory, and can also be interpreted as a form of interethnic fear leading to aggressive behavior. In the eyes of the Palestinian-Arab nurse, the fact that the Jewish nurse could understand Arabic and that her parents had immigrated to Israel from an Arab country made her complaint blatantly political, since it was not motivated by a desire to communicate effectively or by a feeling of being left out of the conversation, but rather appeared to negate and undermine the Arabic language and Palestinian-Arab identity and culture in general. This incident therefore suggests that the underlying reason for the complaint, according to the Palestinian-Arab nurse, was not rational or occupational in nature, but was underpinned by the Jewish–Palestinian divide that plagues Israeli society. In this context, language is more than a means of communication. It provides an occasion for the performance of ethnonational identity and the public rejection of this identity by members of other ethnic groups. In theoretical terms, the speaker protested against the Jewish nurse's use of language to delineate ethnonational boundaries (see Amara 2018), rather than blur them. To understand how and why language becomes a symbolic stage for ethnonational displays and for the constitution of social boundaries and social distance among ethnonational groups, it is necessary to consider the more general meaning of language use, as explained in the scholarship on this issue.

Language is the carrier of cultural knowledge and knowhow, and proficiency grants access to the culture and history of a specific ethnonational group. Addressing language within a broader sociocultural framework, Funkenstein (1989, 4) writes: "No memory, not even the most intimate and personal, can be disconnected from society, from the language and the symbolic system molded by the society over many generations." The author highlights the entwining of language, society, and culture, and views them as part of a system that underpin personal and collective memory and identity. The role of language in constituting national identity is examined by Simpson (2007), who asserts that ethnonational boundaries are sometimes created and supported by language use. In the most comprehensive macrolevel exploration of the role played by language in the context of the Jewish–Palestinian conflict, Amara (2018, 17–18) asserts: "No extraneous element can belong to a given ethnic or national space without meeting certain identifying conditions, among which language is one of the most basic because it constitutes an existential expression, possessing meanings of identity and belonging."

Ethnonational identity is communicated through language use in both oral and written forms from one generation of ethnonational groups to the next. The collective memory is predicated on the use of the same language by all group members, and the production and reproduction of distinct systems of meaning and categories, narratives, and cosmologies that are achieved through oral and written communication (see Kidron and Kirmayer [2019] for the case of language and trauma-related distress in Cambodia). According to Tabouret-Keller (2017), the use of language for communication is always an act of the performance of identity. Thus, ethnonational groups often distinguish themselves from other ethnonational groups by speaking a distinct language in the public sphere. Indeed, public language use, particularly of idioms, accents, and forms of speech, are a central and public marker of ethnonational affiliation. In line with this scholarship, this chapter will treat language within a broad sociocultural and political framework, and argue that language is an important vehicle for constituting and maintaining ethnonational and religious identity and boundaries at work.

Language is not only descriptive but also performative, enacted through speech acts (Bennett 1976). This means that language use can shape human behavior as well as public spaces, mirroring broader social and ethnonational power relations within a given country. As a case about which languages that can be used on public signs in Israel demonstrates, the linguistic landscape in Jewish communities is dominated by Hebrew and English, and Arabic is often excluded in practice (Ben-Rafael et al. 2006). In the public sphere it is also relatively easy to assign people to distinct ethnonational groups based on the language that they speak. Obviously, there is no complete overlap between language use and ethnonational identity, and members of different ethnonational groups often share a common language, as the cases of Russian in the FSU and English in the United States clearly demonstrate. The language shared by members of distinct ethnonational groups may be the result of government coercion, but may also be the outcome of choice necessitated by economic codependence and commercial needs. A key example is immigration and assimilation into the host country, accompanied by acquiring the local language (see Remennick [2003, 2005] for the case of Russian immigrants to Israel).

Three main languages dominate the public sphere in Israel. The first, Hebrew, is the mother tongue of Israeli-born Jews, but it is spoken in various degrees by many of its citizens regardless of their ethnonational identity. Arabic is the second commonly used language in the Israeli public arena. All Palestinian Arabs speak Arabic as a mother tongue, as do many Jews whose parents immigrated to Israel from Arabic-speaking countries such as Iraq or Morocco. Finally, Russian is spoken by most of those who immigrated to Israel from the FSU during the 1990s, about one million in number, along with those who arrived earlier, mainly during the 1970s. These immigrants tend to adhere to Russian culture and education, so much so that in many cases even their grandchildren speak Russian, and many of them attend after school programs in Russian, which are designed in accordance with Russian educational priorities and acquaint them with Russian culture. Most Palestinian-Arab children attend education institutions that teach mainly in Arabic, but learning Hebrew at school is obligatory. The command of Hebrew among Palestinian Arabs varies considerably. In the Jewish sector, learning Arabic is typically not obligatory and the number of Jewish youths speaking Arabic is much smaller than that of Palestinian-Arab youths speaking Hebrew.

Since 2018 teaching Arabic as a second language is compulsory in Israeli junior high schools (see Ministry of Education 2018).

In the public sphere, for example, in shopping malls, Hebrew, Arabic, and Russian are all commonly heard. The use of one's native tongue in the public sphere and in the home is obviously a matter of free choice, yet it is customary for Hebrew to be spoken in all public institutions. This is also the norm in private enterprises, simply because Hebrew is the common language for members of all ethnonational groups in Israel. It is important to note that there is a gap between the status of Arabic as an official language up to 2018 and the implementation of this status in practice. Both Arabic- and Russian-speaking citizens often have to navigate by signs written in Hebrew, to fill in forms written only in Hebrew, and to communicate in Hebrew even if they have a poor command of the language. Nonetheless, it is not uncommon to witness a Palestinian-Arab salesperson in a shop speaking in Arabic with Palestinian-Arab clients or a Russian-speaking salesperson speaking in Russian to Russian-speaking clients.

From a legal standpoint, section 82 of the Palestine Order in Council, 1922, established the official languages of Mandate Palestine as Hebrew, Arabic, and English. The state of Israel continued up to 2018 to maintain a bilingual environment, in which Arabic enjoyed the status of an official language alongside Hebrew and government forms were to be drafted in both languages. Not all government offices and agencies complied with this directive, which created difficulties for those whose mother tongue was not Hebrew. The failure of governmental or municipal bodies to use Arabic in forms or on road and street signs, sometimes resulted in court cases.[1] In 2018, however, the legal situation changed when the Israeli parliament passed the Nationality Law, which, among others, grants priority to Hebrew and defines Arabic as a language possessing a "special status," but no longer that of an "official language." This important legislation, which is strongly contested by Palestinian Arab citizens, as well as by liberal Jews and politicians, occurred after the field studies on which this book was based were terminated. Thus, its impact on the use of different languages in the workplace is not reflected in the research findings and remains to be studied in the future.

Language has an important role in maintaining social distance and inequality between Palestinian Arabs and Jews at work. For example, Remennick (2005), who studied Russian immigrants from the FSU, describes how the use of Russian at work symbolizes ethnic identity, workplace status, and group boundaries. She explains that the use of Russian at work is often contested by Hebrew-speaking

---

1. See, for example, HCJ 4112/99 Adalla v. Tel Aviv Municipality PD 56(5), 393 (2002) (about street signs); Cv/A 105/92 Reem Engineers LTD. v. Nazareth Heights Municipality PD 47(5), 189 (1993) (about billboards).

co-workers, who regard it as indicating the Russian immigrants' wish to distinguish themselves from Israeli culture and their sense of cultural superiority to native Israelis. For their part, her Russian interviewees expressed a desire to improve their command of the Hebrew language as a means of achieving better integration into Israeli society. It is significant that even though my research was conducted more than a decade after Remennick's study, it revealed that Russian was still widely used at work by immigrants from the FSU, some of whom had arrived in Israel in the early 1990s as young children.

Although language constituted a symbolic stage for the performance of ethnonational identity and for the display of the ethnonational cleavage in Israeli society in all the three sectors that were studied, the conflicts and tension surrounding language use were most obvious in the health sector, with its large and ethnically diverse medical teams, as illustrated by the incident cited at the beginning of this chapter. Moreover, physicians and nurses are required by management and by their professional ethos (the Hippocratic oath) to treat all patients equally, but the intensive contact with patients from different ethnonational backgrounds often strained this commitment, in particular when patients expressed racist views against Palestinian-Arab and Russian nurses and physicians or made unpleasant comments when Palestinian-Arab health workers spoke Arabic. The following discussion will therefore first focus on the health sector before examining the more subtle expressions of tension regarding language use in the production and high-tech sectors.

Language Use in the Health Sector

A medley of Hebrew, Arabic, and Russian is heard in the corridors of the two hospitals and in the retirement home, reflecting the use of these languages in the wider society. Yet, language use in the three health institutions is a contested terrain and an object of ongoing negotiations among staff members, between staff members and management, and between staff members and patients and their families. The Palestinian–Jewish cleavage is manifested in many instances when comments about language use are regarded as expressions of the ongoing political conflict. Importantly, health workers in both hospitals tend to speak their native tongues with members of their own ethnic groups in the hospital's corridors. Thus, Palestinian-Arab physicians converse in Arabic when taking a coffee break or having lunch with their Palestinian-Arab colleagues. However, holding conversations in a language other than Hebrew when on duty, particularly in the treatment rooms and in the presence of patients, is generally viewed by both Jewish and Palestinian-Arab medical staff members as harmful to the workflow and sometimes even as an exclusionary act with political overtones.

Despite this wide agreement, during work shifts, and in the absence of members of other ethnic groups, either medical staff or patients, Arabic is also spoken among Palestinian-Arab staff members. This is also true for the Russian staff members. Somewhat unexpectedly, I found Jewish and Palestinian-Arab nurses in the retirement home united in their criticism of Russian nurses who used their native tongue during work hours and in the presence of patients, even if the patient was a Russian speaker. The Russian nurses, who often came under attack for speaking Russian in the wards, nonetheless criticized the Palestinian-Arab nurses for speaking Arabic at work. The use of Hebrew during work shifts was perceived by all groups as politically neutral, since it allowed all parties to participate in the conversation.

To complicate things even further, patients in the three health institutions spoke a variety of languages and if they did not have a sufficient command of Hebrew, members of the medical staff had to communicate with them in their native tongue. For example, in the retirement home a large number of patients spoke Russian and a few Jewish patients spoke Arabic, the languages they had spoken in their countries of origin. Since these patients were generally very old and infirm, they found it difficult to use a language other than their native tongue. Thus, Russian- and Arabic-speaking staff members often spoke these languages with patients while they were feeding or treating them.

Both the large public hospital and the Palestinian-Arab private hospital also had an ethnically diverse medical staff, although with inverse proportions of Jewish and Palestinian Arab workers. In the public hospital the majority of medical staff were Jewish, both native Israeli and immigrants from the FSU. Palestinian-Arab physicians comprised about 20 percent of the medical staff, reflecting their percentage in the general population. In the private Palestinian-Arab hospital the vast majority of staff members were Palestinian Arabs, and the Jewish workers composed a small minority of the workforce. A few of the older Palestinian-Arab physicians in the two hospitals also spoke Russian, since they had received their professional education in the FSU.

Our informants from the three medical institutions distinguished between two arenas of language use and applied separate normative frameworks to each: (1) language use during physicians' patient rounds and encounters with patients inside treatment rooms; and (2) language use during lunch and coffee breaks, and when resting during night shifts.

Language Use in the Presence of Patients

Occupational principles of work organization are often presented in the research literature as contradicting organizational ones (Freidson 1970, 1984). For example, while formal organizations protect knowledge and knowhow by patents in order to maximize their financial gains, occupational communities tend to distribute occupational knowledge and knowhow freely among their members. One of the interesting findings of this study is that an overlap existed between managerial directives and professional norms with regard to speaking Hebrew in the presence of patients. The management of the Jewish retirement home made the most direct efforts to enforce the use of Hebrew in the wards, and specifically in the presence of patients. While the legality of such a rule is questionable, signs written in Hebrew, exhorting staff to "Speak Hebrew at Work" decorated the walls at the entrances to the different wards. Yet, occupational norms did not oppose managerial directives, but rather supported them.

In both the Jewish retirement home and the public hospital, two institutions with a majority of Jewish staff members and ethnically diverse patients, there was wide agreement among the medical staff that Hebrew should be spoken while treating patients. Some members of the medical staff even perceived speaking languages other than Hebrew in the presence of other team members who did not understand the conversation as unethical. The role of language in demarcating ethnic lines, and the occupational norm of speaking Hebrew while treating patients, become clear in the comments of a Russian nurse at the retirement home:

> I don't know who started all this, but the Arabs say, "The Russians speak Russian so we'll also speak [Arabic]." And this is repeated again and again. So we say, "You speak [your language] so we'll do the same." I think that it's unethical if people speak a language that another team member doesn't understand. I try not to do so. But I see a lot of it, also Russians who don't keep the rule and keep on speaking Russian, and it upsets me. When I tell them, "Speak Hebrew!" so they say, "They speak Arabic." And I say, "What, do we need to be like them? To descend to that level?" It's unethical, and very upsetting, but it goes on and on.

According to this Russian-speaking nurse, the use of language other than Hebrew at work resulted in inner tensions between the minority groups of Russian and Arabic speakers. On the one hand it created a shared interest vis-à-vis management, but on the other hand, it led to the constitution of distinctions through constant comparison. Although the speaker was Russian, she was critical of members of her own group as well as of the Palestinian-Arab nurses. Her admonition to her Russian colleagues, that they should not descend to the level of their Palestinian-Arab co-workers who spoke Arabic next to patients transmits a sense of ethnic and national superiority. Indeed, the Jewish and Palestinian-Arab members of the medical staff in the two hospitals studied often thought that their Russian-speaking colleagues felt superior. The Russian nurse cited above labeled the use of Russian and Arabic during work "unethical," probably alluding to its disruption of the work process and to the danger of excluding some team members and patients from vital information. In this case, as well as in many other cases in the two hospitals, occupational norms and needs grounded in work practice were mobilized to support the use of Hebrew at work, thus concurring with managerial directives in this regard. In this case too, concepts from the sociology of work practice such as occupational norms and local division of labor are useful for understanding the daily management of interethnic tensions on the shop floor.

Unlike the retirement home, neither the public nor the private hospital had formal managerial rules regarding the use of Hebrew in the presence of patients. There was, however, a clear informal managerial expectation, as indicated by the response of a young Palestinian-Arab physician in the public hospital when asked about this issue:

> PALESTINIAN-ARAB PHYSICIAN: You are supposed to speak Hebrew [in front of patients].
> INTERVIEWER: In every place? In every situation?
> PHYSICIAN: Yes.
> INTERVIEWER: And if some fail to do so, do you know of anyone who was summoned by management to discuss their behavior?
> PHYSICIAN: No.
> INTERVIEWER: So it doesn't come to that?
> PHYSICIAN: No, no, it doesn't.

This young physician knew about the rule that required him and others to speak Hebrew in the presence of patients, but he also knew that it was not enforced by management. It is likely that the professional norms that supported this managerial directive generated sufficient adherence to the rule and prevented the need to formally discipline Russian- and Arabic-speaking staff who ignored it. The next excerpt, from an interview with a Jewish nurse in the public hospital exemplifies further how norms regulating language use were played out as part of the work routine:

> JEWISH NURSE: There was this situation, when I was participating in a patient round. There was the senior physician who was Arab, and so was the intern, and really, the patient was also Arab. So it's okay that they [the two Palestinian-Arab physicians] spoke in Arabic with her [the patient], it makes sense, it's more comfortable for them. But

afterward they spoke about medical decisions among themselves in Arabic, and I stood there like an outsider, despite my comments about that, it didn't help. So I just left the patient round and didn't participate, something that isn't usually done in our ward.

INTERVIEWER: And you didn't pursue this matter further? You didn't approach the head of your ward and say that you were hurt by this?

NURSE: No. I said, the senior physician came and said, "How come you left? You know that a nurse has to participate during patient rounds!" So I told her that since I don't speak Arabic, I didn't understand what they were talking about anyway.

In this example the Jewish nurse felt left out when her two Palestinian-Arab colleagues spoke Arabic between themselves and with the patient, and ignored her requests to switch to Hebrew so that she could understand the medical discussion. Some practical flexibility regarding the use of Arabic with Arab patients can be detected here. Although the Jewish nurse accepted that it was "more comfortable" for the two physicians to speak Arabic with an Arab patient, and therefore accepted the violation of an occupational norm in this case, she was offended by their use of Arabic when their discussion shifted to professional consultation. Here, she invoked the managerial rule and the occupational norm that required Hebrew to be spoken in medical discussions. The nurse felt so frustrated that she took the unconventional step of leaving the patient round. Her explanation to the senior physician was based on the argument that the workflow and her own professional contribution were hampered by her inability to understand what the physicians were talking about.

In the Palestinian-Arab hospital there were no formal rules regarding language use, and Arabic was the dominant language heard in the corridors. During my visits I hardly heard Hebrew spoken in the corridors and in the waiting areas. But even here, where a majority of the staff were Palestinian Arabs, there was an occupational norm that when a Jewish midwife was present, Hebrew was to be used inside the delivery room, regardless of the ethnonational identity of the woman giving birth. Palestinian-Arab midwives, however, could conduct conversations in Arabic with their patients on other issues. A Jewish nurse in this hospital criticized Russian nurses and physicians for speaking Russian during a delivery, arguing that it disrupted the workflow:

Look, sometimes I don't care if they're talking about their children. It's not that interesting. But, for example, once . . . I was assisting in a birth and I was quite new at the time, I don't think this would have happened today, I think, when people know me already. I was assisting in a birth and I'm delivering the woman, and a midwife is standing next to me, a Russian, and on my other side a physician, also Russian. And the monitor was not okay and it was unclear whether we'd use vacuum or not, and I hear them talking in Russian about the baby I'm helping deliver, and this shouldn't happen! What will I understand? Don't you think I should know what's going on? If you're having a professional consultation, speak the language used here, which is Hebrew, this has to be done, even if I was a Russian speaker. And other than that, in my opinion it's not nice toward the woman [giving birth], who doesn't understand. This really drives me crazy!

While the speaker was tolerant of the use of Russian in private conversation, she was infuriated by its use during a delivery. She felt that the Russian physician, who at the time of this study was no longer working in the Palestinian-Arab hospital, and the Russian nurse had excluded her from decision making and disrupted the delivery process and her ability to learn through practice, since she was a young nurse at the time.

The ethnic diversity of patients sometimes required physicians and nurses to act as translators to the rest of the medical staff if they were treating a patient with little or no command of Hebrew. When a nurse in the public hospital who had immigrated to Israel from the FSU as a child was asked whether Palestinian-Arab patients sometimes preferred to be treated by a Palestinian-Arab nurse rather than her, she replied in the affirmative:

> RUSSIAN NURSE: They preferred, I think, an Arab nurse because of [pause] language problems.
> INTERVIEWER: Yes, just to talk to them?
> NURSE: Yes, but I think that [pause] well, Russian patients prefer a Russian nurse to admit them and treat them, rather than a different nurse. They also say so.
> INTERVIEWER: Because of language?
> NURSE: [Imitates a patient] "You are one of us," "You are one of us."
> INTERVIEWER: Because it's their language and also [gives them] a better sense of security?
> NURSE: Also a sense of security.
> INTERVIEWER: That, they know that you [pause].
> NURSE: Yes. They know that they'll be in good hands.
> INTERVIEWER: Yes.
> NURSE: She's one of us!

INTERVIEWER: And did you ever encounter a situation where someone, let's say Jewish or Russian, it doesn't matter [pause] didn't want an Arab nurse to treat her?

NURSE: Yes.

INTERVIEWER: It happened?

NURSE: Yes.

INTERVIEWER: And what did you do?

NURSE: I clearly stated . . . that this is a public hospital and no one gets to choose, not a nurse and not a physician, and that we have nurses and physicians here from all ethnic groups, and everyone treats everyone, and all have the one same goal, that you'll leave the hospital healthy.

The above cases show how disagreements over language use reflect the deep ethnonational cleavages. Indeed, language use at work should be seen as an integral part of the daily management of the ethnonational and religious conflict between Palestinian and Jews, as reflected in the tensions over this issue even in nonwork situations.

Language Use among Members of the Medical Staff

The wide agreement regarding the use of Hebrew during treatment of patients all but disappeared when it came to conversations among medical staff members when they were not on duty or in sight of patients. Palestinian-Arab members of the medical staff reported comments made by Jewish staff members when they spoke Arabic to their Palestinian-Arab colleagues, and their own sense of resentment toward such remarks, which they perceived as an infringement of their basic right to use their mother tongue, as described by a young Palestinian-Arab physician in the public hospital:

PALESTINIAN-ARAB PHYSICIAN: So, on a couple of occasions when we spoke Arabic, we received a lot of remarks that we shouldn't speak and [pause].

INTERVIEWER: [interrupts] Even when you're by yourselves? Even if you're [talking with] friends?

PHYSICIAN: No, even by ourselves. By ourselves no . . . look, there is, I don't think so, sometimes, but what disturbed me, I'm not saying that if we're part of a [mixed] group, so it's not nice to start speaking in Arabic.

INTERVIEWER: Yes.

PHYSICIAN: But sometimes we were standing aside, and there are two or three [Arabic-speaking colleagues], and we were talking about personal things, and we were standing aside, not as, well, so, even then we received comments.

INTERVIEWER: And how did you feel about these comments? How did you react?

PHYSICIAN: It's infuriating.

This interview reveals the many nuances of the use of Arabic by Palestinian-Arab members of the medical staff. On the one hand, this physician accepted some normative limitations on her natural right to speak her mother tongue at work. She accepted the need to switch to Hebrew when Jewish colleagues joined a group of Arabic-speaking medical staff in order to include them in the conversation. On the other hand, she also expressed a clear view that speaking Arabic in private conversations among her Palestinian-Arab friends was a basic right. Indeed, other Palestinian-Arab physicians and nurses particularly resented admonitions by Jewish members of the medical staff not to speak Arabic in private conversations, which they often perceived as the blatant exercise of hegemonic power by the Jewish majority and a public negation of their distinct ethnonational identity. Interestingly, both Arabic- and Russian-speaking members of the medical staff held similar views in this respect. For example, another young Palestinian-Arab physician described how he reacted when confronted with a request not to speak Arabic at a time when he was not on duty:

PALESTINIAN-ARAB PHYSICIAN: Once, I think it was before I started my internship, I was still doing my training where I was observing, I was doing external shifts [in another hospital], or just at the start of my internship, I was in the delivery room and there was another intern who's a good friend of mine, from way back, from school, from the village both of us come from. We come from the same place and we were really good friends even before we started working here together. And we were just standing in the delivery room, and there is a desk used by the nurses, where two or three midwives were sitting.... We were standing, let's say, standing a few meters away [from the midwives]. I was talking to him [the friend] about something that had happened before, we'd had an [a social] event with friends and we were simply talking about it.

INTERVIEWER: A personal topic, yes?

PHYSICIAN: A totally private issue not related to anything and not related to work or anything, and we were speaking Arabic.

INTERVIEWER: Yes?

PHYSICIAN: I'm Arab and he [his friend] is Arab, so the natural thing for us is to speak our mother tongue and not start talking in all kinds of languages. And when nobody else is participating, this is something totally private that both of us were talking about. And one of the midwives commented that [pause] that is how she told me that, [she] turned around and told me "Sorry! You know that you're not allowed to speak Arabic?"

INTERVIEWER: Not allowed?

PHYSICIAN: Yes, "You're not allowed to speak Arabic."

INTERVIEWER: OK, interesting.

PHYSICIAN: And at that point, I sometimes have a short fuse [laughs] so the minute I heard that I said, okay, and I started to raise my voice, and say "What are you talking about, is this an official or unofficial language," and I'm talking to a friend, and both of us have the same mother tongue, and we're talking about something that's got nothing to do with work, and why do you even bother to listen to what I'm saying to him? And . . . so, this is one incident that, by the way, happens all over the country.

The claim made by the Jewish midwife that the two young Palestinian-Arab physicians were not allowed to speak Arabic between them was unfounded and surprising, and it may have been based on a very broad interpretation of the rule that inside treatment rooms Hebrew is the common language that all members of the medical staff should use when treating patients. On this occasion, there were no patients in the delivery room, and the two physicians were conducting a private conversation not far from the midwives' desk. The fact that they were very young and new at the hospital might also partly explain the midwife's curt tone. The speaker was clearly offended by her blunt attempt to prevent his use of Arabic. At the time of the interview Arabic was still an official language in Israel, along with Hebrew, as the speaker had reminded the midwife. He had also clarified that this was a private conversation among friends, thus indirectly acknowledging the general rule that professional conversations should be conducted in Hebrew to ensure high-quality treatment. The strong reaction of the Jewish nurse might also be understood as a show of strength directed against physicians, who at times play down the role of nurses and emphasize the difference in their statuses.

A Russian nurse from the Jewish retirement home, expressed understanding for those who used their native language during work hours, but she also revealed how language use played a part in broader ethnic politics among the diverse medical staff:

> Since I'm from Russia, I speak Russian when I'm working on a shift with another Russian, even though it's forbidden and despite the complaints. So I don't get upset if Arabs speak Arabic and Ethiopians speak Amharic. It doesn't disturb me. But other people, for example, we have a career, she speaks Russian to everyone, but if an Arab is next to her and speaks Arabic, she complains about him.... Obviously it's easier to speak your native language, it's easier to express your thoughts, easier to communicate. But there are those who are disturbed by this. The Israelis [*sic*, referring to Jews born in Israel] get upset if any other language than Hebrew is spoken, it doesn't matter whether it's Russian, Arabic, or Amharic, or even Philippine. In my opinion, the Arabs don't mind which language is spoken next to them, but they'll criticize you in order to spite you, and especially if someone just forced them to speak Hebrew rather than Arabic.

Despite the fact that management issued formal directives requiring the use of Hebrew at work, both Palestinian-Arab and Russian nurses spoke their native tongue at work and generally supported the right of minority groups, like the few Ethiopian Jews in the medical workforce, to do so. Yet, when political tensions were high, these conventions were more likely to be broken and members of minority groups were more likely to complain about each other. The Russian nurse also claimed that Hebrew-speaking Jews, the majority of the workforce, were more likely than others to complain to management about the use of Russian or Arabic at work.

Although there was no formal policy regarding language use in the private hospital, when either a Jewish or a Russian nurse was on duty or the patient was Jewish, the norm was to communicate in Hebrew. The Palestinian-Arab and native-born Jewish nurses expressed the strongest resentment against Russian nurses who talked among themselves in Russian or who spoke Russian to the few Russian patients in the maternity ward. For example, after complaining about a Russian physician and a Russian nurse who used to speak Russian between them even in the presence of other nurses who did not speak Russian, a Palestinian-Arab nurse in the private hospital emphasized the more considerate behavior of her Palestinian-Arab colleagues:

> We Arabs are ashamed to behave in this manner, and when a Jewish nurse is among us, we try to use the common language [Hebrew] and not let the Jewish nurses feel left out in such situations. Today, for

example, when X [names a Jewish nurse] is with us on a shift, we even tell our jokes in Hebrew, so that she won't feel left out. It's unpleasant to simply ignore her presence. It's not polite.

When asked whether ethnic origin affected relationships among the nurses in the maternity ward, a Jewish nurse in the private hospital first described a certain bond between the native-born Jewish and the Russian nurses, specifically on political issues and at times of political violence, a bond that also exists in the broader political arena (Kraus and Yonay 2018). But then the speaker went on to criticize the Russian nurses for speaking Russian in the presence of people who did not understand the language, such as herself, and thus excluding them from the conversation:

> Sometimes, I'll tell you that a group of Russians can speak Russian among themselves, and they, the fact that I'm there doesn't bother them, something that won't happen with the Arabs. I do understand Arabic already, but usually the Arabs, when they see someone who doesn't speak Arabic, they will immediately switch to Hebrew. But with the group of Russians, they don't care who's next to them. They talk among themselves, sometimes about professional matters. They don't, I can't say they're bothered about whoever's next to them.

Although she noted that the boundaries between the Jewish and the Russian nurses became blurred on matters of politics, and the two groups typically united in support of the actions of the Israeli state, she claimed that the Hebrew-speaking Jews and the Palestinian Arabs sometimes joined forces against Russian colleagues who not only spoke Russian on shifts, but were also reluctant to switch to Hebrew when non-Russian speakers were present. The fact that, according to this nurse, Palestinian-Arab members of the medical staff were more likely than their Russian counterparts to switch to Hebrew in the presence of others might also be linked to the ethnonational conflict. While the reluctance of Russian workers to switch to Hebrew could be interpreted as a lack of courtesy or a sense of cultural superiority over the "natives," such reluctance on the part of Arabic-speaking members of the medical staff could be understood as expressing hostility rooted in the political conflict and therefore be viewed as more offensive.

Language use and indication of national pride sometimes went hand in hand. Jewish and Russian nurses at the private hospital also cited instances when Palestinian-Arab patients alluded to the broader political conflict by expressing their displeasure at not being addressed in Arabic in an Arab hospital, as cited in chapter 1. In these cases language denoted pride in a wide range of ethnon-ational symbols, such as the ownership of the hospital, its existence within a

Palestinian-Arab city in Israel, and the dominance of Palestinian Arabs in management, the workforce, and among patients. The role played by language in performing ethnonational identity at work was also visible in the Israeli high-tech sector, although in a less blatant form than in the health sector, and with distinct manifestations determined by the context.

Language Use in the High-Tech Sector

During my first visit to one of the multinational high tech firms, an HR employee accompanied me from the lobby to the interview room assigned to me for that morning. We went through a maze of corridors, surrounded by dozens of cubicles, each accommodating two or three R&D engineers, who were sitting back-to-back working in front of their computers. Small groups of workers were standing in the corridors chatting, while others were taking coffee breaks in the few well-supplied kitchenettes scattered along the long corridor. During this short walk I was amazed by the number of languages I heard around me—Hebrew, Arabic, English, Russian, and even Swedish. Although this multilingual environment could potentially introduce various ethnonational tensions into the daily work, of all the three research contexts, the high-tech companies manifested the lowest level of tension related to language use. The interviewees in the two multinationals mentioned only a few incidents of explicit tension between Palestinian-Arab and Jewish workers surrounding language use. An extreme example, which also sheds light on the reason for the low level of ethnonational conflict in these firms, was reported by a Palestinian-Arab engineer, when he was asked whether a co-worker had ever commented on his use of Arabic at work. He replied that he himself had never encountered such an incident, but that his friend, who worked in a different R&D team, had experienced a very unpleasant incident when he was talking on the phone in Arabic with a Palestinian-Arab colleague:

> PALESTINIAN-ARAB ENGINEER: I remember someone, my friend from another team, someone who works with him said to him "Why are you talking to your friends in Arabic?" So, they had some [prior] problems between them, and then this guy says to him: "What are you telling your friend [on the phone]? That he can come and blow my house up?"
>
> INTERVIEWER: Whoa!
>
> ENGINEER: Yes, and then my friend was in shock, "What are you saying?"
>
> INTERVIEWER: And all this happened here in the company?

ENGINEER: Yes, here in the company. So [my friend] told him: "What, are you crazy to talk like that?" And then the people who were in the office, they wanted to close the matter, to ignore it. They wanted to take [the offending person] out because they knew that he'd done something that is [pause], like, you don't talk like that ever! So when this reached the group manager, the [offending] guy was sent home! Fired from work! They told him, "We don't need people like you" [pause]. It was a real shock to my friend.

This was a rare instance of such an exchange in an environment in which racist comments were unusual and unacceptable. For this Jewish engineer the very sound of Arabic appeared to be associated with fear and terror. As the Palestinian-Arab engineer noted, the two had had previous unpleasant encounters, but this was the most openly racist one and clearly shocked his colleague as well as the Jewish team members who heard it. The fact that some of the latter wanted to take the offender outside, in an attempt to calm him down and possibly minimize this racist incident, may indicate a spirit of camaraderie among the Jewish engineers, albeit mobilized for the wrong cause. The Palestinian-Arab engineer's complaint about the incident, however, and top management's swift response by firing the offending engineer, probably reassured the Palestinian-Arab engineer and his friend that the company was committed to diversity management and was ready to enforce its opposition to racism at work. Indeed, engineers and other high-tech workers in both of the multinational companies studied reported the existence of formal guidelines and clear norms that helped to prevent or minimize any racist reaction to the use of languages other than English or Hebrew.

The interviewees in the two high-tech companies made a distinction between written communication, which had to be conducted in English, and formal meetings, in which Hebrew was usually spoken. Nonetheless, if even one participant in a meeting did not speak Hebrew, the meeting would be held in English, which meant that, unlike the other research contexts, English, not Hebrew, was the default language. A Jewish engineer, was asked if there was a company policy regarding language use, and she chose to speak about written communication:

JEWISH ENGINEER: There are no formal directives. The only directive we have here is to use English in written communication.
INTERVIEWER: Okay.
ENGINEER: Since it [written communication] goes out to many places.
INTERVIEWER: Yes, I also noticed that David [the HR manager] sent me an email in English. It surprised me.

ENGINEER: Yes, yes, because it [the email] can land in Sweden, China, Japan, so [pause] they don't want [pause] something to be incomprehensible.

The logic behind the management directive to use English in written communication was clear to employees, and we witnessed no resistance to this rule among them. When it came to informal work encounters, most interviewees had no objection to their colleagues' use of their mother tongue, whether Russian or Arabic, as was confirmed by a Jewish team manager in one of the multinational companies:

INTERVIEWER: Does it ever happen that when people talk in the corridor, you know, during breaks in the kitchenette, people speak, let's say Russian, and someone can come by and comment "Speak Hebrew" or something like that?

JEWISH MANAGER: No, not really. We have lots of guys who are Russian, some of them don't speak Hebrew.

INTERVIEWER: I see.

MANAGER: So they speak Russian among themselves, and that's fine. And we speak English to them, that, everyone [understands]. And there are Arab guys who speak Arabic. Let them speak whatever [language] they want.

This team manager expressed a liberal view of language use when compared with the situation in the health institutions, but the logic behind this approach was clearly functional. High-tech workers, according to David, can speak any language they want, as long as they can understand each other, even though Hebrew and English have a leading role in formal contexts. As in the case of the medical teams, the high-tech workers made a clear distinction between formal and informal encounters, as a veteran Palestinian-Arab engineer, explained:

I've noticed that people speak their mother tongue, let's say Arabic or Russian, among themselves, and also when they're good friends. But in the more [formal] spaces, let's say, when colleagues or people who don't know the language [are around], or when they work, work formally, they do use Hebrew. I've noticed that they're strict about it lately.

While the use of Arabic or Russian in social conversation was regarded as natural, Hebrew served as the dominant language in formal meetings, except, as noted, when a non-Hebrew speaker was present, which was quite common, and all participants resorted to English. When asked if the use of English during some meetings disturbed her, another Palestinian-Arab engineer replied:

> PALESTINIAN-ARAB ENGINEER: No, it doesn't disturb me. During work meetings we speak Hebrew as long as everyone understands.
>
> INTERVIEWER: An American?
>
> ENGINEER: Not necessarily American. It can be a Malaysian, or someone else who doesn't speak Hebrew, so everyone quite naturally switches to English.
>
> INTERVIEWER: And this happens often, I assume?
>
> ENGINEER: It happens very often, yes.

For the growing numbers of Palestinian-Arab engineers in the high-tech firms, hearing Arabic in the corridors created a sense that their distinct culture was present and accepted by their employing organization. One of the first Palestinian-Arab engineers to work in one of the multinational companies described her pleasure at hearing Arabic in her work environment:

> PALESTINIAN-ARAB ENGINEER: Something has changed. Listen, I've been here for thirteen years and when I first started working here, there were only three Arab women working in the company.
>
> INTERVIEWER: You don't say! Amazing.
>
> ENGINEER: Now the number has jumped incredibly. First of all I look [around] and I hear the language [Arabic]. It's not that strange anymore and [pause] all of a sudden I've got people to talk to!
>
> INTERVIEWER: You've got people to talk to [laughs].
>
> ENGINEER: Exactly, exactly, I didn't have anyone just to talk to, not in my own language!
>
> INTERVIEWER: Not in your language.
>
> ENGINEER: And all of a sudden it's not strange, it's acceptable, there are lots of people who speak the language and you really feel [pause] you see the [growing] numbers and the truth is also the quality, good people! [pause] Still only a few are in managerial positions; I don't see that we're moving up [pause] into the managerial positions although, let's say, personally, I'd like to.

It is clear that hearing and then using Arabic in casual conversation at work bears a symbolic meaning for this engineer, fostering a sense of well-being and belonging. The ability to speak and hear her mother tongue as she walks through the corridors seems to bolster her trust in the multinational company's ability and willingness to absorb Palestinian-Arab workers on the cultural level as well, allowing them to perform their distinct identity. Indeed, as noted, language use as a signifier of broader ethnocultural identity is a recurrent theme in the research literature (Amara 2018; Funkenstein 1989). At the end of this interview excerpt the engineer nonetheless expressed her disappointment that there were so few Palestinian-Arab engineers in managerial positions, pointing out that there was still room for further improvement.

While management tried to regulate language use to various degrees in the health and high-tech sectors, on the production line such regulations were in the process of being elaborated by the workers themselves.

Language Use on the Production Floor

Language use was not a main point of contention between Palestinian Arabs and Jews on the production floor. Hebrew- and Russian-speaking Jews composed a small minority among the production workers, and Arabic was the dominant language heard on the shop floor. The workers were organized in small groups along different stations of the production line, and communication between stations was rare, partly because of the physical distance between stations, amounting to ten meters or more. Additionally, management had no specific guidelines for language use, leaving the issue to be negotiated among the workers. Unlike the case of the health sector, the production workers had little formal training and no sense of an occupational community, so there were no professional guidelines to use Hebrew while working in a mixed group. Thus, Palestinian-Arab workers switched from Arabic to Hebrew when a Jewish co-worker joined their group, but then returned to Arabic for social conversations with their Palestinian-Arab friends. They were likely to switch back to Hebrew if they wanted to communicate with their Jewish co-worker about his work. Jewish workers acted likewise when two of them were assigned to the same workstation. The pragmatic approach to daily management of language use is demonstrated by the response of a Palestinian-Arab production worker when asked whether Russian-speaking workers sometimes spoke Russian among themselves, and whether he ever made comments about that:

> PALESTINIAN-ARAB PRODUCTION WORKER: When they [the Russian workers] sit together on breaks, for example, they keep to themselves, and the reason's clear. They like to talk to each other in their own language. You see, they like to sit by themselves.
>
> INTERVIEWER: Yes?

PRODUCTION WORKER: But that's, that's fine.

INTERVIEWER: During work shifts and at the machines, does it happen that sometimes they speak Russian and then you ask them to speak Hebrew so that you can understand?

PRODUCTION WORKER: Most of the time no, speaking [Russian] I mean. They [management] don't usually put two Russians together, they diversify.

INTERVIEWER: [interrupts] And how do they talk? Do they have to use Hebrew?

PRODUCTION WORKER: If they want to talk so they speak Hebrew, because they have to.

INTERVIEWER: And what do you speak? Hebrew?

PRODUCTION WORKER: We speak Hebrew, yes.

INTERVIEWER: So during shifts and by the machines Hebrew is mainly spoken?

PRODUCTION WORKER: If we're, let's say if I'm talking to an Arab [co-worker] I speak Arabic.

INTERVIEWER: Even if a Russian-speaking man is next to you? You speak Arabic?

PRODUCTION WORKER: If our conversation concerns him, as well as us, so then we speak Hebrew so that he can understand.

INTERVIEWER: Yes.

PRODUCTION WORKER: But if the conversation has nothing to do with him, we speak Arabic.

On the production line, in distinction from the health and high-tech sectors, religious belief was sometimes used as a rationale for the use or the rejection of a particular language in a particular place. In one instance, a religious Muslim worker claimed that his religious belief forbade him to listen to Hebrew songs that were transmitted over loudspeakers near the production line during the night shift. Indeed, as we shall see in the next chapter, workers in the production plant often used religion to display their distinct ethnonational identity.

Language as a Symbolic Stage

The findings presented above lend support to existing scholarship that analyzes language use within a broad sociocultural context (Funkenstein 1989) and treats language as a symbolic stage for the performances of ethnonational identity (Amara 2018). This chapter has placed language use in the context of work organization and highlighted the multifaceted meanings attributed to it in different sectors of the Israeli economy. In all of the three sectors language use provided a symbolic stage on which ethnonational identity was displayed and, as such, could sometimes create tensions. The ethnonational divide in Israeli society shaped the attitude and reactions to language use by members of other groups. The medical sector exhibited the highest level of friction with regard to language use, mainly as a result of the large and heterogeneous medical teams and the intensive interactions with patients and their families who also come from diverse ethnonational backgrounds. In the high-tech sector, only a few racist incidents related to language use were reported, and these were swiftly and decisively dealt with by management, which reinforced the Palestinian-Arab engineers' belief that their company was committed to equal treatment and their full integration into the company. Similarly, when Arabic became part of the daily soundscape in the multinationals, it created a sense of cultural inclusion on the part of the Palestinian-Arab engineers, showing how language use can shape public spaces (Ben-Rafael et al. 2006). Finally, in the production sector, where Palestinian-Arab workers dominated the workforce, language use was regulated from below by emergent norms that gave workers flexibility and confined the use of Hebrew to the production line when there was a need for a common language of communication.

The deep insult and frustration felt by some Palestinian-Arab employees in the health sector when their Jewish co-workers asked them to refrain from talking in their mother tongue demonstrates that they viewed such comments as a rejection of their distinct ethnonational identity. Some Jewish workers, sometimes supported by managerial directives, wished to impose the rule that Hebrew should be spoken at work, partly as a display of Jewish hegemony in the state of Israel. The case of the Jewish nurse in the retirement home, who understood Arabic but nonetheless complained about her Palestinian-Arab co-worker who spoke Arabic in front of patients' families, angered the Palestinian-Arab workers precisely because the complaint represented a rejection of Arab culture. Indeed, the hegemony of the Hebrew language sometimes united Russian- and Arabic-speaking employees in their effort to protect their basic right to speak their native tongue, and hence display their unique identity through language use. By contrast, creating a multilingual environment provided members of ethnonational minorities with a sense of belonging and acceptance by the employing organization, as vividly illustrated by the joy experienced by the Palestinian-Arab engineer on gradually hearing more Arabic in the corridors of her high-tech firm.

As we have seen, regulations regarding language use varied in the different sectors. In the two hospitals and the retirement home, language use was regulated not only by managerial directives but also, and probably mostly, by occupational norms, which required the use of Hebrew as the preferred language during medical treatment to ensure that all members of the medical staff received the necessary information. Professional norms also influenced managerial directives in the high-tech sector, where English was used as the default language but Hebrew was spoken in meetings if it was understood by all participants. The most relaxed and least regulated environment was the production line, where language use was determined by the workers themselves according to their practical needs.

RELIGION AT WORK

Although the Palestinian–Jewish conflict is primarily national and territorial, and the Jewish-Israeli political leadership has refrained from presenting the conflict as a fundamentally religious one, it has strong religious overtones. Both nations appeal to religious sentiments or invoke the sacred texts, the Torah and the Koran, when justifying their claim to the land of Palestine/Israel. Most of the founding fathers of modern Zionism were secular European Jews, yet they often referred to the special connection between the Jewish people and the land of Israel, based on a historical reading of the Bible. Moreover, since the 1967 war the Jewish settlers in the occupied territories proclaim their right to settle there by invoking God's promise to Abraham and their religious attachment to places sacred to Judaism such as the Western Wall in Jerusalem and the Cave of the Patriarchs in Hebron. Since the latter is believed to be the burial site of Abraham, Isaac, Jacob, and Sarah, among others, it is also sacred to Muslims. Palestinians also cite their religious attachment and right to sacred sites such as Haram esh-Sharif, the Noble Sanctuary, on top of what the Jews call the Temple Mount in Jerusalem. On both sides of the ethnonational cleavage, religious and right-wing parties such as the Islamic Movement on the Palestinian side and the New Right Party and the Jewish Home Party on the Jewish-Israeli side base their resistance to any form of compromise between Jews and Palestinians on religious grounds. Religion, therefore, is clearly an active ingredient of the Israeli–Palestinian conflict.

The fierce political struggle between Palestinian Arabs and Jews within the 1948 borders and also in the territories occupied in the 1967 war is a defining

feature of Israeli society, and the religious aspects of this conflict are part and parcel of the political landscape and debate in the Israeli public sphere. For example,
studies of the historical trajectories of the Islamic movement in Israel (Ali 2004;
Suwaed and Ali 2016) find that religion was mobilized to gain political power by
both Palestinian Arabs and Jews. On the Palestinian-Arab side, the Islamic movement in Israel offered a wide range of educational and social services to mainly
poor Palestinian-Arab citizens, and this support was translated into increased
political power. As Ali (2004) puts it: "Social engagement represented also a
good example of the integration of the socio-political aspects with the religious
one." He notes that the combination of religion and politics, operating through
the provision of social services and education, was also mobilized by the right-
leaning Jewish Shas political party (Association of Torah-Observant Sephardim),
founded in 1984.

While recent studies have highlighted the increasing role played by religion
in contemporary Israeli politics, little is known about how religion and religious
beliefs play out on the shop floor inside Israeli work organizations. This chapter fills this lacuna by providing a situated account of the way Palestinian-Arab
and Jewish workers in the three sectors relate to and employ religion as part of
their daily activities and discussions at work. Such an analysis can provide the
foundations for a middle-range theory capable of connecting the micro and the
macro in relation to the role of religion in the management of ethnonational and
religious conflicts at work.

For members of all religious affiliations, religious holidays and memorial days
are important markers of identity and culture and are accompanied by distinct
ceremonies, dress codes, and traditional foods. They also hold the potential of
being points of contention for rival ethnonational groups, especially in a country with such deep tensions as Israel. This chapter inquires into how religion
is expressed by workers coming from different backgrounds and also examines
whether religion and religious holidays become a source of friction between
Palestinian-Arab and Jewish workers or whether they might have a more positive role of bringing members of these two groups of workers closer together.

Work organizations, which are immersed in the broader sociocultural context and institutional setting, can be viewed as microcosms of ethnocultural
trends in society in general. For example, work organizations choose which
holidays to celebrate and which memorial days to commemorate at work, while
ignoring others, and these choices reflect the power relations in society between
majority and minority groups. For obvious reasons, the holidays and memorial days of the hegemonic group in Israeli society, the Jews, are most likely to
be celebrated at work. Nonetheless, the question remains to what extent the
holidays of the Palestinian-Arab citizens of Israel, whether Muslim, Christian,

or Druze, are also acknowledged and celebrated by Israeli work organizations, and in what manner.

The decision regarding which religious holidays and memorial days, whether religious or civic, should be celebrated in the workplace is of particular significance in deeply divided societies, and especially those in which religion and nationality intersect so strongly such as Israel or the countries of the former Yugoslavia. In a war-torn or ethnically divided country, this decision has strong ethnonational overtones, since the civic or religious memorial day or religious holiday of one group sometimes has an adverse meaning for members of rival ethnonational and religious groups. The Israeli Day of Independence, which is one of the cases discussed below, is a particularly vivid example of this problem. On May 15, 1948, one day after the declaration of the establishment of the state of Israel, the British left Palestine and the 1948 war officially erupted. That date is when the Palestinians commemorate the Nakba, the "Day of the Catastrophe," a term coined in August 1948, during the war, by the Lebanese historian Constantine Zureik (see Kabha 2010, 144) to denote the great political and military defeat of the Palestinian Arabs and their Arab allies. The Nakba resulted in the displacement, both outside and inside the borders of the newly established Israeli state, of a large proportion of the Palestinian-Arab population and the demise of their collective desire to constitute an independent Palestinian state on the entire area of British Mandate Palestine. What for the Jews is a joyous national holiday celebrating the establishment of a national home in a sovereign state is for the Palestinians a painful national disaster. This chapter explains how the celebration of religious holidays at work serves as an occasion for a public display of religious, cultural, and even national identity, and how ignoring the holidays of minority groups undermines their sense of belonging to their employing organization. It reveals striking differences between the three sectors studied: the prominence of religious discourse and friction in the production plant and the mobilization of religion to express political views; the Palestinian-Arab engineers' desire for recognition of their religious affiliation in order to gain a sense of cultural inclusion in the two multinational high-tech firms; and the more positive role played by religion in the three health institutions, where religious diversity was perceived as having certain benefits and even enhancing relations within the medical teams.

Expressing Religious Beliefs in the Production Plant

As we have seen in previous chapters, religion figured prominently in the daily encounters between the Jewish and the Palestinian-Arab production workers.

The heated discussions triggered by violent events related to the Palestinian–Jewish conflict outside the production plant often shifted from the political to the religious sphere. The use of religious arguments in political debates is a unique feature of the interethnic relations among production workers and has no empirical parallels in the high-tech or health organizations, where religion remained a suppressed issue in public discussions. This could also be explained by the larger percentage of production workers on both sides of the ethnonational cleavage who defined themselves as religious. Thus, many of the interviewees in the production plant indicated their distinct religious affiliation as part of their self-presentation, even when they were not specifically asked about their religious background, and most of the Jewish interviewees wore a yarmulke (skullcap, an indication of Jewish religious observance) and referred to their religious upbringing and formal education. Moreover, the heated religious debates that were a defining feature of daily life on the production floor were not limited to the Jewish-Muslim cleavage but also took place among Palestinian-Arab Christians, Muslims, and Druze who comprised the majority of the labor force and engaged in passionate discussions about religious belief, the Bible, the Koran, and even the secretive Druze religion.

The tendency to invoke religious beliefs when talking about pressing political events is well demonstrated by the following excerpt from an interview with a Palestinian-Arab production worker, who defined himself in the beginning of the interview as a religious Muslim. He had obtained an academic degree in education and worked for a short time as a teacher in the south of Israel. However, having been unable to find a job in his profession on moving back to the Galilee in northern Israel, where he had been born and raised, he had been obliged, by economic necessity, to find employment as a production worker. After changing a few jobs, he had settled down in his current employment, where he had worked for over five years. His education, as well as his strong religious faith, was a source of pride for this production worker, and he expressed a sense of disappointment at his inability to find work as a teacher. In the following excerpt, he described how, following a suicide bombing, he had overheard a heated argument between a Jewish and a Palestinian-Arab worker and had come to the rescue, as he put it, of his Arab colleague:

INTERVIEWER: What did he [the Jewish co-worker] say to you?

PRODUCTION WORKER: "Arabs, what are you looking for here? You are this and you are that, and we [the Jews], God promised us this land, and God said: 'It's ours.'" He [the Jewish co-worker] is religious.

INTERVIEWER: Religious, yes?

PRODUCTION WORKER: Religious, I was simply passing by and found him talking to someone else, that is [pause].

INTERVIEWER: [interrupts] An Arab?

PRODUCTION WORKER: An Arab who isn't educated and doesn't know [pause].

INTERVIEWER: Yes?

PRODUCTION WORKER: So he [the Jewish co-worker] tried to confront me, I had already been [working] here for six months at the time.

INTERVIEWER: Six months.

PRODUCTION WORKER: And he [the Jewish co-worker] didn't know me. No one knew me other than management, what I'd studied and what I have. I was offended that while I'm drinking my coffee he [the Jewish co-worker] starts confronting the other [Arab] guy, who doesn't respond. Maybe he was afraid, and maybe he didn't know what to say, so I [pause].

INTERVIEWER: [interrupts] intervened?

PRODUCTION WORKER: I intervened after [pause] I saw that he [the Jewish co-worker] was being offensive. I'm one of those people for whom religion is very important. Right, I don't have a beard, but I'm a person who cares a lot about religion, and I don't let anybody talk, whether about our prophet or someone else. This is for me a red point [probably meaning a red light]. So when he [the Jewish co-worker] spoke, this red point started flickering, and I attacked him from a religious perspective. Their [Jewish] religion, I attacked it! The religion itself, since I've studied!

INTERVIEWER: And how did he react?

PRODUCTION WORKER: He remained silent.

INTERVIEWER: [He] didn't complain to management?

PRODUCTION WORKER: He tried to, but they [management] sent for us and told us [pause].

INTERVIEWER: [interrupts] The two of you?

PRODUCTION WORKER: They told us to leave religion out of it, yes. By the way, they [management] don't allow things to come to religion or politics. Here in our plant it's forbidden to talk about religion or politics.

This excerpt exemplifies the way in which religion can be mobilized to strengthen political positions in an argument. In this discussion the Jewish worker claimed property rights over the land of Israel, based on promises made by God to the Jewish people. He was then challenged with religious counterarguments by the educated Muslim worker, who asserted that his studies had given him the tools to attack the Jewish religion. This excerpt also reveals that, despite management's directive not to talk about religion or politics at work, probably because they are considered to be explosive topics, such conversations did occur, especially following violent events outside the workplace. Thus, it might be concluded that management's enforcement of its own rules was partial, particularly when it came to religious discussions among the production workers. Even though the participants in this argument were summoned by management, the speaker did not mention any subsequent sanctions.

For some of the Palestinian-Arab workers, particularly Muslims, religion was also a means for expressing opposition to the Zionist state, and particularly to national memorial days such as the Memorial Day for Fallen Soldiers and Holocaust Memorial Day. Although these are not religious holidays per se, their performance is infused with elements from the Jewish religion. Protest often took the form of ignoring the siren that is sounded on these days, which gives the signal to cease all activity and solemnly stand in honor of the dead.

One interviewee, a female Jewish production worker promoted to the marketing department around the time of the interview, described what she experienced as a disturbing event when a few of the Palestinian-Arab workers engaged in what she dubbed "a rowdy behavior" talking in loud voices during the siren on Holocaust Memorial Day. She did not refer to their religious belief, but only to their ethnonational identity. The same incident, however, was also mentioned in an interview with a Palestinian-Arab worker who identified himself as a Christian Arab. His account not only differs somewhat from the Jewish worker's depiction but also demonstrates the religious differences among the Palestinian-Arab workers themselves:

> A few Arab workers, veterans, they started working here before me, they didn't stand in one place during the siren [to commemorate Holocaust Memorial Day]. They are religious Muslims, and they didn't stand still. They walked around the plant, and then, one production [Jewish] worker, I'm not sure if she's still in the plant, she went over and scolded them: she said: "What does this [behavior] mean? You need to respect the people around you here." But he [one of the Palestinian-Arab co-workers] replied: "I don't want to stand," and then added "You can't make me stand." Yes, he is one of the religious Muslims. Yes, he did it. But there were other people who, just before the siren, went and hid somewhere around the plant. They went elsewhere and sat down, as though to say: "We don't want to stand up."

This account was less emotional than that of the Jewish worker and did not describe their behavior as rowdy, but simply as a rejection of the dictate to stand for a minute's silence. What is interesting is that he reiterated that these were religious Muslims, implying that he attributed their behavior to their religious belief. He also mentioned less provocative forms of resistance, such as going to hide in remote areas of the plant during the siren to avoid participation in the ritual.

The failure to adhere to this norm of showing respect to the victims of the Holocaust, a catastrophe with universal implications, may seem puzzling. One explanation might be that the genocide of the Jews is often presented in Israel as the driving force behind the constitution of the state. Thus, in the long shadow of the Holocaust, the state of Israel is depicted by its proponents as a haven for persecuted Jews around the globe that will protect them from a second catastrophe. In this sense the Holocaust is also mobilized to strengthen the Jewish identity of the state of Israel. The refusal of a few Muslim workers to stand in silence during the siren on Holocaust Memorial Day may therefore be related to the association between this horrific historic event and the establishment of the state of Israel, although the Christian Arab worker described their behavior as having a religious rather than a political basis.

Another point of contention between Palestinian-Arab and Jewish workers in which religion played a role was the celebration of the Memorial Day for Fallen Soldiers and Israeli Independence Day, which are observed on two consecutive days in the spring. Both these holidays are charged with emotional and political content that exacerbates the existing tensions between Jewish and Arab citizens of Israel. Not only does Israel's independence mark the occurrence of the Nakba, but the commemoration of fallen Israeli soldiers who died in wars with Arab states or in military conflicts with Palestinians is an extremely sensitive issue for Israel's Palestinian-Arab citizens. The findings suggest that religion was one of the means for expressing resistance to the Zionist state and its symbols, as described in the following interview with one of the Palestinian-Arab workers, who presented himself as an observant Muslim:

> INTERVIEWER: On the memorial day for fallen soldiers, when the siren is heard, the Jews stop working and stand in honor of the fallen, is that right?
>
> PALESTINIAN-ARAB PRODUCTION WORKER: Right, they stand up, yes.
>
> INTERVIEWER: They stand up? And what do you do, the Arabs?
>
> PRODUCTION WORKER: I don't stand up, since according to our religion we are not allowed to stand up. For our prophet Muhammad, may he rest in peace, we don't stand up. So you don't stand up for anybody else. This is the logic that I follow that is based on my own religious belief.
>
> INTERVIEWER: So none of you stand up [during the siren]?

PRODUCTION WORKER: No, some do but we don't.

INTERVIEWER: There are some Arab workers who do stand up?

PRODUCTION WORKER: Yes, some do stand up to show sympathy. I don't, not because I'm a racist, I don't stand since according to my religion I'm not allowed to stand up. You know in our religion the prophet Muhammad prevented us from standing up even during mourning.

INTERVIEWER: I don't know. So you don't stand up [during the siren] for religious reasons.

INTERVIEWER: Yes, for religious reasons and not any other. . . . and I also try to leave the [production] floor where they are all standing, to respect and not to hurt them. I mean I do respect them and leave the floor.

The speaker makes a clear connection between his strong religious belief and his refusal to stand in honor of the fallen soldiers. His explanation that "this is the logic that I follow that is based on my own religious belief" may be seen as implying that not all Muslims accept his interpretation. In fact, the interviewer, who was an observant Muslim herself, had never heard of such a prohibition on standing up as a sign of respect. Whether or not this is the case, what is relevant here is the role of religion in workplace relations. Clearly, in this example religion was mobilized to resist a very powerful Israeli symbol, the memorial day for fallen soldiers, most of whom are Jews and also Druze and Bedouin soldiers (Orgad 2007).

One veteran Palestinian-Arab worker, who defined himself in the interview as a not very religious Muslim, described the preparations in the production plant for Israel's Independence Day. He related that after he had been assigned by management to hang Israeli flags around the plant, two of his co-workers, both of whom he characterized as very religious Muslims, refused to help him with the task. According to his account, these workers did not want to even touch the Israeli flag, which bears the Jewish symbol of a blue Star of David. What is interesting in the following excerpt, as in the previous interview, is the speaker's attempt to explain his co-workers' behavior by their deep religious sentiments, rather than their political opposition to Zionism:

You see the Israeli flag here? I'm in charge of these flags. And when I wish to hang them, well you need assistance, since I can't do it by myself. So I call X [names a Palestinian-Arab co-worker] and tell him: "Come on, what do you think, do I intend to marry this flag? This is work, come on and let's hang it." He doesn't agree [to help me] not even to hold the rope of the flag. He doesn't want to do it and he tells

> me: "No way, I can't touch it." And the guy in charge of the warehouse [where the flags are usually stored] too. When I order flags from him he brings them to me [to hang around the plant]. So once he brought me the small [Israeli] flags, and to make him angry, I said: "Bring me the larger flags, these [the smaller ones] won't do." This guy is 100 percent religious, and he told me: "The flags are over here. When you need, then come and get them. I can't bring them over to you."

It was a Palestinian-Arab, not a Jewish, worker who made the link between resistance to the Israeli flag and the religious belief of his two co-workers. For this self-declared moderate Muslim, hanging the flags was merely a task he had to perform at work, and not a symbolic "marriage," as he put it, referring to his lack of an emotional bond to the flag. By contrast, for the two religious Muslim workers, the Israeli flag represented something repulsive, something that could not be touched. It should be borne in mind that Muslim belief does not prevent followers from touching or hanging Israeli flags. This excerpt therefore exemplifies how religion and nationality are often intertwined in Israeli daily life, and how ethnonational sentiments can be expressed through religious arguments.

The role of religion in channeling ethnonational tensions between Jewish and Palestinian-Arab production workers could be seen in other interviews as well. A veteran Palestinian-Arab worker described an incident in which a religious Muslim worker expressed resentment at the Hebrew songs that one of the Jewish line managers used to stream through the loudspeakers during work shifts:

> I remember that once, you know, we also have problems with workers, a religious Muslim worker came to me and asked to turn down the volume of the Hebrew songs that were played over the loudspeakers during the night shift. I went to X, his [Jewish] manager, who responded by saying "He doesn't have to listen." Just like that, he threw a bomb and just carried on.

By describing his friend as a religious Muslim, the speaker hinted that the request was predicated on religious grounds and that listening to Hebrew songs somehow offended this friend's religious belief. The metaphor of a bomb that he uses to describe the dismissive reaction of the Jewish line manager to this request implies that this cultural clash can be compared to a military conflict in which the Jews are the aggressor.

According to a few other accounts, religion was used by management to control interethnic relations at work. Management was accused of employing a kind of "divide and rule" strategy in which they sought to intensify the antagonisms between Muslims, Christians, and Druze in the workforce in order to prevent the development of class consciousness. One example of such a strategy was described by one of the more experienced production workers, a Christian by faith:

> Listen, management, they're not stupid, they're smart. They saw how we all worked together, all of us Arabs were united only a few years ago, we were like one hand in the plant. We started, not that we were against the Jews, but we'd talk to one another and they [management] would see us [Palestinian-Arab workers]. Then they started to use [the strategy of] divide and rule. For example, they had these elections to choose the "best worker." Look how far they went ... they led to a situation in which each worker would choose a worker from his own [religious] group. But they [management] really divided us and they caused prejudice and suspicion among us. Now we Christians stayed neutral, and they [management] asked us "Why are you neutral?" And we answered: "Because this is called 'divide and rule,' we don't want to choose a Christian or a Muslim or a Druze worker, we simply don't want to choose anyone." In the end a guy from X village won, he left the factory not long ago. . . . They were able to divide us for some time, but now we're back to being friends. We're much closer now. We all understood that these elections were made to divide us, and the end result was actually stronger bonds among us.

This worker described a sense of solidarity that had developed among the Palestinian Arabs in the plant, which the Jewish managers perceived as threatening and tried to disrupt. He also noted that it took time for the Palestinian-Arab workforce to overcome the divisions exacerbated by management policy and to reunite. Nonetheless, the religious cleavage continued to disrupt working relations among the Palestinian-Arab workers, as described below in an interview excerpt with another Christian worker who, not long before the interviews took place, had had a fierce argument about religion with a Druze counterpart:

> I had this argument with a Druze worker, and I wanted to file a complaint about him at the police station. I had a quarrel with him, you know the Druze have something that is a form of life after death where your soul is reincarnated, and all of that. . . . Now I was speaking to someone who asked me "What is this idea?" and I started to explain to him, and then another guy comes and says: "'Why are you speaking about our religion?" . . . And he threatened to shoot me! But then someone from his village [also a Druze] came and told him, "Reincarnation doesn't belong to the Druze, it appears all over the world."

This is an extreme example of how religion could become a point of contention among the Palestinian-Arab workers, and not only between them and the Jewish workers.

Even though Palestinian Arabs constituted a majority of its workforce, the production plant failed to celebrate any of the Muslim or Christian holidays, and the interviewees made no reference to any special policies relating to Ramadan, a major Muslim holiday during which Muslims fast from dawn till sunset for an entire month, at the end of which there is a three-day celebration. The production workers perceived this neglect as another indication of management's broader disregard for their distinct cultural and religious identity. This neglect is surprising in light of the prominent role of religion in the daily management of workplace relations in the plant. In contrast to the production sector, religion played a distinctively different role in the two other research contexts.

Responding to Employees' Religious Needs in the Israeli High-Tech Sector

Both the Jewish and the Palestinian-Arab engineers agreed that the policy of the two multinational firms was to create a work environment that disregarded any cultural or religious differences between members of the diverse workforce. "Color-blind" (Bonilla-Silva 2017) policies, discussed in chapter 2, fall under the label of diversity management, and refer to human resource practices deliberately designed to ignore the racial and ethnonational background of employees. The ideology of diversity management is most explicit in the high-tech sector and is hardly mentioned by interviewees in the production and health sectors. According to some critical studies that analyze the notion of color blindness, such policies often lead to the reaffirmation of the cultural dominance of the majority group within a given society (see Hackler [2017] for the case of black citizens in the United States). Israel is no exception. Jews often hold prominent managerial positions in work organizations, even in branches of foreign multinationals, and their own cultural norms and codes of conduct become natural or taken-for-granted scripts of behavior and managerial policy. The resulting organizational culture might then reflect the hegemonic cultural and religious attributes of the majority group, and minority group members might feel left out. This means that the neglect of Muslim and Christian holidays is sometimes the result of lack of attention to the deeper meaning of diversity management, and not necessarily an explicit act of discrimination or rejection of other religions.

As we have seen in chapter 3, the vast majority of Palestinian-Arab engineers supported diversity management policies and expressed high satisfaction with

their treatment as equals among equals. In this sense they favorably acknowledged a merit-based promotion policy and the basic principle that ethnonational
origin had no influence on hiring and promotion decisions. Yet, and seemingly
paradoxically, they also wanted to be acknowledged and treated as members of
a different religion and culture within Israeli society. For example, Palestinian-
Arab engineers who worked for the American multinational firm repeatedly
complained in interviews that their employing organization was predominantly
Jewish. Some of the interviewees even felt that their distinct religious and cultural affiliation as Muslims or Christians was suppressed or simply ignored by
management, much like Ailon and Kunda's (2009) findings. When asked which
holidays were celebrated at work, a veteran Palestinian-Arab engineer in the
American multinational looked back at her experience in both her previous and
her current employment:

> Since I started to work for companies in the [Israeli] high-tech sector,
> their whole focus is on Jews and Jewish holidays, Jewish events, and this
> is as if another population of workers simply doesn't exist. And then
> all the holidays and gifts and [pause], all the culture is around the Jew-
> ish calendar, and the other things [other religious holidays] are simply
> ignored, totally ignored [pause]. My [team] manager, well, I send him
> an email, "I'm on vacation, I have this holiday" and just every time,
> again and again, he asks me afterward "What is this holiday? What is Eid
> al-Adha? What is Eid al-Fitr [major Muslim religious holidays]." Each
> time the same question! Get to know me already! [raises her voice], get
> to know our holidays [bursts into laughter]. Get to know the holidays
> of people who work with you. And to my organization I say, "Give them
> [the non-Jewish employees] a small gift, even a symbolic one. Put them
> in the spotlight, give them a day off."

This engineer was frustrated and even angry that only Jewish holidays were celebrated at her place of work and that the religion and associated culture of the
Palestinian-Arab employees were ignored, as though these were purely Jewish
organizations. She also expressed indignation at what she saw as her team manager's patent lack of interest in learning about the meaning of her religion and
religious holidays, which she regarded as implying a rejection of her religious
identity as a Muslim. She explicitly demanded that management should formally recognize Muslim holidays through small gifts to their employees on these
occasions, as is customary on some Jewish holidays. Thus, to mark the Jewish
New Year all employees in the Israeli multinational were given gifts and money
vouchers, which sometimes included a bottle of wine, even though, as one of the
Muslim engineers pointed out, Muslims are forbidden to consume any alcohol.

For some Palestinian-Arab employees, however, working in the Israeli high-tech sector offered an opportunity to learn more about Judaism and Jewish holidays, as described by a young Palestinian-Arab engineer from East Jerusalem:

> During Passover they prevent us from eating bread [at work], and I think that just after Passover they have this day when they bring different types of cheese and food to all the workers [probably referring to Shavuot, celebrated a few weeks after Passover]. Every holiday has its own atmosphere. They really live the spirit of the holiday. During Purim they have a fun day in all the company, I mean they bring candies and the little kids come and everybody dresses up.

This engineer, who had grown up and been educated in East Jerusalem, spoke Arabic as a mother tongue and English as a second language, but very little Hebrew. His previous exposure to Jewish culture had been very limited, and he expressed a sense of curiosity and even amazement at the degree to which the Israeli multinational celebrated Jewish holidays, which gave the organization a clear Jewish identity. While describing the organizational attention and financial support given to Jewish holidays, this account made no mention of any effort to celebrate Christian or Muslim holidays.

Another Palestinian-Arab engineer was very critical of the way the Israeli multinational ignored Ramadan. When asked if Jewish holidays are celebrated at work, he responded:

> Yes, they even make them [the Jewish workers] fancy dinners [during Jewish holidays]. During Ramadan we fast for a whole month, and it's difficult, and it would mean something . . . if my team manager sent an e-mail saying, "May your fast be easy" and it doesn't cost anything, and we don't want gifts or anything else.

This engineer clearly sought recognition and a sense of inclusion of her Muslim identity and resented, and was possibly offended by, the fact that her team manager simply ignored the Ramadan fasting period, with all the difficulties experienced by the Muslim workers who continue to work as normal while fasting from dawn to dusk. The phrase "they even make them fancy dinners" highlights her resentment at her work organization's willingness to satisfy the religious and cultural needs of the Jewish workers while neglecting the distinct identity and needs of the Muslim workers.

Nonetheless, the Palestinian-Arab engineers in the two multinationals did not attribute the dominance of Jewish holidays in their workplace to racism or prejudice, but rather to a lack of cultural sensitivity. A common thread that ran through the interviews was the need of the Palestinian-Arab engineers to be

acknowledged as part of the cultural environment of the employing organization. It is clear that alongside their support for merit-based promotion and equal
treatment for all employees, regardless of ethnonational or religious affiliation,
they also sought a sense of inclusion as Muslims and Christians.

Addressing the religious needs of Muslim workers was another point of tension in the two multinationals. Muslims are required to pray for a few minutes
five times a day. While the American multinational offered its Muslim workers
a dedicated prayer room, the Israeli multinational asked them to use any room
that happened to be free when they wished to pray. The veteran engineers in
the Israeli multinational accepted this arrangement, but the younger engineers,
especially those from East Jerusalem, who were more likely to identify themselves
as observant Muslims in the interviews, wished to receive a dedicated room for
Muslim prayer. These engineers had started working for the Israeli multinational
firm only three years prior to the interviews, mainly in the quality assurance
department that has lower occupational status than the R&D units. One of them
described their efforts to secure a permanent room:

> INTERVIEWER: Does your organization have a prayer space for Muslims?
> PALESTINIAN-ARAB ENGINEER: That's exactly the question I asked when
> I arrived here. Jews have a [permanent] space to pray, just left of
> the main entrance. I think they pray around noon, but these are not
> Muslim prayers, but Jewish prayers. So when I approached the HR
> manager, she answered: "If you're interested we can ask if you can
> use the same space, if there is more than one of you who wishes to
> pray." Well, before I used to choose one of the vacant meeting rooms,
> and I would close the door and pray, and if we were more than one
> person, we'd choose a larger space, a vacant conference room. But
> there is no dedicated space, and they offered us to pray there [in the
> Jewish prayer room].
> INTERVIEWER: But that space is dedicated to Jewish prayer?
> ENGINEER: For Jews, and we declined their offer out of respect and we
> told them "We better not, this is yours, so you continue praying here
> and we'll manage." And my friend Ahmed and myself, we'd again go
> to a meeting room or a conference room and close the door and pray,
> and then we'd tidy up the room and go.

It should be noted that management accepted the Muslims' need to pray during
working hours, but refused to allocate a permanent space for the prayers, a privi-
lege that only the Jewish workers enjoyed. While the interviewee claimed that
the Muslim workers refused to accept the HR manager's offer to use the Jewish

workers' prayer room because of their respect for the Jews' religious needs, their refusal might also indicate that they regarded the assignment of a dedicated room for prayers as a symbol of cultural acceptance of them as Muslims.

It would seem logical to assume that the American multinational firm would be more attuned to the religious needs of its Muslim workers when compared to the Israeli multinational because diversity management was more deeply ingrained in its structure and work processes and its top management at head-quarters had no reason to favor the religious needs of Jews over those of the Muslim workers. It would also seem reasonable to attribute the Israeli multinational's failure to recognize its Muslim employees' needs to the ongoing conflict between Jews and Palestinian Arabs. Nonetheless, it was precisely the Israeli multinational that expressed greater sensitivity during the month of Ramadan, when, accord-ing to the account of two Palestinian-Arab engineers, it allowed Muslim workers to leave one hour early so that they could arrive home in time for the Iftar dinner with family and friends that breaks the fast for that day.

But what can be considered an inclusive policy toward workers of all religious affiliations? A Palestinian-Arab HR manager described the policy of her previous employer, a company that had been established by a group of experienced Jew-ish high-tech entrepreneurs with the explicit goal of hiring a large workforce of Palestinian-Arab engineers in order to help them gain professional experience at work and later integrate them into the Israeli high-tech sector. These entrepre-neurs considered that Palestinian-Arab engineers were discriminated against in the thriving Israeli high-tech sector and that they required assistance, particularly when launching their engineering careers right after graduation. It was her expe-rience in that company that had indeed paved her way into the HR department of a large multinational firm:

> INTERVIEWER: In X company [her previous employer], what was your policy [regarding religious holidays]? Which holidays did you mark at work?
>
> PALESTINIAN-ARAB HR MANAGER: We said, we are X company, a com-pany that was founded on the basis of respect for the other [eth-nonational groups], and to respect others you need to respect the individuals who compose these "others." So everyone celebrates their own holidays and receives their own gifts.
>
> INTERVIEWER: Nice idea. Can you give me an example?
>
> HR MANAGER: So on the Jewish New Year, the Jews celebrate and they receive a gift. We [the HR department] organize an event at which one of the Jewish workers explains to everyone else what the Jewish New Year is. Why do the Jews celebrate the day? [We] put honey and

apples [traditional Jewish New Year foods] out in the kitchen and everyone, everyone including the Arab [employees] are part of the Jewish New Year event. But those who are given the gift and the day off are the Jewish workers. We speak about diversity, and we want to translate diversity into praxis. So we use Christmas to expose people to what Christmas means, what the traditions are, and what we did, we took Jewish people [from the high-tech firm] and we invited them to walk around the market [in Nazareth] and we showed them what Christmas is.

In her previous company, instead of ignoring the distinct religious backgrounds of different employees, as the "color-blind" approach does, in her capacity as HR manager she had striven to make religious holidays an occasion for mutual acquaintance. The fact that Jews were a minority in that company (although most of the managers were Jewish), because of its explicit goal of recruiting Palestinian-Arab engineers and technicians, might explain management's willingness to celebrate all major religious holidays at work and to use them as opportunities for their employees to become acquainted with each other's diverse religious and cultural identities. National holidays were also celebrated in the company, but the sensitive and positive use of the celebration of religious holidays, designed to bring members of different ethnonational groups closer together, only highlights the failure of the two multinational companies in this study to take steps to deepen cultural awareness among their employees.

Religion in the Health Sector

Of all the three research contexts, religion was of least significance in the three health institutions. Religion or religious cleavages were rarely mentioned by the interviewees, and, unlike the production workers, the Palestinian-Arab physicians did not present themselves as religious. Only a few of the Jewish physicians interviewed mentioned their religious belief, and only one wore a yarmulke. Moreover, religion and religious holidays did not emerge as a point of interethnic contention or as platforms for expressing political views or distinct national identities. According to these accounts, the public performance of religious identity was even viewed as having a beneficial role, such as the flexibility that religious diversity allowed in managing work shifts during religious holidays, since Jewish staff members could work extra shifts during Christian or Muslim holidays, and non-Jewish members of the medical teams could reciprocate during the Jewish holidays. Thus, members of different religious groups could celebrate their holidays without disrupting the workflow, and this interdependency encouraged social solidarity. The second positive role of religion in the medical sector was the custom of sharing traditional foods with fellow members of the medical teams, mainly just after religious holidays. Thus, religious holidays became an occasion for learning about each other's religion and culture.

These experiences were reported by Palestinian-Arab medical staff in both the public and the private hospital. For example, a veteran Palestinian-Arab nurse in the public hospital, Christian by religion, described how she was able to take time off during the Christmas holiday:

> PALESTINIAN-ARAB NURSE: For the head nurse [she knows that] I have my holiday on Christmas, and no one ever argues with me about that, and I don't argue either. This is my holiday!
>
> INTERVIEWER: This is yours? [pause]
>
> NURSE: It's because I work on their [Jewish and Muslim] holidays.
>
> INTERVIEWER: Exactly, it's good for everybody?
>
> NURSE: I respect them. On their holidays I work the whole holiday. There's no way I'd make a fuss or fail to do so. But on my holidays, everybody calls me and sends me [holiday] greetings, I feel that I'm treated very well.

A Palestinian-Arab physician depicted a similar situation in the public hospital:

> PALESTINIAN-ARAB PHYSICIAN: Every time that we [Muslims] have a holiday, they [the Jewish and Christian co-workers] say, for example: "What about the cakes?" so I bring the cake with me the next morning. In this respect things are really good here.
>
> INTERVIEWER: And how about those fasting through the month of Ramadan?
>
> PHYSICIANS: They have to work one hour less.
>
> INTERVIEWER: They can arrive later or leave earlier?
>
> PHYSICIAN: I don't know, I'm also Muslim but I don't fast, so I never found out how to get the reduced shift time during Ramadan.
>
> INTERVIEWER: And how about the Christian members of the medical teams? Someone told me that they do many shifts during the Jewish holidays, and then during Christmas they are given time off?
>
> PHYSICIAN: That's true, totally true, and really good. Since I don't want to work on my holidays, we have the same problem. On Passover we [the non-Jewish members of the medical staff] work extra shifts and also during the [Jewish] New Year. And this year we enabled many of

the Jewish co-workers, mainly the religious Jews among them, not to work during the October [Jewish] holidays.

INTERVIEWER: Do you feel that they also reciprocate? That this is a fair system?

PHYSICIAN: Yes, I get my holiday when we have our holiday [referring to Eid al-Fitr], then I get six days, including one day before the holiday and one day after.

It therefore seems that in the health sector religious holidays encourage coop-eration among members of different ethnonational and religious groups, rather than becoming a point of friction as in the case of the production workers, and to a lesser extent in the high-tech sector. Traditional holiday food is the way members of the medical team express their distinct religious identity, much to the enjoy-ment of their co-workers from other religious groups. Moreover, although the public hospital marked Jewish holidays such as the Jewish New Year or Passover with official celebrations, the non-Jewish employees, unlike their counterparts in the high-tech sector, did not complain that their holidays were overlooked. One possible explanation is that work shifts are so demanding that the hospital's management and medical team members do not usually have time to participate in the holiday celebrations at work and confine them to their private sphere.

Comparing the Role of Religion across the Research Settings

The findings of this chapter indicate that religion indeed plays a role in the daily management of workplace relations in the ethnically divided state of Israel, but that this role varies across the three research contexts. In the production plant, religion was tightly entwined with political views. It was an important part of the self-identity of workers and also provided a platform for expressing political opinions. Production workers, both Jews and Palestinian Arabs, justified territo-rial claims over the land of Israel/Palestine by referring to divine promises and citing the Bible and the Koran. On some occasions, Palestinian-Arab production workers employed religion to refrain from participating in what they perceived as Zionist ceremonies. The importance attached to religion in the production plant was highlighted by the claim made by a Palestinian-Arab worker that man-agement employed religion in a "divide and rule" strategy that aimed to control the workforce by deepening existing religious cleavages among Christians, Mus-lim, and Druze workers. Thus, religion was reportedly used to undermine the class struggle and to weaken the bargaining power of a unified Palestinian-Arab workforce. Nonetheless, issues of class consciousness and class struggle have little empirical manifestation in the interviews, which might suggest that the deep ethnonational and religious cleavage overshadows a shared class position. The above instance, however, directs our attention to attempts made by some production workers to overcome these cleavages and to work together to improve their working conditions.

This chapter demonstrated that religion had the potential to escalate political arguments and to make them even more emotional and difficult to resolve. Yet, the fact that both the Jewish and Palestinian-Arab production workers who participated in political discussions were religious people and often grounded their political arguments in the sacred texts also created a common ground. I conclude that political arguments were often more substantive, egalitarian, and open between majority and minority group members in the production sector than in medicine or high-tech. One can argue that religion provided a way to bypass the clear ethnonational hierarchies that dominate Israeli politics and allowed deeper mutual understanding among the production workers, despite opposing political views on the Israeli–Palestinian conflict.

The interrelation between religion and politics was all but absent in the high-tech sector, where Palestinian-Arab engineers sought recognition of their religious identity in order to gain a sense of inclusion in the dominant Jewish culture of their employing organization. When discussing religion in the workplace, the Palestinian-Arab engineers challenged the color-blind policies of the two multinationals by expressing a desire that their co-workers acknowledge their distinct religious beliefs and customs. Interestingly, the issue of facilities for prayer became a source of tension in the Israeli multinational only when the new recruits from East Jerusalem, and not the veteran Palestinian-Arab engineers, requested a permanent prayer room, like the room dedicated for Jewish prayer. This demand might reflect a growing confidence in the legitimacy of expressing Muslim belief at work, but it might also simply indicate that the engineers and technicians from East Jerusalem were more religiously observant. In the American multinational, management set aside a permanent prayer room for the Muslim employees. As to special considerations during the month of Ramadan, it was the Israeli multinational that granted Muslim workers one hour off every day so that they could arrive home in time for the Iftar dinner, a practice that was also reported in the public hospital.

Finally, the medical workers, both Jewish and Palestinian-Arab, rarely spoke about religion and rarely presented themselves by their religious affiliation. Instead, the physicians and the nurses described the religious diversity in positive terms, since it allowed flexibility in managing time off for Christian, Jewish, Druze, and Muslim physicians and nurses on their religious holidays. Moreover, the custom of bringing traditional holiday food to work and sharing it with their colleagues brought members of medical teams closer together, at least in this narrow sense. What is striking is that religion in both the high-tech and health sectors was not employed by the Palestinian-Arab professionals to express political views or resistance to Zionist symbols. This might be explained by the more general inclination in high tech and medicine to refrain from political arguments at work. It might also be related to the higher level of education required by those sectors and the smaller proportion of deeply religious people among their employees (for the negative correlation between level of higher education and religiosity, see the seminal study of Albrecht and Heaton 1984).

Religion and religious holidays can also serve to bring members of opposing groups closer together, by exposing them to each other's traditions. Despite this potential, religion was more a point of contention than a point of convergence. The only positive example, although limited in scope, was reported in the medical sector. But despite the deep ethnonational and religious cleavage, workers from opposing sides to the conflict did find ways to constitute ties across the divide. Some of these workplace ties even persisted outside the workplace and over extended periods of time. The next chapter delves deeper into the nature and duration of these more meaningful relations between Jewish and Palestinian-Arab workers.

BUILDING BRIDGES ACROSS THE ETHNONATIONAL DIVIDE

The considerable geographical and sociocultural segregation of Palestinian Arabs and Jews in Israel has deep historical roots. In the mid-1970s, a debate developed among historians of the British Mandate in Palestine over the nature and extent of social relations between the Arab and Jewish communities of that period. Some historians and sociologists (e.g., Horowitz and Lissak 1977) argued that a "dual society," composed of distinct Jewish and Arab communities already existed at that time. According to this model each community had its own cultural, economic, and social worlds, with little interaction between them. They were already geographically separated, had established separate educational systems, and enlisted international support from distinctively different allies across the globe.

Other historians argued that interactions between Palestinian Arabs and Jews under the British Mandate were significant and more frequent than described by the first model. Some studies of everyday life have identified personal and social connections between Jews and Palestinian Arabs and the common social ground they shared vis-à-vis their British rulers (e.g., Alyagon-Darr 2019). This model is confirmed by the work of certain labor historians, who depict how the British Mandate administration employed thousands of local Palestinians and Jews in the public sector, including the Haifa port, the oil refineries, and the railway and postal authorities. In his seminal historical study of Palestinians and Jews at work in Mandate Palestine, Lockman (1993) describes a few instances of cooperation between Jewish and Palestinian Arab members of the railway workers' unions under the British Mandate, which arose from the weakness of the unions against the mighty employer—the colonial British government. As indicated in the introduction, Lockman also gives examples of personal amicable relations both between Jews and Palestinian Arabs who worked together and between the leaders of the unions, including attendance at co-workers' funerals and one documented instance when Jewish and Palestinian-Arab union leaders relaxed together on the Tel Aviv beach after a meeting with the Mandatory railway management (618). There is, however, scant research on Palestinian–Jewish cooperation and friendship in work organizations after the establishment of the state of Israel, apart from a few studies of collegial relationships among Palestinian-Arab social workers and psychologists (e.g., Katz et al. 2005). This chapter seeks to tackle this gap in the literature by focusing on amicable relations across the ethnonational cleavage today, in the first quarter of the twenty-first century, in the three sectors studied. Previous chapters depicted such ties within the context of work itself, for example in the case of interdependencies created by local divisions of labor in the medical sector. This chapter will explore other cases in which such ties led to meaningful personal relations among workers and their families in the world outside the workplace.

While the research literature on this topic is scarce, survey data provide some evidence regarding the willingness of Palestinian Arabs and Jews to accept members of the other group as personal friends. For example, in a 2021 survey, Hermann et al. (2022, 137) found that 78 percent of Palestinian-Arab respondents expressed a willingness to establish a personal friendship with a Jewish person, compared with only 58 percent of the Jewish respondents. An interesting finding of this survey was the negative correlation between the Jews' level of religious observance and their willingness to create a friendship with a Palestinian Arab. By contrast, educational attainment was found to increase the Jews' tendency to form such relationships (139).

The daily experience of working together offers ample opportunities for people to get to know one another. We have already established that personal ties are indeed forged at work, based on various attributes such as personality, mutual interests, or simply interdependence demanded by the task at hand. The question remains to what extent these ties endure once Palestinian-Arab and Jewish workers end their work shift and leave their employing organization.

Besides the natural curiosity regarding friendships across the ethnonational divide, especially in a country mired in violent political conflict, there are strong theoretical reasons for studying interethnic personal ties. An analysis of day-to-day working practices in ethnically mixed settings reveals that workers tend to buffer their immediate work environments from external political pressures and sometimes even constitute friendly ties inside the workplace with co-workers from other ethnonational affiliations. The examples presented in chapter 2 regarding the coping strategy of "split ascription" indicate, however, that workers do not necessarily translate microlevel social ties and the reduction of interethnic prejudice that occurs within mixed teams into a more positive view of macrolevel structures. This explicit disconnect between microlevel encounters and macro-level structures can start laying the ground for the foundation of a middle-range theory designed to address the failure of microlevel accounts of intergroup preju-dice reduction to be translated into reduced macrolevel conflicts among oppos-ing groups (Darr 2018; see also Pettigrew 2008, 195), a critical issue in studies of interethnic relations in conflict zones (e.g. Hargie and Dickson 2003; Hewstone et al. 2006).

Chapter 2 also showed that workers tend to describe their ties with their work colleagues from other ethnonational groups as neutral or even positive at times. Yet, the distinction they make between the direct work environment and struc-tural elements of their employing organization, as reflected in split ascription, makes it less likely that reduced intergroup prejudice at work will have an impact on the macrolevel conflict. While the nurses cited in chapter 2 are ready to insu-late their immediate work environment from fierce ethnonational conflict, they are reluctant to change their basic attitudes toward that conflict, and they assert their reluctance by projecting the deep schisms in Israeli society onto organiza-tional structures and formal processes. As a structural attribute, perceived dis-crimination is hard to resist or change but is easy to accept as a fact of life. As explained in chapter 2, these findings suggest that split ascription is an effective situational coping strategy within the workplace, but that it is not an engine of change that can remedy deeply entrenched ethnonational divides in war-torn countries.

This chapter continues the analysis beyond the framing of split ascription and argues that the potential of social ties forged at work to reduce levels of intereth-nic tension in broader social spheres should also be explored. It asks if workplace ties spill over into the private sphere and, if so, whether they have the potential to alter interethnic relations outside the workplace. Could the spillover of such ties on a large enough scale form the basis for reducing the level of interethnic con-flict in the country as a whole? Thus, the following analysis should also be seen as an attempt to explore another venue for a middle-range theory that connects workplace ties with the broader ethnonational and political conflict between Pal-estinian Arabs and Jews in Israel.

This chapter identifies important, often surprising, differences between the health, high-tech, and production sectors with regard to the spillover of amicable ties from work to the private sphere. It was precisely the production workers who reported the most enduring social ties across the ethnonational divide, on both the personal and family levels, despite the fierce political and religious arguments that characterized the workplace. Medical workers, specifically the interns and the younger nurses, expressed interest in allowing social ties forged at work to spill over into the private sphere, but this interest was often hampered by the heavy workload, the long shifts, and the demands of family life, especially caring for young children. It was the engineers and technicians in the high-tech sector who reported the lowest level of interethnic ties, within and without the workplace, despite their shared membership in a strong professional community of highly educated engineers, and the application of explicit diversity management policies in their employing companies.

In all the sectors, social activities outside of work can be classified into three categories. The first comprises activities organized by management such as retreats, fun days, and trips to various places in the country. The second category consists of grassroots social initiatives that include all or most members of the work team, for example organizing a barbecue in a public park. The third category relates to more private and voluntary social encounters between two or three members of the workforce, such as going out together for a drink. All these activities sometimes involved family members. Attending colleagues' weddings, an activity that looms large in the examples below, can be seen as combining formal and grassroots elements. All three categories will be discussed below in each of the sectors, but the focus will be on personal and voluntary social ties that originate at work and are maintained in the private sphere. The conclusions will compare the findings across the sectors and draw more general insights about the transformative potential of amicable social ties on the macro level.

Amicable Ties among the Production Workers

Management of the production plant organized trips twice a year, which included workers and their families. At times, these events lasted two days, with the company paying for a hotel. Interestingly, Palestinian-Arab workers who spoke about these events in interviews, generally described them as a positive initiative by management, but downplayed their impact on the constitution of social ties across the ethnonational divide, as in the following interview with a Palestinian-Arab production worker who was asked about such trips:

> PALESTINIAN-ARAB PRODUCTION WORKER: Yes, sometimes they take us on trips, with sleepover.
> INTERVIEWER: Yes? Where did you go?
> WORKER: Jerusalem.
> INTERVIEWER: Everyone? Including families?
> WORKER: Yes, together with our families.

INTERVIEWER: And do you feel that Jewish and Arab workers bond together on such trips?

WORKER: The truth is, that being with my family, I don't really know where all the younger people go, or what they do. I feel that they don't bond together, that is, the Arabs go in one group and the Jews in another.

This account, which was echoed by other workers, casts doubt on the ability of work trips to enhance social bonds among Jewish and Palestinian-Arab workers. Yet, production workers did testify to deep and meaningful grassroots social ties that were typically created at work, during regular shifts, and later extended to the private sphere. A veteran Palestinian-Arab worker described how, while working for a previous employer, he had forged close ties with Jewish co-workers:

PALESTINIAN-ARAB WORKER: I can tell you that the bond [with Jewish co-workers] was very strong, I mean, [in my previous employment] I used to hang out with Jewish [co-workers], we'd sit together, have fun. They were all Jewish, I'd go out with them with two other Arab colleagues of mine.

INTERVIEWER: You'd go out with them?

WORKER: Yes, we'd sit, have a drink, laugh together, all was fine.

INTERVIEWER: You didn't feel like an outsider?

WORKER: No, the Jewish workers would come and invite me to join them, we'd sit and talk, just like friends. I didn't feel that I'm an Arab among Jews, or that anyone dislikes me because I'm Arab.

This worker stressed a sense of friendship among this group of people who chose to spend time together while setting aside, at least temporarily, the ethnonational tensions that sometimes flared up at work. Indeed, some of the Palestinian-Arab workers who reported friendly ties across the ethnonational divide, also engaged, according to their accounts, in fierce arguments with their Jewish friends. They claimed that their friendship with the Jewish workers was maintained despite these arguments.

Another Palestinian-Arab worker also reported voluntary social activities with co-workers whom he described as Jewish friends at the production plant: "I sometimes go to dinner together [with a Jewish co-worker] and then go out to the pub or to the disco. Sometimes I even sleep overnight at his house." A Palestinian-Arab shift manager who had worked for over fifteen years at this plant also described a close personal relationship he had developed with one of the Jewish workers. The interview was carried out in the main building where all the administrative staff was working, and the door was half open:

> PALESTINIAN-ARAB PRODUCTION WORKER: [to the interviewer] Did you see that blonde woman who just passed by the door? Holding a baby?
>
> INTERVIEWER: Yes, just now.
>
> WORKER: I've been working with her for about four and a half years. Listen, she, also I, I regard her as my sister, and she treats me like a brother.
>
> INTERVIEWER: Really?
>
> WORKER: Yes, I tell you, I even visited her house, and she visited us, she's from the kibbutz originally, but what a woman!
>
> INTERVIEWER: Yes?
>
> WORKER: You don't find such people.
>
> INTERVIEWER: Sometimes good things happen.
>
> WORKER: Last year I was in Mecca.
>
> INTERVIEWER: Yes?
>
> WORKER: When I returned, even though she knows that with us [Muslims] it's forbidden, she hugged and kissed me [laughs]. . . . I even met her husband and she met my wife.

This worker exemplified the strength of this relationship by saying that despite that fact his friend had disregarded a religious norm by greeting him with a hug upon his return from Mecca, he had not been angry with her but rather perceived her behavior as a token of their friendship.

Workers in the production sector had the deepest acquaintance with each other's family life and were far more likely than their counterparts in the health and high-tech sectors to be involved and to lend support to co-workers during difficult times. A Palestinian-Arab production worker, who described himself as an observant Muslim, reported how he still kept in touch with the widow of a Jewish colleague whom he had considered a personal friend:

> PALESTINIAN-ARAB PRODUCTION WORKER: There was a religious Jewish worker who was an old friend of mine. He passed away a year and a half or two years ago.
>
> INTERVIEWER: He worked here?
>
> PRODUCTION WORKER: He used to work here. We were very good friends, his wife and his daughters would visit us at home and we visited their house. This man passed away, and today his wife called me. They are religious and live in a religious moshav [agricultural village].

This excerpt reveals a remarkably deep friendship between the two workers, which even continued after the Jewish worker's death. The fact that the Jewish family was religious, which the speaker stressed twice, is especially interesting since religion is often perceived as deepening ethnonational divides in Israeli society. We have already seen that talk about religious matters could lead to heated political discussions in the production plant, but this case, where both parties were religious, might indicate that religious belief also had the potential to bring Jewish and Palestinian-Arab workers closer together.

One of the Jewish workers, a religious young man who had recently finished his military service, described a friendship that had developed between him and an older Palestinian-Arab worker, who had become his informal mentor when he took his current job. He described in the interview how the Palestinian-Arab workers explained to him how to perform different work tasks and how to keep safety regulations. This act of kindness had helped him integrate into the workplace and had formed the basis for their friendship. As described in chapter 2, the Jewish worker mentioned that they coordinated their smoking breaks, had personal discussions and occasionally went out for a drink in the nearby city when they were off work.

All these examples demonstrate that despite the fierce political arguments, at times intertwined with religious beliefs, some production workers formed deep and amicable ties with Jewish co-workers that extended to the private sphere and involved their families. The proportion of Palestinian-Arab workers who reported such relations with Jewish workers in their current or past employment was impressive. Nine of the twelve Palestinian-Arab workers mentioned Jewish friends. The type of friendship varied and included going out together for coffee or a drink in the evening and meetings with the families of both sides. Some of these ties were reported to exist over long periods of time. As we shall see in the following sections, such close ties were rarely reported in the medical sector, and were simply nonexistent in the two multinationals in the Israeli high-tech sector.

Amicable Social Ties among Members of Medical Teams

As noted above, both Jewish and Palestinian-Arab members of medical teams expressed their willingness to organize shared social activities and to constitute ties with members of other ethnonational groups, but these intentions often encountered difficulties associated with shift work, which prevented some of the medical workers from participating. This section discusses the attitudes of three occupational groups in the three health institutions studied: (1) interns in the public hospital; (2) senior physicians in the public hospital; and (3) nurses in all three institutions. Although the differences between these groups are minor, they do deserve attention as they demonstrate how the potential to develop closer bonds is sometimes rooted in variables such as shared work practice, age group, and local division of labor.

Interns in the Public Hospital

The public hospital studied employed thousands of health workers, including junior and senior physicians, nurses, and nursing assistants. The very size and heterogeneity of the workforce provide a fruitful basis for comparing amicable social ties among interns, senior physicians, and nurses. The group that reported the closest ties that persisted outside the hospital was that of the young interns.

The liminal status occupied by the interns—somewhere between student and senior physician—might explain their greater desire to initiate social events as these created a sense of group solidarity. The interns themselves pointed to their long working shifts, which at times, such as over the weekend, could extend to twenty-six hours, as promoting social cohesiveness and even friendships. According to their accounts, it was these long shifts, in which they constantly consulted with one another, shared responsibility, and had the joint experience of having to learn on the job, along with the demanding exams that they went through together, that brought them closer. Their intense interaction at work might account for their willingness to participate in organizing formal social events sponsored by the hospital. The interns were also more likely to initiate grassroots activities such as meeting with other interns outside the hospital, than senior physicians or nurses.

Every ward in the public hospital was allocated a budget for social activities and could decide what form they would take. A Palestinian-Arab intern, who had been working at the hospital for five years, described these formal activities, but also alluded to an array of other social events initiated by the interns themselves:

> PALESTINIAN-ARAB INTERN: We've got ward activities, fun days that we hold. These activities are most important for interns. We had a few fun days; I was even on the organizing committee. It's important not to meet only here [at the hospital] and discuss work, but also to talk about other things, to meet colleagues' families.
>
> INTERVIEWER: And how about coffee places, or other things you like to do?
>
> INTERN: Cafés, yes,
>
> INTERVIEWER: Do you ever go to colleagues' weddings?

INTERN: Yes, sure, all the Jewish interns are older than me, they've got military service and they start [medical school] only afterward. So I'm not married yet, but I'm getting married in six months

INTERVIEWER: Congratulations!

INTERN: Yes, and I intend to invite everyone, and I assume that they'll all come.

This speaker presented a favorable view of the formal social events, which he implied, are intended particularly for interns, possibly to help them develop a sense of solidarity and shared support during their difficult work. He also mentioned informal social gatherings and attending weddings of his Jewish colleagues and felt close enough to his fellow interns, whether Jewish or Arab, to invite them to his own wedding and expect all of them to attend. Since interns are of the age when marriage usually takes place, wedding parties, which there is a high obligation to attend, also provide opportunities for strengthening more lasting social ties.

Senior Physicians in the Public Hospital

The senior physicians also described amicable ties across the ethnonational divide but noted that most of these were created during the internship and dwindled over time. For this reason, most examples in the interviews with the senior physicians referred to formal events such as weddings and funerals. Some of the senior physicians portrayed a very similar picture to that of the interns, while others argued that with time and seniority social ties with peers become more formal. An example of social activities both within and outside the hospital setting was offered by a senior Palestinian-Arab physician, who had graduated from the internship program at the hospital, gone abroad for a two-year residency, and returned to the hospital as a senior physician:

SENIOR PALESTINIAN-ARAB PHYSICIAN: We work together, three doctors on each shift. . . . It's not as if we work separately, since during shifts we spend a lot of time together, we take breaks together, and have lunch or dinner [at the hospital's canteen] together. If we have the time, we go for a coffee, also outside of the ward, we go out and have fun together from time to time.

INTERVIEWER: Really, so you get to spend time outside the ward with Jewish and Arab colleagues?

PHYSICIAN: Yes, we go out together. This is because relations among us are good. I can even say that I have [Jewish] friends. We spend lots of time together at the ward but also outside the hospital.

This physician attributed the personal relations to the intensive work with his colleagues and their constant need to consult with and depend on one another. His use of the word *friends* to describe some of the Jewish physicians emphasized that these social ties were not confined to the hospital, although he did not explicitly refer to social events involving families.

Other senior physicians, both Palestinian-Arab and Jewish, also expressed a positive attitude toward social ties with members of the other ethnonational group, but tended to describe them as taking place in more formal settings, as in the following account by a Jewish senior physician:

> INTERVIEWER: Do you sometime meet [Palestinian-Arab] colleagues for coffee outside the hospital?
>
> JEWISH SENIOR PHYSICIAN: We meet more at formal events.
>
> INTERVIEWER: More formal? Let's say weddings?
>
> PHYSICIAN: Yes, or various events organized by the ward.
>
> INTERVIEWER: I see.
>
> PHYSICIAN: Yes, and at soccer games, we sit together, at home games of [names a local soccer team].
>
> INTERVIEWER: In the stadium?
>
> PHYSICIAN: Yes, so we meet in places like that.
>
> INTERVIEWER: Do you bring your kids with you?
>
> PHYSICIAN: Yes, sometimes we do.

This account indicated that meetings with colleagues outside the hospital were less spontaneous than in the case of the interns. Even the occasional outings to soccer games, which are less formal than weddings but also require planning, suggest that these relations fall short of the warm and long-lasting personal ties among a few of workers' families in the production plant. While young Palestinian-Arab and Jewish physicians did develop personal ties, senior physicians reported that over time these ties were restricted to more formal events such as weddings and funerals and the boundaries between workplace relations and private life became more sharply drawn.

Nurses in All Three Health Institutions

The nurses' accounts of lasting amicable relationships with members of other ethnonational groups varied across the three medical institutions. Nurses in the private Palestinian-Arab hospital reported the highest level of grassroots social initiatives and also a few cases of personal friendships across the ethnonational divide that extended beyond working hours. Nurses in the public hospital expressed a real interest in constituting ties with members of the other ethnonational group but described various obstacles that prevented them from doing so. Finally, nurses in the retirement home reported that they socialized with members of the other group only at formal events such as weddings but did not mention any amicable social bonds that continued to exist outside the workplace.

A veteran Palestinian-Arab midwife in the private hospital described some of the social activities organized by nurses in the maternity ward:

> We'd organize a day trip, we love going out on trips together. Usually all of us participate, except those who are on shift duty that day. Typically, we hold a lottery, we write our names on pieces of paper, and then draw the names of those who'll work. Sometime we organize a barbecue, and we hold it at convenient hours, so that those who worked on the night shift can sleep after their shift and still join us, and those who work on the evening shift can be with us before going to work.

Other accounts of nurses in this hospital also focused on the logistical difficulties of organizing social events that involved all members of the medical teams. Another Palestinian-Arab midwife from this institution indeed differentiated between such events and more spontaneous meetings with her small group of midwives, composed of both Palestinian Arabs and Jews, which were more feasible:

> It's very difficult because our work here is very demanding. We always make plans to go out together, but then it takes ages until we actually do so, go out to have fun. You need to check all the time: who's on shift duty and when? Who'll do the work when we're away? This is why it's extremely difficult to meet with the whole medical team. Including physicians. But it's easier for me to meet with the midwives since we work eight-hour shifts, and the rest of the day is ours. For example a month ago we organized and went out together for coffee after the morning shift, just like that, we made a plan and carried it out.

The nurses in the large public hospital depicted a somewhat different picture of socializing outside the hospital. One of the veteran Jewish nurses confirmed the willingness of many nurses in her department to take part in social activities:

> JEWISH NURSE: They [the Palestinian-Arab nurses] are very open to social ties with their Jewish counterparts, we have good relations. [In our ward] we have two young nurses, an Arab and a Jewish nurse, who are single, and they sometimes go out at night to have, what do

you call this food [pause] sushi, and drink beer, I mean they go out together.

INTERVIEWER: Did you ever go to the wedding of one of your Arab co-workers?

NURSE: Yes.

INTERVIEWER: Yes?

NURSE: I went to a number of weddings. Just recently we had X's [names a fellow Palestinian-Arab nurse] wedding, but I didn't go because I was in mourning. But before that I attended the wedding of one of the physicians.

While this nurse described a friendship between two younger nurses in her ward that extended beyond the workplace, she seemed to imply that this was an exception. Indeed, the vast majority of nurses claimed that shift work presented a real barrier to creating enduring friendships among members of the medical team. Thus, one nurse from the public hospital succinctly summarized the main obstacle to social activities outside the hospital, regardless of the ethnic origin of the people involved: "First of all, the shifts, and we are so tired from work that [laughs] we don't even have time for our family!"

A few nurses in the public hospital even drew a clear distinction between collegial relations at work and deeper personal friendships in general, as in the following excerpt from an interview with a Palestinian-Arab nurse:

PALESTINIAN-ARAB NURSE: [Speaking about personal ties with other members of her medical team] The relations among us are good, but I've got a lot of experience, and I've learned not to have friends at work.

INTERVIEWER: Okay. So you'd rather not have [friends] at work?

NURSE: No, at work it's nice, but outside of work, I don't know, that's my personal attitude.

INTERVIEWER: So you don't drink coffee with your colleagues outside of work?

NURSE: The truth is that it's very hard to coordinate. We work shifts 24/7, and every time we want to, even when we really want to, it doesn't work out.

INTERVIEWER: And do you attend events held by your colleagues?

NURSE: Sure.

INTERVIEWER: Of Jewish members of the team?

NURSE: Sure, weddings, at these events we're okay. . . . But the truth is that when I got married they [Jewish colleagues] didn't come.

> INTERVIEWER: Really?
>
> NURSE: Yes, they were afraid to visit village X [where she lives].
>
> INTERVIEWER: But why? Were those politically tense or violent times?
>
> NURSE: No, and there were nurses that I've worked with for seven years who didn't attend my wedding. That really hurts.

This nurse's opposition to forming personal friendships at work may have been the result of her disappointment with her Jewish colleagues who had failed to attend her wedding because, she explains, "They were afraid." The geographical separation between the Jewish and Palestinian-Arab citizens of Israel means that many Palestinian-Arab villages and towns around the country have no Jewish residents. The only places where Jews and Palestinian Arabs live alongside each other are mixed cities such as Haifa and Jerusalem, and even there many neighborhoods have a clear ethnonational identity. The fear of visiting her village that this nurse attributes to her Jewish colleagues may reflect a more general fear and distrust of the large Palestinian-Arab minority on the part of Jews in Israel. She thus relates the failure of her Jewish colleagues to attend her wedding to the broader Israeli–Palestinian conflict, which reveals the profound impact that the conflict is perceived to have, even on the personal and social levels. This interview provides further evidence of how the workplace acts as an important arena of broader political, ethnonational, and religious divides.

In the Jewish retirement home, there were no reports of social activities organized by management, and also no evidence of grassroots social initiatives. The only occasions on which Jewish and Palestinian-Arab co-workers met outside the hospital were at weddings and funerals. One of the Palestinian-Arab nurses described one such instance:

> PALESTINIAN-ARAB NURSE: Yesterday we were all together, most of the medical team in my ward, at a wedding.
>
> INTERVIEWER: Who got married?
>
> NURSE: X [names a co-worker]
>
> INTERVIEWER: Really, how nice,
>
> NURSE: Yes, she got married yesterday.
>
> INTERVIEWER: So all of you were at the wedding?
>
> NURSE: Not exactly, but most of us [mentions the names of eight nurses, four Jewish and four Palestinian-Arab].

Such events are not only more formal and structured but also relatively rare and entail a greater social obligation to attend. Since they are conducted according to the religious and cultural norms of each ethnic group, they also provide an opportunity for nurses to learn about each other's customs and to observe their colleagues' lives outside the familiar workplace context. It is precisely these events, which are marked by formal ethnic differences, that provide an important basis for deeper social acquaintance between the different groups in all three medical institutions.

The interviews with the nurses in the three medical institutions therefore reveal that it was only in the private Palestinian-Arab hospital that more informal social activities took place, despite the desire expressed by a few nurses in the public hospital to constitute deeper ties with their co-workers in general, and with members of the opposite ethnonational group in particular. The fact that Jewish nurses formed a minority within the private hospital, which was located inside a large Arab city, might have contributed to their greater willingness to engage socially with their Palestinian-Arab counterparts. Moreover, many of the Palestinian-Arab nurses had previously worked in large public hospitals where they had been in a minority. Most of these hospitals are located in large Jewish cities. It could be argued that the Palestinian-Arab nurses consequently sympathized with the situation of the few Jewish nurses and tried to ease their sense of alienation, which they themselves had experienced as a minority group in previous jobs. Indeed, Aftema's (2017) study of the infrastructure and construction sector also provides evidence that in Israeli workplaces owned by Palestinian Arabs with a minority of Jewish workers there is a greater tendency to form meaningful personal ties between the two groups that extend into the private sphere.

Social Ties in the High-Tech Sector and the Paradox of Diversity Management

The ideology and practice of diversity management governed daily life in the two multinational firms and appeared in many interviews with Palestinian-Arab and Jewish engineers. While conducive to a sense of fairness in promotions, at least in regard to top management, the diversity management policies also created the "color-blind" phenomenon (Bonilla-Silva 2017), which in fact impeded the Palestinian-Arab engineers' sense of inclusion by ignoring their distinct culture and religion. Paradoxically, the interviews indicate that an ideology designed to constitute basic equality in the workplace tends to reinforce the dominance of the majority group and the willingness of employees to accept this situation as the natural order of things. This chapter highlights another paradox of diversity management—its apparently negative effect on the ability to form enduring amicable ties across the ethnonational divide. It might have been expected that a social environment encouraging workplace equality would have facilitated social ties, regardless of the ethnicity or nationality of the people involved. Similarly, the engineers' high level of education and shared belonging to a strong professional community with distinct norms and standards could have been expected to encourage amicable ties across the ethnonational divide. Yet, even though both Jewish and Palestinian-Arab engineers acknowledged the fairness of promotion policies, and even alluded to personal ties with Jewish students during graduate school, this did not seem to result in the formation of real friendships at work. While most interviewees mentioned formal and largely positive ties with peers at work, none of them could describe meaningful relations that continued to exist outside of the work settings and also involved spouses and families. Moreover, it turned out that Jewish and Palestinian-Arab engineers knew relatively little about the private life of their colleagues from the other ethnonational group.

Like their counterparts in the production and medical sectors, engineers and technicians often referred to formal social events such as organized trips and weddings. While some of them attended weddings of team members from the other ethnonational group, they did not express any social bond or sense of friendship arising from these encounters. Thus, a Palestinian-Arab engineer, who had worked for twelve years in the American multinational, gave a description of these events that was typical of interviews with members of both ethnic groups:

> INTERVIEWER: Do you get to go out with peers, not for formal events that the firm organizes, but to have coffee with friends from work or to go out together to a restaurant with your spouses, I mean things that you organize voluntarily?
>
> PALESTINIAN-ARAB ENGINEER: In a team that I worked in many years ago, yes, but not in my current or my previous team. A long time ago we had a socially cohesive group.
>
> INTERVIEWER: I see, that was a group of both Arabs and Jews?
>
> ENGINEER: We were Arabs and also Russians and Jews, we were two Arabs in the team, and we did go out together, but not anymore.
>
> INTERVIEWER: Are you invited on various occasions by other team members?
>
> ENGINEER: You mean weddings and such? Yes, sometimes.
>
> INTERVIEWER: And do you go to weddings?
>
> ENGINEER: Yes, but without spouses.
>
> INTERVIEWER: Without spouses, why's that?
>
> ENGINEER: I really don't know. In my husband's firm, I do go [to weddings] with him. It's a smaller firm with more personal ties.
>
> INTERVIEWER: And here, you're expected to attend, but without spouses?

> ENGINEER: Yes, to go, but on your own. Maybe it also depends on how
> long your team has been together.

According to this depiction, formal events such as weddings were simply considered as work-related obligations. She mentioned the norm of not including spouses in wedding invitations, but was not sure of its origin. She did, however, contrast it with the warmer atmosphere in her husband's organization, where spouses were invited and, more generally, social ties were closer. Even having coffee together, a practice cited by nurses and young physicians, was something from the distant past, which did not occur in her two last teams. This excerpt indicates some possible explanations for the lack of personal ties, including the size of the company as compared with the smaller company her husband worked for, where amicable social ties were more frequent. Indeed, she implied that the cohesiveness that had developed among members of a team she had once worked on and their habit of spending leisure time together were unusual. Finally, she suggested that the possibility of constituting long-lasting ties also depended on the length of time the team members had worked together. The fact that the reshuffling of teams was common practice in the multinationals may have been detrimental to the formation of more meaningful personal ties among team members.

One Palestinian-Arab engineer, a young woman who was an observant Muslim, explained that she refrained from attending weddings because men and women mingled together at such events, which was against her religion: "They invite me but they know that I can't attend, I mean a ceremony where women and men are together, so when I'm invited to a wedding where this is the situation I simply apologize that I can't attend."

A Palestinian-Arab engineer in the American multinational did try to initiate more personal ties with a Jewish co-worker by inviting him to his home and was frustrated and disappointed by his reluctance to visit him:

> One of my [Jewish] team members, he lives just next to my village, on a
> moshav only a two-minute drive from my home. And I tell him: "Come
> and visit us." And then he answers jokingly, "I'm afraid I'll be killed." You
> know, he hears about all kinds of shooting incidents in my village. Me
> and this person argue a lot, and I try to tell him that we don't want these
> shooting incidents in my village . . . and I also tell him that if he comes
> to visit me, no one will harm him, these shootings are internal, among
> Arabs. But he's afraid, because it's an Arab [village].

He clearly attributed the Jewish engineer's reluctance to visit him to the Arab-Jewish conflict and to the extensive news reporting on such incidents, and the resulting fear and prejudice that shape the way in which his Jewish co-worker perceives life in an Arab village. This explanation recalls the comment by the nurse in the public hospital whose Jewish colleagues had failed to attend her wedding because "they were afraid." According to these accounts, the Jewish-Arab conflict casts a dark shadow even over personal ties at work.

Can Amicable Workplace Ties Spill over to the Private Sphere?

This chapter set out to explore whether strong social bonds constituted at work spill over to the broader private sphere and thereby might have the potential to reduce interethnic tensions in the political sphere. Sadly, the interviews revealed the scarcity of amicable social ties across the ethnonational divide, especially in the medical and the high-tech sectors. Although recent survey data reveal that the majority of the Palestinian-Arab and Jewish respondents in the sample are willing to make friends with members of the other group (Hermann et al. 2022), our findings suggest otherwise. Real friendships across the ethnonational divide were scarce. Rather than generating hope that the experience of positive interethnic relations in the workplace has the power to overcome the fear and prejudice generated by interethnic conflicts in war-torn countries, this chapter discovered an unexpected and possibly detrimental outcome of the ideology of diversity management prevalent in the high-tech sector. Contrary to the positive correlation that Hermann et al. (2022) found between the level of education and willingness to accept Palestinian Arabs as personal friends, in the Israeli high-tech sector friendship ties were absent. The section on the high-tech sector pointed to a few underlying factors that might hinder the development of meaningful ties beyond the workplace, such as the tendency to constantly shift workers from one team to another. An important research hypothesis that can be derived from the high-tech data is that instead of promoting friendships in and outside of work, diversity management, with its formalization of social encounters, seems to distance people of different ethnonational origins from each other and inhibit meaningful engagement and more intimate ties. This hypothesis can be empirically examined in future studies.

The production section proved to be an interesting exception. Although the sometimes aggressive arguments between Palestinian-Arab and Jewish workers on political and religious issues that have been described in previous chapters might have been expected to hamper the formation of friendships in this sector, the findings suggest the opposite. The deepest ties, which also extended to workers' families, were reported in the production sector. This might be because precisely the informality and frankness of the arguments engendered more open communication, which enabled people to become more deeply acquainted. Another possible explanation, which requires additional empirical support, is that the production workers were mostly religious. It seems that religious beliefs can not only polarize but also bring together Palestinian-Arab and Jewish workers. The mobilization of religious arguments by both sides in political discussions might provide a shared platform for mutual understanding. These explanations are reinforced by a comparison with the high-tech sector where social ties are much more formal and structured, political arguments are rare and at times even censured, and the ideology of diversity management prevails. The paradox exposed in this chapter is that an environment that fosters basic equality and merit-based promotions seems to be less, rather than more, conducive for the creation of meaningful social ties across the ethnonational divide. Indeed, the formal nature of social interaction in high tech might hamper the constitution of social ties in general, since engineers might refrain from open discussions with members of other ethnonational groups that are liable to cause tension and entail managerial sanctions. Additionally, as in the case of cultural inclusion, the "color-blind" policy might cause majority group members to remain in their comfort zone, or their familiar social environment, and not respond to attempts on the part of minority group members to enhance social bonds with their Jewish colleagues.

Discussion and Conclusions

The workplace has emerged in this book as an important arena for the performance of broader interethnic and interreligious tensions. Workers from diverse backgrounds who work together in a country torn by fierce ethnonational strife cope daily with the shop floor manifestations of the conflict. The findings support the general claim that broader tensions permeating the workplace and workers' grassroots coping strategies are an important dimension of any study of war-torn countries and regions. On the job, members of rival ethnonational and religious groups work side by side, depend on one another, and cooperate. Sometimes they must serve hostile and even racist clients or patients. The antagonism generated by violent events outside their workplace often percolates into their work environment and threatens the coexistence, social ties, and cooperation required by the local division of labor among members of mixed work teams. The long-standing and often bloody Jewish–Palestinian conflict is a glaring example of such ethnonational rivalry, compounded by religious sentiments, which also appears, in various degrees and forms, in many other countries and regions. Events in Israel/Palestine, home to sites that are sacred to Judaism, Christianity, and Islam, attract, however, particular attention both from the media and world leaders and have been extensively researched in an array of academic disciplines. Political sociologists, scholars of stratification and inequality, and historical sociologists, have all contributed important insights in their respective areas of interest.

This book set out to explore an important aspect that has received less attention in the scholarship—how this conflict is manifested within the workplace and its impact on day-to-day relations among workers from diverse ethnonational backgrounds in different sectors of the economy. This study offers a theoretical framework focusing on tensions that permeate the workplace, the forms that these tensions take at work, and the strategies devised by workers to deal with them. The findings are grounded in the case of the Palestinian–Jewish conflict, but are applicable to many countries around the world that are plagued by such conflict, either for historical reasons as in Northern Ireland, the former Yugoslavia, and the United States, or as a result of the recent waves of immigration to Europe from Africa, Afghanistan, and Syria.

The book has demonstrated that the fierce ethnonational conflict between Palestinian Arabs and Jews in Israel indeed has strong manifestations in the workplace. Political events and ethnically motivated violence in the public sphere quickly find their way into the workplace and impact different facets of daily life on the shop floor. During such times, interethnic and religious tension are more likely to erupt, and Palestinian-Arab workers, members of the minority group, are more likely to be exposed to explicit and implicit hostility, and to what Shoshana (2016) dubs "everyday racism," on the part of some Jewish co-workers. In the health sector, Palestinian-Arab physicians and nurses are sometimes the target of offensive and even racist remarks by patients and their families as well, which also strains relations within the mixed health teams. In all the research sites, Palestinian Arabs described the suspension of regular ties across the ethnonational divide during tense periods. At such times they felt that some of their Jewish counterparts perceived them as part of a hostile collective rather than as individual colleagues with whom they have personal relationships. This situation is very hard for minority group members to grasp or accept, and yet it serves as another reminder that even personal workplace ties are shaped in the shadow of the broader Jewish–Palestinian conflict. If we accept the dictum that the strength of social ties is tested during difficult times, the suspension of these ties during violent occurrences outside the workplace signals to the Palestinian-Arab workers that their relations with many of their Jewish colleagues are fragile. Studies of workplace tensions in Northern Ireland between Protestant and Catholic workers also show that external political events strain workplace relations, and workers tend to curtail workplace ties across the religious-national cleavage and to treat co-workers from the other group as one mass of hostile people (Hargie, Dickson and Nelson 2005; Dickson et al. 2009). An important general conclusion is that daily working life and workplace relations between members of different groups should be treated as an integral part of the study of any active ethnonational and religious conflict.

The empirical core of the book comprises an exploration of the following questions: How does an ongoing and sometimes violent ethnonational-religious conflict manifest itself in the workplace? What facets of organizational life are impacted by the broader conflict? How do workers in different work environments experience politically charged periods and what strategies do they adopt to cope with the tensions these create? Are these interethnic tensions manifested differently in the production, health, and high-tech sectors that were studied? The grounding of the research within the field of the sociology of work practice provided the theoretical tools to seek answers to these questions. The sociology of work practice encourages sensitivity to shop floor practices and interactions, promotes grounded workplace studies, and directs research attention to grassroots sense-making processes developed by workers and to their coping strategies with shifting situations in their workplace (e.g., Burawoy 1979). This theoretical emphasis underpins the discovery that workers develop a wide range of grassroots strategies to cope with external pressures that impact workplace relationships. The coping strategies of workers in mixed work teams appear in all the different research sites of this study and span different facets of the manifestations of the conflict. The following pages are designed to provide answers to the main research questions and to highlight the main conclusions, which are organized into five analytical categories: (1) cross-sector differences in the manifestations of interethnic tensions; (2) grassroots coping strategies; (3) the professional community as a mitigator of external tensions in the medical sector; (4) a reassessment of contact theory and diversity management in light of the findings; and (5) workplace relations as a potential engine of social change.

Cross-Sector Differences in the Manifestations of Interethnic Tensions

Interethnic tension is palpable in all the sectors that were studied, but to varying degrees and with an array of empirical manifestations. The comparative research design enabled a fine-grained analysis of similarities and differences across the Israeli health, production, and high-tech sectors. This comparative framework revealed how the impact of external ethnonational and religious conflict can be mediated by factors germane to the sociology of work practice, such as the distinct content and organization of work, the skill levels and educational attainment of workers, and the institutional contexts of the various sectors and work environments.

All the Palestinian-Arab workers in the three sectors expressed a clear view that their ethnonational identity had an influence on their career trajectories, as well as their career expectations. This conclusion suggests that skills, occupational training, and level of education are not perceived by the Palestinian-Arab interviewees as the only factors that shape the promotion decisions of Israeli managers, who are predominantly Jewish. This is but another indication of the deep impact of ethnonational conflicts on workplace relations and perceptions of managerial decisions. Nonetheless, the comparative design exposed important differences across the research sites. The effect of the Jewish–Palestinian conflict on career expectations and trajectories was most apparent in the production sector, where the Palestinian-Arab workers perceived their career opportunities to be nonexistent. Many of them explicitly pointed to their Palestinian identity in the context of the ongoing conflict as the reason for their complete lack of hope of being promoted. To add to their frustration, they reported specific instances where young Jewish workers with shorter tenure, less experience, and fewer skills were promoted to work in the "offices." Much of the literature on prejudice and racism in workplace promotion uses the metaphors of "glass ceiling" and "shadow structures" to denote real barriers for promotion that are transparent for minority group members (Kanter 1977; Maume 1999). The impenetrable barrier that the production workers encountered when trying to move up the hierarchy was, however, visible and concrete, forcing them into a horizontal pattern of employment, where they shifted employer every few years, but with no career gains. While in many countries majority group members tend to promote members of their own group, the findings suggest that in countries with an ongoing ethnonational-religious conflict, prejudice and racism in promotion are exacerbated by the fear and deep lack of trust that exist among the rival groups.

The Jewish–Palestinian conflict also weighs heavily on the prospect of a Palestinian-Arab engineer and technician hired by companies in the Israeli high-tech sector, which is tilted toward the defense industry, with the IDF being a major client. The Israeli army demands security clearance for all employees involved in military projects, and employers are aware that Palestinian Arabs are less likely to receive such clearance. This situation has changed somewhat since the late 1990s, with the arrival of multinational companies in Israel following the 1993–94 Oslo Accords. These multinational companies opened research and development operations, as well as production facilities in the semiconductor area. The Israeli high-tech sector has been slowly opening to Palestinian-Arab workers over the past two decades, and the interviewees in this study could already share their own work experience and relate to their career expectations and actual career trajectories. They expressed a firm belief in top management's desire to promote them and were aware of the benefits of the diversity management ideology it propagated, which guided some aspects of daily work. Yet, they still described difficulties in advancing their careers, which they attributed to discrimination based on their ethnonational background. The Palestinian-Arab engineers directed most of their criticism to middle-range, rather than top, management, as the main obstacles to a managerial career, although most of them did not accuse their Jewish team managers of outright racism. Instead, they highlighted their tendency to hire and promote people with a similar background to theirs, for example, military service in one of the elite intelligence units of the IDF. Since the vast majority of Palestinian Arabs do not serve in the army, they do not fit this profile.

Palestinian Arabs currently make up about 4 percent of the workforce in the high-tech sector. Based on current growth trends, the percentage of Palestinian-Arab engineers might eventually better represent their 20 percent share of the general population, but the road to such representation is still long. By contrast, Palestinian-Arab nurses constituted already in 2009 15.8 percent of the total number of Israeli nurses. Recent data suggest that in 2021 the percentage of Palestinian-Arab nurses stood at 27 percent (Central Bureau of Statistics 2021). This difference reflects the fact not only that the Israeli medical sector has been open to Palestinian Arabs for much longer than the high-tech sector but also that this is a predominantly public sector, in which promotion guidelines and procedures are more formal and accessible to workers, and more subject to administrative and judicial scrutiny. The health workers indeed reported the least difficulties in managing their careers despite the tensions sometimes created by the political conflict. Nurses, however, expressed greater reservations regarding their chances for promotion than physicians, who were more optimistic about their prospects of climbing up the hierarchy and becoming heads of wards or departments or even hospital directors.

Can management influence the ways in which Jewish and Palestinian-Arab workers experience the manifestations of the ethnonational conflict? A comparison between the situations in the health sector, where there is relatively little managerial involvement in regulating such tensions, and the high-tech sector, where there are clear managerial directives in this regard, indicates that management can indeed play a crucial role. An important finding of this study is that Palestinian-Arab physicians and nurses preferred at times to ignore offensive comments by patients and even to accommodate racist requests, simply to refrain from conflict. The lack of clear managerial policy can explain this strategy of choosing silence over voice. In the government hospital, where one would expect to find a strict stance against prejudice and racism in the public sphere, many gray zones exist, specifically regarding such behavior on the part of patients. Indeed, when medical workers were not sure that they could rely on managerial support, they were less likely to confront racist patients. In contrast, Palestinian-Arab engineers in the two multinationals cited managerial policy designed to curb racist incidents, and specific instances when top management quickly intervened. This swift managerial reaction was lauded by a few of the Palestinian-Arab engineers. While there were few documented racist comments, this management support encouraged them to confront offending co-workers.

Important differences across the sectors also emerge in relation to the manifestation and performance of religious belief at work. This study reveals a desire shared by all Palestinian-Arab workers, regardless of sector, to achieve better cultural and religious inclusion in their employing organization, and specifically, that their religious belief and holidays be integrated into the social fabric of everyday life in the Israeli workplace. However, in all three sectors they claimed that their religion and religious holidays were regularly ignored by Jewish top and middle managers. Some of them identified their employing organization as a Jewish institution, including the American multinational high-tech firm, precisely because it only celebrated Jewish holidays. The Palestinian-Arab workers also felt that their Jewish co-workers showed little interest in their religion and the folklore associated with Muslim or Christian holidays, which fueled their broader sense of exclusion from the culture of their work organization.

While the desire for cultural and religious inclusion appears in all three sectors, the findings identify striking differences in the ways Palestinian Arabs manifest and perform their religion at work. Of all the three sectors, the public display of religious belief was most apparent and widespread in production. Religion is an important component of the self-identity of many production workers, both Jews and Palestinian Arabs, and during the interviews they referred to themselves and others as religious people, even without being asked, and sometimes even described peers as "very religious." Religious belief, however, was not restricted to personal identity but fulfilled another function in this sector. It was often mobilized by Palestinian-Arab production workers as a symbolic tool for resisting Zionism and what they perceived as Zionist symbols, such as Israeli and Jewish memorial days. In this sense religion becomes a resource in the daily management of the ethnonational conflict at work. For the production workers, religion was often tightly entwined with political views, and religious arguments and references to their respective sacred texts were reportedly used in heated political debates more frequently than in the medical institutions or the two high-tech multinationals. For example, both Jewish and Palestinian-Arab production workers justified territorial claims over the land of Israel/Palestine during shop floor arguments by invoking divine promises and citing the Bible and the Koran. Furthermore, religious differences form the basis for schisms within the Palestinian-Arab workforce itself. One Palestinian-Arab interviewee argued that management employed the religious cleavages among Muslim, Christian, and Druze employees to make it more difficult for the largely Palestinian-Arab workforce to present a united front vis-à-vis management. Here, religious schisms were reportedly exploited by management to prevent the formation of organized class action.

The public manifestation of religious belief in political arguments was all but absent in the high-tech sector, where religion was presented within a broader cultural framework. Instead of political arguments, Palestinian-Arab engineers sought managerial and public recognition of their religious identity to gain a sense of inclusion in what they perceived as the dominant Jewish culture of their employing organization. Religion was rarely part of the self-presentation of Palestinian-Arab or Jewish engineers, and many of the Palestinian-Arab engineers refrained from speaking about their religious beliefs. When they did speak about religion in the workplace, they employed it to challenge the color-blind policies of the two multinationals by expressing a desire that their co-workers acknowledge their distinct religious identity and show interest in Muslim and Christian holidays and customs. Even though the American multinational could be assumed to be more attuned than the Israeli multinational to the religious needs of the Muslim workers because of its lack of involvement in the ongoing conflict and its greater sensitivity to cultural diversity, the findings offer a more nuanced picture. On the one hand, it was only in the American multinational that a permanent prayer room was set aside for the Muslim employees. Indeed, in the Israeli multinational the request for a dedicated room for Muslim prayer, like the room set aside for Jewish prayer, was made only recently by the new East Jerusalemite recruits, and not by the veteran Palestinian-Arab engineers, who mostly came from northern Israel. This demand might reflect a growing confidence in the legitimacy of expressing Muslim belief at work, but it might also simply indicate that the engineers and technicians from East Jerusalem are more religious than their counterparts from the Galilee. On the other hand, it is the Israeli multinational, and not the American one, that grants Muslim workers one hour off every day during Ramadan, so that they can arrive home in time for the Iftar dinner that breaks the daily fast.

A few of the Palestinian-Arab physicians in the public hospital also reported that they were allowed to leave work an hour earlier during Ramadan. During interviews, both Jewish and Palestinian-Arab workers in the medical sector indicated their ethnic, but not religious, affiliation when describing themselves. In this sector, religious diversity in the mixed teams of physicians and nurses was generally regarded as a positive factor, since it allowed flexibility in managing vacations for Muslim, Christian, Jewish, and Druze medical staff on their respective religious holidays. Moreover, the custom of bringing traditional holiday food to work and sharing it with their colleagues, which was popular in the health institutions, created a certain sense of intimacy among members of the medical teams. What is striking is that in the health sectors the Palestinian-Arab professionals did not employ religion to express political views or to request a sense of cultural inclusion, but instead as a means for enhancing social solidarity among all co-workers. While this book has highlighted the main points of tension between rival ethnonational groups in the Israeli workplace, and an array of manifestations of these tensions, it also identified the main strategies used by workers to cope with these tensions.

Grassroots Coping Strategies

This book identifies split ascription as a key example of a grassroots coping strategy, whereby a distinction is drawn between interethnic relations within the work team, which workers in all the three sectors depicted as neutral or even positive, and the structural elements of their employing organizations, such as promotion procedures and training processes, which members of minority groups perceived to be discriminatory. They explained this discrimination as deeply embedded in the broader Israeli–Palestinian conflict and as reflecting ethnonational and religious schisms within Israeli society. The projection of these schisms onto organizational structures and formal processes allowed minority group members to attribute discrimination to their employing organization rather than their co-workers. For example, that some of the Palestinian-Arab nurses interviewed dubbed public hospitals in Israel "Jewish places" indicates their belief that the discriminatory treatment they have experienced there is deeply ingrained in organizational structures and is unlikely to change because it reflects the situation in broader Israeli society as a result of the Israeli–Palestinian conflict. Similarly, the Jewish nurse who was told by the nun-manager of the private Palestinian-Arab hospital, "This is ours, not yours," and who understood the comment to mean that the facility was a Palestinian-Arab and Christian institution, but not a Jewish one, believed that discrimination is a defining structural feature of the hospital and also expressed little hope for change.

The coping strategy of split ascription seems to reject a sense of structuration (Giddens 1984)—a dialectical relationship between social agency and social structure—that is central to sociological thought. The interviews with minority group workers in all the sectors reveal a perceived and explicit disconnect between workplace agency and social interaction, on the one hand, and the structural and more formal elements of the employing organization, on the other. Although workers in all the three sectors displayed a willingness to artificially insulate their immediate work environment from the conflict, they were reluctant to change their basic disposition toward it, despite their amicable or neutral relations with co-workers from the other ethnonational group. This disconnect inhibits the creation of a middle-range theory explaining the translation of microlevel accounts of intergroup prejudice reduction into reduced macrolevel tensions among opposing groups (see Pettigrew 2008, 195), a critical issue in studies of interethnic relations in war-torn countries (for the case of Northern Ireland, see Hargie and Dickson 2003; Hewstone et al. 2006). The notion of split ascription provides a missing link in explaining the inability of positive workplace encounters across the ethnonational divide to genuinely reduce broader prejudice and racism at work, let alone in society as a whole, despite the repeated depiction of workplace ties as positive or neutral. Instead, minority group members tend to attribute discrimination to the organizational, or structural, level, rather than to co-workers.

Language use in the Israeli workplace is a point of contention across the ethnonational divide and in all sectors. To deal with this tension, workers develop grassroots coping strategies that regulate language use and provide normative guidelines for its daily management. Previous scholarship teaches us that language use should be examined within a broad sociocultural framework (Funkenstein 1989), that language provides a stage for the performance of ethnonational identity and a shared sense of belonging (Amara 2018), that language use can also shape the public sphere and its soundscapes, and as in the case of public signs, can reflect broader ethnonational hierarchies (Ben-Rafael at al. 2006). All these theoretical elements had an empirical presence on the shop floor. The findings show that within the broader framework of the conflict, language use forms an important arena for the manifestation of ethnonational identity in all three sectors, and that the use of Arabic or Russian in the Israeli workplace can lead to tensions. In particular, Jewish co-workers' disparaging comments on the use of Arabic at work tended to increase during tense political times, which demonstrates how the issue of attitudes toward language is also linked to the broader conflict. To cope with this potential source of tension, a normative framework existed in all three research contexts, according to which workers of all ethnonational groups understood and accepted the premise that Hebrew should be spoken among all workers when work practice required coordination and mutual understanding. At the same time, both Russian- and Arabic-speaking workers expected the Jewish workers and Jewish management to respect their right to converse in their native tongue with peers of the same ethnic group when such communication did not harm the workflow, affect the quality of work, or present safety issues. As we have seen, this perceived right was not always respected by majority group members, a fact that caused frustration and conflict among Jewish and Palestinian-Arab workers, mostly among the medical workers and more rarely in the high-tech companies. In the high-tech sector, the book found, management provided clear and formal guidelines for language use in different situations, thus preventing it from becoming a point of contention. Indeed, one of the Palestinian-Arab engineers who were interviewed explicitly testified that hearing Arabic in the company's soundscape symbolized cultural inclusion.

The preference for using the Hebrew language, health workers pointed out, is based on medico-ethical considerations. In the three health institutions, professional norms and socialization often provide the blueprints for such local arrangements. To begin with, all health workers agreed that for the sake of saving human lives, the use of Hebrew during medical treatments was essential, since it provided a common ground for all members of the medical team. The general aim in the health institutions is to provide quality care, and to achieve this goal all members of the medical staff must fully communicate and comprehend all necessary information. Since most patients, regardless of their ethnonational origin, understand Hebrew, the desire to keep them informed also determined the use of Hebrew during medical treatment. Violation of this norm was deeply resented by Hebrew-speaking medical workers, as in the case of the Jewish nurse who left the room in anger when a Palestinian-Arab physician and nurse both spoke Arabic with a Palestinian-Arab patient during the doctors' round, thus effectively leaving her out of the conversation.

Grassroots arrangements, however, do not always suffice to prevent tensions related to language use. Problems arose when, for example, Jewish members of medical teams made negative remarks about their Palestinian-Arab counterparts' use of Arabic at work even in situations that were not directly related to medical practice. The Palestinian-Arab nurses and physicians were offended by what they perceived as blatant attempts to prevent them from using their mother tongue, and some of them experienced these comments as a wider rejection of their distinct ethnonational identity and culture by majority group members. This is but another indication of the broad interpretive space that surrounds language use. The Palestinian-Arab production workers also reported that when safety issues were at hand, they shifted to Hebrew to ensure that Jewish and Russian workers understood the conversation. Moreover, the Jewish and Russian production workers did not complain about the extensive use of Arabic on the production floor and perceived this situation as natural, given the majority status of the Palestinian Arabs in this plant.

Promotion is desired by all workers, and the findings demonstrate that ethnonational and religious background impact the career aspirations and trajectories of minority group members. In face of the prejudice, and even racism, that were reported to affect promotion decisions in all the three sectors, minority group members devised an array of coping strategies. A unique coping strategy, germane to the high-tech sector, is related to career decisions made by minority group members in the context of the broader ethnonational conflict. Most

Palestinian-Arab engineers choose promotion on the technical rather than managerial career ladder, primarily because of the perceived obstacles to obtaining a managerial position, which means that they become recognized technical experts within their area rather than team managers. Some of the interviewees cited their futile attempts to become team managers, pointing the blame mainly at their Jewish team managers rather than higher management policy. A few Palestinian-Arab engineers attributed their decision to pursue a technical career not only to organizational obstacles, but also to their own insecurity and fear of managing a team with a majority of Jewish workers. Such fears are likely the result of long socialization into the role of minority group members, as well as the geographical and sociocultural separation between Palestinian Arabs and Jews within Israeli society (Kraus and Yonay 2018). The preference of Palestinian-Arab engineers to pursue technical rather than managerial careers means the potential loss of managerial talent that could benefit the Israeli economy. From the minority group members' perspective, merit-based promotion in their labor market and work organizations was overshadowed by ethnonational tensions and insecurities.

Professional Community as a Mitigator of External Tensions in the Medical Sector

The constitution of occupational communities (Van Maanen and Barley 1984) in different lines of work is a common area of study within the sociology of work practice. Scholars often differentiate occupational communities by their strength, with professional communities representing the strongest form. The professions have a government-backed monopoly over their line of work, control of academic education and certification, and internal ethical committees. Given these special traits, the professions are most likely to mitigate fierce ethnonational tensions at work, since they provide members with a long socialization process, a strong professional identity, and professional norms and ethics.

Several chapters in this book support the claim that strong occupational communities serve as moderators of external conflict in a war-torn country. Thus, in the health sector, when patients or their families expressed racist or derogatory remarks toward Palestinian-Arab physicians and nurses, the latter expected the Jewish members of their professional community to support them. The clear professional norms of medical staff, calling for equal treatment for all people regardless of gender, ethnicity, or political views, help physicians and nurses ignore such racial slurs, while the lengthy socialization process into the profession of medicine—in medical school and during the internships—strengthens the sense of mutual solidarity and professional identity among all the physicians, regardless of their ethnonational background. It is this perception of a shared professional community that underlies the Palestinian Arabs' clear expectation that their Jewish colleagues will come to their aid when they witness racist behavior on the part of patients or their families, and their disappointment when, as in some of the cases documented, this expectation is not fulfilled.

The findings further indicate that physicians can maintain a positive interethnic dialogue even during periods of heightened tensions. Many of the young physicians in the hospital that were interviewed had attended the same medical school and spent the six years of internship in the same hospital, working side by side for very long shifts. The division of expert labor in hospitals also creates interdependency, as young physicians often consult one another on medical decisions regarding the treatment of their patients. The long-standing acquaintance with each other and their close cooperation enhance mutual trust and create a solid social infrastructure that helps to mitigate the external political tensions. By contrast, nurses reported that external political circumstances had a greater impact on social relations within their teams. One explanation might be that, as members of a semiprofession, they have a weaker sense of occupational community and a shorter period of shared socialization when compared to the physicians.

In the scholarship, engineering is considered a profession with unique characteristics that differentiate it from traditional professions such as medicine and law. Unlike other professions, engineers are trained to show loyalty to their employing organization, over and beyond their loyalty to their professional community. They are also socialized to view managerial careers within their employing organizations as an integral part of their professional careers (Ritti 1982). Thus, organizational rather than occupational norms and values often take center stage in engineers' daily work. These facts might explain why engineers in the two multinational firms failed to report any significant sense of being part of a professional community. Furthermore, compared with the physicians, engineers made little implicit or explicit reference to their professional community as a mitigating factor in workplace relations. This was even more evident in the production sector where there are no occupational community and occupational norms that can moderate political disputes. Indeed, as the interviews have shown, production workers engaged in charged political exchanges in which religious arguments were often invoked, which made them more emotional. These findings suggest that a strong professional community can provide workers from diverse backgrounds with shared identity and ethical guidelines for managing ethnonational tensions within the workplace arising from the broader conflict in the surrounding society. Future large-scale comparative research can improve our understanding of the role played by different types of occupational communities in mitigating interethnic and interreligious conflict at work.

A Reassessment of Contact Theory and Diversity Management

The comparative design of this study, the variety of facets of workplace relations influenced by the external conflict that it considered, and its sensitivity to grassroots coping strategies provide a basis for reassessing whether diversity management (Ashkanasy et al. 2002; Jackson et al. 1995) and social contact theories (Allport 1954; Pettigrew 2008), the two leading theoretical approaches to analyzing interethnic workplace relations, are adequate for interpreting workplace encounters across the ethnonational cleavage in war-torn countries. The notion of split ascription reveals that these approaches do not yield a complete picture of worker responses to interethnic tensions during politically charged periods because they disregard the grassroots strategies workers deploy to manage interethnic relations. Consistent with contact theory, the application of split ascription in the three research contexts illustrates that the intense social engagement and interdependency created by local divisions of labor function to reduce interethnic prejudice and to maintain a neutral work environment (Pettigrew and Tropp 2006). Split ascription diverges from contact theory, however, in suggesting that interaction, even when managed correctly, does not genuinely reduce prejudice and racism at work. Instead, discrimination is attributed to the organizational, or structural, level rather than to co-workers. While this finding is consistent with diversity management's assertion that discrimination can be inscribed into formal organizational structures, split ascription theory draws attention to grassroots coping strategies and is therefore better suited to incorporating interactional elements into interethnic workplace models. Stated differently, the emphasis of diversity management on formal organizational structures and processes reduces its sensitivity to grassroots coping strategies that lie at the core of interethnic relations at work and the daily, shop floor management of the conflict in war-torn countries.

There is a vast literature on diversity management, which includes academic as well as applied research. This literature identifies obstacles to the fair and equal treatment of workers of different genders and ethnonational origins and offers mainly structural and formal remedies, which include both procedural and educational dimensions. For example, many diversity management scholars advocate formal and public procedures for promotion, as well as structured cultural awareness workshops for all workers and managers in ethnically mixed work environments (Mor Barak 2014). This study found, however, that, when transplanted into the Israeli context, diversity management is limited to its formal procedural aspects. The aspects of diversity management concerned with cultural education and awareness are all but absent from the daily work environments of the two high-tech multinational companies that were studied. This partial transplantation of diversity management is puzzling, since mutual exposure and sensitivity to the culture and religion of members of other ethnonational groups is paramount precisely in war-torn countries. While the findings fail to provide a clear explanation for this paradox, I suggest that the reason lies in the fierce ethnonational conflict itself, which makes top and middle management reluctant to promote intergroup cultural awareness. Since the imposition of cultural awareness workshops is potentially a sensitive and politically controversial issue, management may prefer to confine itself to the formal and procedural aspects of diversity management and neglect its cultural elements. Here, the principal of color blindness, also inherent in diversity management theory, helps majority group members ignore the distinct identity of minority group members, their cultural and religious background, and their living conditions.

Paradoxically, in the production sector, where diversity management policies were completely lacking and workers were most vulnerable from an economic standpoint, the Palestinian-Arab workers felt more at ease to express their distinct Palestinian identity, religious affiliation, and political views than those in the medical or the high-tech sectors. The book documents heated political debates in which Palestinian-Arab production workers freely expressed their views on violent events outside the workplace, and the opposing Palestinian-Arab and Jewish political interests were placed on an equal footing. By contrast, medical and high-tech workers refrained from political debates and explicitly stated that politics and political discussion should be kept outside the workplace whenever possible. These different behaviors could perhaps be explained by the composition of the workforce in the various sectors—whether the Palestinian-Arab workers constitute the minority or the majority group in a particular workplace. Palestinian-Arab workers felt more secure when they were in the majority in the Palestinian-Arab hospital or the production plant and were therefore more willing to expose their political views in discussions with their Jewish co-workers. Another possible explanation, which was provided by a Palestinian-Arab interviewee, is also related to workforce composition, but is purely economic. He argued that because of their weaker position in the labor market, Palestinian-Arab workers are more flexible than their Jewish counterparts and are willing, for example, to come to work at short notice, an advantage that makes management more reluctant to fire them. Thus, the very dependence of management on the Palestinian-Arab production workers allows them greater freedom to express their political views without fear of the consequences. The opposite could also be argued: since Palestinian-Arab production workers had hardly any expectations of being promoted, they had less to lose and were therefore more likely to feel at liberty to express their political views. As they themselves testified, religion played a prominent part in their self-identity, unlike their counterparts in the medical and the high-tech sectors, and their deep religious belief might explain their greater willingness to openly voice political views. According to this explanation, politics is simply a platform for expressing religious belief at work. These hypotheses need to be empirically tested by future research on these issues.

Workplace Relations as an Engine of Social Change

It would be tempting to assume that mutual acquaintance among co-workers of different ethnonational and religious groups has the potential to ease political tensions in broader society, but the question of whether positive workplace relations spill over into the private sphere has rarely been studied. This book has tried to close the gap by specifically investigating whether workplace relations can become an engine of social change in war-torn countries, and whether amicable or neutral social bonds constituted at work can reduce the intensity of the broader ethnonational conflict.

The findings of this study indicate that this is highly unlikely. There were few instances of enduring and amicable social ties across the ethnonational cleavages, with the surprising exception of the production sector. Whereas the sometimes acrid and outspoken arguments on political and religious issues that were reported to take place between Palestinian-Arab and Jewish production workers might have been expected to inhibit the formation of friendships in this sector, the findings suggest the opposite. The deepest ties, ones that also extended to workers' families, were reported in the production sector, rather than the high-tech sector, where social ties are much more formal and structured, political arguments are rare and at times even censured, and the ideology of diversity management prevails. Precisely the informality and frankness of the arguments in the production sector may have engendered more open communication, which enabled people to become more deeply acquainted. Hence, an environment that fosters basic equality and merit-based promotions seems to be less, rather than more, conducive to the creation of meaningful social ties across the ethnonational divide.

I suggest that the formal nature of social interaction in the high-tech sector, encouraged by management with its prescribed behavioral scripts, might hamper the constitution of social ties in general, since engineers might refrain from open discussions with members of other ethnonational groups that are liable to cause tension and entail managerial sanctions. Additionally, as in the case of cultural inclusion, the color-blind policy, which encourages workers to ignore gender or race differences, might actually make majority group members reluctant to deal with issues related to ethnicity since they are considered taboo. As was described in a few of the interviews, this may cause majority group members to ignore attempts on the part of minority group members to enhance social bonds.

The book therefore found that the influence of amicable or neutral workplace relations rarely extends beyond the immediate work environment, which suggests that such relations do not provide an engine of change that can remedy deeply entrenched ethnonational and religious divides. Notwithstanding this conclusion, the daily management of ethnonational and interreligious conflicts at work deserves increased research attention since it is precisely at work that members of rival ethnonational groups meet regularly, experience tensions that infiltrate the workplace from the outside, and actively perform their distinct ethnonational identities and sometimes express their political views. The workplace, with its particular socioeconomic structure, should therefore be part and parcel of every study of ethnonational and religious conflict.

The book has highlighted multiple ways in which the sociology of work practice can enrich our understanding of the workplace manifestation of broader ethnonational and religious conflict. Yet, the sociology of work practice, which tends to attribute less importance to the impact of fierce political conflicts on workplace occurrences, could also benefit from better integrating such variables into workplace studies. This book has demonstrated that ethnonational and religious conflict influences a wide range of factors that shape daily interactions and local divisions of labor among workers in different sectors. Skill acquisition and occupational training, career trajectories, and even language use at work are shown to be partly determined by the tensions created by the wider social and political context.

The variety of grassroots coping strategies identified by the book draws attention to a hidden, yet central, dimension of the daily management of fierce ethnonational conflicts that otherwise remains outside the purview of dominant theories of interethnic relations at work. By uncovering the main points of contention and the main grassroots coping strategies, this study has endeavored to contribute to a deeper understanding of the motives and behavior of workers from diverse ethnonational backgrounds. My hope is that it will encourage further studies that put the spotlight on the daily workplace manifestations of ethnonational conflicts, with greater sensitivity to the manifold ways in which workers manage their daily relations with their colleagues in face of the broader political, social, and religious schisms that threaten to divide them.

References

Aftema, Fadwa. 2017. "Being a Jewish Minority in an Arab Organization: On Jewish-Arab Employee Relations in 'Merchavim'" [in Hebrew]. MA thesis, University of Haifa.

Ailon, Galit, and Gideon Kunda. 2009. "The One Company Approach: Transnationalism in an Israeli-Palestinian Subsidiary of a Multinational Corporation." *Organization Studies* 30 (7): 693–712.

Albrecht, Stan L., and Tim B. Heaton, T. B. 1984. "Secularization, Higher Education and Religiosity." *Review of Religious Research* 26 (1): 43–58.

Ali, Nohad. 2004. "Political Islam in an Ethnic Jewish State: Historical Evolution, Contemporary Challenges and Future Prospects." *Holy Land Studies* 3 (1): 69–92.

Allport, Gordon W. 1954. *The Nature of Prejudice*. Reading, MA: Addison-Wesley.

Alyagon-Darr, Orna. 2019. *Plausible Crime Stories: The Legal History of Sexual Offences in Mandate Palestine*. Cambridge: Cambridge University Press.

Amara, Muhammad. 2018. *Arabic in Israel: Language, Identity and Conflict*. London: Routledge.

Anteby, Michel. 2008. *Moral Gray Zones: Side Production, Identity, and Regulation in an Aeronautic Plant*. Chicago: Chicago University Press.

Arnesen, Eric. 2017. "Race and Labour in a Southern US Port: New Orleans, 1860–1930." In *Dock Workers: International Explorations in Comparative Labour History 1790–1970*, vol. 1, edited by Sam Davies, Colin J. Davis, David de Vries, Lex Heerma van Voss, Lidewij Hesselink, and Klaus Weinhauer, 38–57. London: Routledge.

Ashkanasy, Neil M., Charmine E. J. Härtel, and Catherine S. Daus. 2002. "Diversity and Emotions: The New Frontiers in Organizational Behavior Research." *Journal of Management* 28 (3): 307–38.

Bar-On, Dan. 2001. "The Silence of Psychologists." *Journal of Political Psychology* 22 (2): 331–45.

Bechky, A. Beth. 2006. "Talking About Machines, Thick Description, and Knowledge Work." *Organization Studies* 27 (2): 1757–68.

Ben-Rafael, Eliezer, Elena Shohamy, Muhammad Hasan Amara, and Nira Trumper-Hecht. 2006. "Linguistic Landscape as Symbolic Construction of the Public Space: The Case of Israel." *International Journal of Multilingualism* 3 (1): 7–30.

Bennett, Jonathan. 1976. *Linguistic Behaviour*. Cambridge: Cambridge University Press.

Bernstein, Deborah S. 1995. "Jews and Arabs in the Nesher Cement Enterprise" [in Hebrew]. *Cathedra* 76: 82–102.

——. 1996. "The Palestine Labor League and the Hebrew Labor Policy Trap" [in Hebrew]. *Megamot* 37 (3): 229–53.

——. 1998. "Strategies of Equalization, a Neglected Aspect of the Split Labour Market Theory: Jews and Arabs in the Split Labour Market of Mandatory Palestine." *Ethnic and Racial Studies* 21 (3): 449–75.

——. 2000. *Constructing Boundaries: Jewish and Arab Workers in Mandatory Palestine.* Albany: SUNY Press.

Berry, Orna, and Yigal Grayeff. 2009. "Emerging Markets: Israel's Technology Industry as an Economic Growth Engine." *Communications of the ACM* 52 (12): 25–27.

Bonilla-Silva, Eduardo. 2017. *Racism without Racists: Color-Blind Racism and the Persistence of Racial Inequality in America.* 5th ed. Lanham, MD: Rowman & Littlefield.

Burawoy, Michael. 1979. *Manufacturing Consent: Changes in the Labor Process under Monopoly Capitalism.* Chicago: Chicago University Press.

Campbell, Jim, and Patrick McCrystal. 2005. "Mental Health Social Work and the Trouble in Northern Ireland: A Study of Practitioner Experience." *Journal of Social Work* 5 (2): 173–90.

Central Bureau of Statistics. 1995. *Labor Force Survey*, no. 1057 [in Hebrew]. Jerusalem: State of Israel.

——. 2012. *Labor Force Survey*, no. 1565 [in Hebrew]. Jerusalem: State of Israel.

——. 2016. *Statistical Abstract of Israel* 67 [in Hebrew]. Jerusalem: State of Israel.

——. 2019. "Press Release" [in Hebrew]. July 23.

——. 2021. *Labor Force Survey*, no. 1815 [in Hebrew]. Jerusalem: State of Israel.

Chaifetz, Lesha R. 2002. "The Promised Land: An Examination of the Israeli High-Tech Industry." *University of Pennsylvania Journal of International Economic Law* 23: 385–414.

Corbin, Juliet, and Anselm Strauss. 1998. *Basics of Qualitative Research: Techniques and Procedures of Developing Grounded Theory.* London: Sage.

Darr, Asaf. 2006. *Selling Technology: The Changing Shape of Sales in an Information Economy.* Ithaca: Cornell University Press.

——. 2009. "Palestinians and Jews at Work: On the Sociology of Work Practice in Israel and Its Contribution to the Analysis of the Conflict" [in Hebrew]. *Israeli Sociology* 10 (2): 287–306.

——. 2018. "Palestinian-Arabs and Jews at Work." *Work, Employment, and Society* 35 (5): 831–49.

——. 2020. "Shared Work Spaces: Jewish and Arab Workers in Israel." Policy Research 142 [in Hebrew]. Jerusalem: Israel Democracy Institute.

Dashti, Yossi, Dafna Schwartz, and Ayala Malach-Pines. 2008. "High Technology Entrepreneurs, Their Social Networks and Success in Global Markets: The Case of Israelis in the US Market." *Current Topics in Management* 13 (8): 131–44.

Department of the Chief Economist of the Ministry of Science. 2017. *Weekly Economic Report*, August 27. Jerusalem: Ministry of Science.

Desivilya, Helena Syna. 1998. "Jewish-Arab Coexistence in Israel: The Role of Joint Professional Teams." *Journal of Peace Research* 35: 429–52.

De Vries, David. 1991. "The Labor Movement in Haifa, 1919–1929: A Study in the History of Urban Workers in Mandatory Palestine" [in Hebrew]. PhD diss., Tel Aviv University.

——. 1993. "Work and Authority Struggles among Industrial Workers in Palestine: The Workers of the Nesher Cement Factory in the 1920s" [in Hebrew]. *Yahadut Zemanenu* 8: 177–215.

——. 1994. Proletarianization and National Segregation: Haifa in the 1920s." *Middle Eastern Studies* 30 (4): 860–82.

——. 2004. "British Rule and Arab-Jewish Coalescence of Interests: 1946 Civil Servants' Strike in Palestine." *International Journal of Middle East Studies* 36: 613–38.

———. 2014. *Strike Action and Nation Building: Labor Unrest in Palestine/Israel 1899–1951*. New York: Berghahn Books.

———. 2017. "Nationalism and the Making of Dock Labour in British-ruled Palestine." In *Dock Workers: International Explorations in Comparative Labour History 1790–1970*, vol. 1, edited by Sam Davies, Colin J. Davis, David de Vries, Lex Heerma van Voss, Lidewij Hesselink, and Klaus Weinhauer, 231–51. London and New York: Routledge.

Dickson, David, Owen Hargie, Aodheen O'Donnell, and Christel McMullan. 2009. "*Learning to Deal with Difference in the Workplace*." In *The Challenges of Peace: Research as a Contribution to Peace-Building in Northern Ireland*, 37–52. Belfast: Northern Ireland Community Relations Council.

Ewon, Andrew I. 2013. "Managing and Valuing Diversity: Challenges to Public Management in the 21st Century." *Public Personnel Management* 42 (20): 107–22.

Feinstein, Yuval, and Maha Shehade Switat. 2019. "Keep a Stiff Upper Lip or Wear Your Heart on Your Sleeve? Ethnic Identity and Emotion Management among Arab/Palestinians in Israel." *Sociology* 53 (1): 139–55.

Freidson, Elliot. 1970. *Profession of Medicine: A Study in the Sociology of Applied Knowledge*. New York: Harper and Row.

———. 1984. "The Changing Nature of Professional Control." *Annual Review of Sociology* 10: 1–20.

Funkenstein, Amos. 1989. "Collective Memory and Historical Consciousness." *History and Memory* 1 (1): 5–26.

Gabbay, Uri, Eynav Erlich, Chir Abdelrazek, and Carmi Kriger. 2019. *Human Capital in The High-Tech Industry*. Jerusalem: The Israeli Innovation Authority.

Giddens, Anthony. 1984. *The Constitution of Society: Outline for the Theory of Structuration*. Cambridge, UK: Polity Press.

Gluckman, Max. 1964. *Closed Systems and Open Minds: The Limits of Naivety in Social Anthropology*. Chicago: Aldine.

Goffman Ervin. 1974. *Frame Analysis: An Essay on the Organization of Experience*. New York: Harper Colophon.

Gonos, George. 1977. "'Situation' vs. 'Frame': The 'Interactionist' and the 'Structuralist' Analysis of Everyday Life." *American Sociological Review* 42 (6): 854–67.

Gozansky, Tamar. 2014. *Between Expropriation and Exploitation: Status and Struggles of Arab Workers in Palestine and Israel* [in Hebrew]. Tel Aviv: Pardes.

Hackler, Nuri. 2017. "Publicity Designed Color Blindness: Whiteness as a Realized Public Value." *Administrative Theory and Praxis* 39 (3): 175–92.

Halpern, R. 1992. *Down on the Killing Floor: Black and White Workers in Chicago's Packinghouses, 1904–1954*. Urbana: University of Illinois Press.

Hargie, Owen, and David Dickson, eds. 2003. *Researching the Troubles: Social Science Perspectives on the Northern Ireland Conflict*. Edinburgh: Mainstream Press.

Hargie, Owen, David Dickson, and Seanenne Nelson. 2003. "Working Together in a Divided Society: A Study of Intergroup Communication in the Northern Ireland Workplace." *Journal of Business and Technical Communication* 17 (3): 285–318.

Hargie, Owen, David Dickson, and Aodheen O'Donnell. 2006. *Breaking Down Barriers: Sectarianism, Unemployment, and the Exclusion of Young People from Northern Ireland Society*. Community Relations Council through the European Union Programme for Peace and Reconciliation in Northern Ireland and the

Border Region of Ireland (Peace II Measure 2.1). Jordanstown: University of Ulster.

Hermann, Tamar, Or Anabi, Yaron Kaplan, and Inna O. Sapozhnikova. 2022. *A Conditional Partnership: Jews and Arabs, Israel 2021*. Jerusalem: Israel Democracy Institute.

Hewstone Miles, Ed Cairns, Alberto Voci, Juergen Hamberger, and Ulrike Niens. 2006. "Intergroup Contact, Forgiveness, and Experience of 'The Troubles' in Northern Ireland." *Journal of Social Issues* 62 (1): 99–120.

Horowitz, Dan, and Moshe Lissak. 1977. "The Growth of a Dual Society." In *From Settlement to the State: Jews of Israel during the Mandate Period* [in Hebrew], edited by Dan Horowitz and Moshe Lissak, 19–30. Tel Aviv: Am Oved.

Hultin, Mia. 2003. "Some Take the Glass Escalator, Some Hit the Glass Ceiling: Career Consequences of Occupational Segregation." *Work and Occupations* 30 (1): 30–61.

Ibarra, Herminia. 1992. "Homophily and Differential Returns: Sex Differences in Network Structure and Access in an Advertising Firm." *Administrative Science Quarterly* 37 (2): 422–47.

Ivancevich, John M., and Jacqueline A. Gilbert. 2000. "Diversity Management: Time for a New Approach." *Public Personnel Management* 29 (1): 75–92.

Jackson, Susan E., Karen E. May, and Kristina Whitney. 1995. "Understanding the Dynamics of Diversity in Decisions Making Teams." In *Team Effectiveness and Decision Making in Organizations*, edited by Richard A. Guzzo and Eduardo Salas, 204–61. San Francisco: Jossey-Bass.

Kabha, Mustafa. 2010. *The Palestinians: A People Dispersed* [in Hebrew]. Tel Aviv: The Open University Press.

Kanter, Rosabeth Moss. 1977. *Men and Women of the Corporation*. New York: Basic Books.

Katz, Israel, Marzouk Halabi, Gabi Neiman, Jaber Asakla, Yuval Fiorko, Rolly Rosen, Carlos Stieglitz, Shahira Shelby, and Michael Sternberg. 2005. "On the Dialogue between Palestinians and Jews in the Israeli Organizational Arena" [in Hebrew]. *Organizational Analysis* 11: 59–46.

Kellerman, Aharon. 2002. "Conditions for the Development of High Tech Industry: The Case of Israel." *Tijdschrift voor Economische en Sociale Geografie* 93 (3): 270–86.

Kelly Erin, and Frank Dobbin. 1996. "How Affirmative Action Became Diversity Management: Employer Response to Antidiscrimination Law, 1961–1996." *American Behavioral Scientist* 41 (7): 960–84.

Kidron, Carol, A., and Laurence J. Kirmayer. 2019. "Global Mental Health and Idioms of Distress: The Paradox of Culture-Sensitive Pathologization of Distress in Cambodia." *Culture, Medicine and Psychiatry* 43: 2111–235.

Kirkwood, Jerald. 2009. "Motivational Factors in a Push-Pull Theory of Entrepreneurship." *Gender Management: An International Journal* 24 (5): 346–64.

Kraus, Vered, and Yuval P. Yonay. 2018. *Facing Barriers: Palestinian Women in a Jewish-Dominated Labor Market*. Cambridge: Cambridge University Press.

Lamont, Michèle. 2000. *The Dignity of Working Men: Morality and Boundaries of Race, Class and Immigration*. New York: Russell Sage Foundation.

Le Page, R. B., and Andrée Tabouret-Kelle. 1985. *Acts of Identity: Creole-Based Approaches to Language and Ethnicity*. Cambridge: Cambridge University Press.

Levy, Nissim. 1998. *The History of Medicine in the Holy Land: 1799–1948* [in Hebrew]. Tel Aviv: Hakibbutz Hameuchad.

Lewin-Epstein, Noah, and Moshe Semyonov. 1994. "Sheltered Labor Markets, Public Sector Employment, and Socioeconomic Returns to Education of Arabs in Israel." *American Journal of Sociology* 100 (3): 622–51.

Lockman, Zachary. 1993. "Railway Workers and Relational History: Arabs and Jews in British-Ruled Palestine." *Comparative Studies in Society and History* 35 (3): 601–27.

Lupton, T. 1963. *On the Shop Floor: Two Studies of Workshop Organization and Output.* London: Pergamon Press.

Lupton, Tom, and Sheila Cunnison. 1964. "Workshop Behaviour." In *Closed Systems and Open Minds: The Limits of Naïvety in Social Anthropology*, edited by Max Gluckman, 103–28. Chicago: Aldine.

Manna, Adel. 2017. *Nakba and Survival: The Story of the Palestinians Who Remained in Haifa and the Galilee, 1948–1956* [in Hebrew]. Tel Aviv and Jerusalem: Van Leer Institute Press and Hakibbutz Hameuchad.

Maume, D. J., Jr. 1999. "Glass Ceiling and Glass Escalators: Occupational Segregation and Race and Sex Differences in Managerial Promotions." *Work and Occupations* 26 (4): 483–509

Ministry of Education. 2018. "Permanent Order No. 0132, 9.7.2018." Jerusalem: Ministry of Education.

Mor Barak, Michàlle E. 2005. *Managing Diversity: Towards a Globally Inclusive Workplace.* Thousand Oaks, CA: Sage.

———. 2014. *Managing Diversity: Toward a Globally Inclusive Workplace.* 3rd ed. Thousand Oaks, CA: Sage.

Morris, Benny. 1987. *The Birth of the Palestinian Refugee Problem.* Cambridge: Cambridge University Press.

———. 2013 (1948). A History of the First Arab-Israeli War. [in Hebrew] Tel Aviv: Am Oved.

Orgad, Liav. 2007. "The Arab Minority in Israel and the Compulsory Military Service." [In Hebrew] *Hamishpat* 11: 381–407.

Orr, Julian, E. 1996. *Talking about Machines: An Ethnography of a Modern Job.* Ithaca: Cornell University Press.

Pettigrew, Thomas F. 2008. "Future Directions for Intergroup Contact Theory and Research." *International Journal of Intercultural Relations* 32 (3): 187–99.

Pettigrew, Thomas F., and Linda R. Tropp. 2006. "A Meta-Analytic Test of Intergroup Contact Theory." *Journal of Personality and Social Psychology* 90 (5): 751–83.

Preminger, Jonathan. 2020. "Meritocracy in the Service of Ethnocracy." *Citizenship Studies* 24 (2): 247–63.

Pudney, Stephen, and Michael Shields. 2000. "Gender and Racial Discrimination in Pay and Promotion for NHS Nurses." *Oxford Bulletin of Economics and Statistics* 62 (1): 801–35.

Ramon, Shulamit, Jim Campbell, Jane Lindsay, Patrick McCrystal, and Naimeh Baidoun. 2006. "The Impact of Political Conflict on Social Work: Experiences from Northern Ireland, Israel and Palestine." *British Journal of Social Work* 36 (3): 435–50.

Remennick, Larisa. 2003. "Career Continuity among Immigrant Professionals: Russian Engineers in Israel." *Journal of Ethnic and Migration Studies* 29 (4): 701–21.

———. 2005. "Resetting the Rules of the Game: Language Preferences and Social Relations of Work between Russian Immigrants and Veteran Professionals in an Israeli Organization." *Journal of International Migration and Integration* 6 (1): 1–28.

Ritti, Richard. 1968. "Work Goals of Scientists and Engineers." *Industrial Relations* 7 (2): 118–31.

Saar, Amalia. 2016. *Economic Citizenship: Neoliberal Paradoxes of Empowerment*. New York: Berghahn Books.

Sa'di, Ahmad H. 1995. "Incorporation without Integration: Palestinian Citizens in Israel's Labour Market." *Sociology* 29 (3): 429–51.

Sa'di, Ahmad H., and Lewin-Epstein, Noah. 2001. "Minority Labour Force Participation in the Post-Fordist Era." *Work, Employment and Society* 15 (4): 781–802.

Sanchez, Juan I., and Petra Brock. 1996. "Outcomes of Perceived Discrimination among Hispanic Employees: Is Diversity Management a Luxury or a Necessity?" *Academy of Management Journal* 39 (3): 704–19.

Saxenian, Annalee. 2002. "Silicon Valley's New Immigrant High-Growth Entrepreneurism." *Economic Development Quarterly* 16 (1): 20–31.

Schine, Edgar, and John Van Maanen. 2013. *Career Anchors Participation Workbook*. 4th ed. San Francisco: John Wiley.

Schjoedt, Leon, and Kelly G. Shaver. 2007. "Deciding on an Entrepreneurial Career: A Test of the Pull and Push Hypotheses Using the Panel Study of Entrepreneurial Dynamic Data." *Entrepreneurship Theory and Practice* 31 (5): 733–52.

Semyonov, Moshe. 1988. "Bi-Ethnic Labor Markets, Mono-Ethnic Labor Markets, and Socioeconomic Inequality." *American Sociological Review* 53 (2): 256–66.

Semyonov, Moshe, and Noah Lewin-Epstein. 1985. *Hewers of Wood and Drawers of Water: Noncitizen Arabs in the Israeli Labor Market*. Ithaca: Cornell University Press.

Shalev, Michael. 1992. *Labour and the Political Economy in Israel*. Oxford: Oxford University Press.

Shoshana, Aviho. 2016. "The Language of Everyday Racism and Microaggression in the Workplace: Palestinian Professionals in Israel." *Ethnic and Racial Studies* 39 (6): 1052–69.

Simpson, Andrew. 2007." Language and National Identity in Asia: A Thematic Introduction." In *Language and National Identity in Asia*, edited by Andrew Simpson, 1–31. Oxford: Oxford University Press.

Smooha, Sammy. 1978. *Israel: Pluralism and Conflict*. Berkeley: University of California Press.

——. 2001. "Arab-Jewish Relations in Israel as a Jewish and Democratic State." In *Trends in Israeli Society* [in Hebrew], edited by Ephraim Yaar and Zeev Shavit, 231–63. Tel Aviv: Open University.

——. 2012. *Still Playing by the Rules: The Index of Arab-Jewish Relations in Israel* [in Hebrew]. Haifa: University of Haifa and the Israel Democracy Institute.

Suwaed, Muhammad, and Nohad Ali. 2016. "Education, Identity and Ideology: The Islamic Movement and Moslem Religious Education in Israel." *Journal for the Study of Race, Nation, and Culture* 22 (4): 426–49.

Swed, Ori, and John Sibley Butler. 2015. "Military Capital in the Israeli Hi-Tech Industry." *Armed Forces and Society* 41 (1): 123–41.

Tabouret-Keller, Andrée. 2017. "Language and Identity." In *The Handbook of Sociolinguistics* edited by Florian Coulmas, 315–26. London: Blackwell.

Van Maanen, John, and Stephen R. Barley. 1984. "Occupational Communities: Culture and Control in Organizations." *Research in Organizational Behavior* 6: 287–365.

Weber, Max. 1946. "Bureaucracy." In *From Max Weber: Essays in Sociology*, edited by H. Gerth and C. Wright Mills, 196–262. Oxford: Oxford University Press.

Yiftachel, Oren. 1992. *Planning a Mixed Region in Israel: The Political Geography of Arab-Jewish Relations in the Galilee*. Aldershot: Avebury.

Yonay, Yuval, and Vered Kraus. 2001. "Strategies of Economic Endurance: Israeli Palestinians in the Ethnic Economy and the Public Sector." *Research in Social Stratification and Mobility* 18: 207–47.

RECOMMENDED FURTHER READING

Aboud, Nader. 1995. "Jewish-Arab Cooperation in the Trade Unions at the Beginning of the Mandate." In *Arabs and Jews during the Mandate Period: A New Look at Historical Research* [in Hebrew], edited by Ilan Pappé, 125–40. Givat Haviva: Institute for Peace Studies.

Almor, Tamar, and Gilad Sperling. 2008. "Israeli, Born Global, Knowledge Intensive Firms: An Empirical Inquiry." In *Handbook of Research on European Business and Entrepreneurship: Towards a Theory of Internationalization*, edited by Léo-Paul Dana, Isabelle M. Welpe, Mary Han, and Vanessa Ratten, 316–36. Cheltenham, UK: Edward Elgar.

Amir, Yehuda, Rachel Ben-Ari, Aharon Bizman, and Miriam Rivner. 1982. "Objective versus Subjective Aspects of Interpersonal Relations between Jews and Arabs." *Journal of Conflict Resolution* 26 (3): 485–506.

Asali, Muhammad. 2010. "Jewish-Arab Wage Gap: What Are the Causes?" *Defense and Peace Economics* 21 (4): 367–80.

Asante, Molefi, and Alice Davis. 1985. "Black and White Communication: Analyzing Work Place Encounters." *Journal of Black Studies* 16 (1): 77–93.

Avnimelech, Gil, and Morris Teubal. 2004. "Venture Capital Start-up Co-evolution and the Emergence and Development of Israel's New High Tech Cluster: Part 1, Macro-Background and Industry Analysis." *Economics of Innovation and New Technology* 13 (1): 33–60.

Bacharach, Samuel, Peter A. Bamberger, and Dana Vashdi. 2005. "Diversity and Homophily among White and African-American Peers." *Academy of Management* 48 (4): 619–44.

Barclay, David R. 1992. "Diversity in the High-Tech Workplace: Commitment from the Top Makes It Work." *IEEE Spectrum* 29 (6): 24–27.

Baum, Nehami. 2010. "After a Terror Attack: Israeli-Arab Professionals' Feelings and Experiences." *Journal of Social and Personal Relationships* 27 (5): 685–704.

Behar, Robert. 2016. "Inside Israel's Secret Startup Machine." *Forbes* 197 (7): 86–95.

Bekerman, Zvi. 2002. "The Discourse of Nation and Culture: Its Impact on Palestinian-Jewish Encounters in Israel." *International Journal of Intercultural Relations* 26: 409–27.

——. 2007. "Working with 'Others'" [Hebrew]. *Organizational Analysis* 11: 22–28.

——. 2012. "Teachers 'Contact' at the Integrated Bilingual Schools in Israel." *Policy Futures in Education* 10 (5): 552–62.

Ben-Tovim, Neelie, and Noam Kost. 2017. *Students in High-Tech Professions: National Target and Practical Recommendations* [Hebrew]. Jerusalem: National Economic Council.

Breschi, Stefano B., Francesco Lissoni, and Gianluca Tarasconi. 2014. *Inventor Data for Research on Migration and Innovation: A Survey and a Pilot*. Economic Research Working Paper no. 17. Geneva: World Intellectual Property Organization.

Chakravartty, Paula. 2006. "Symbolic Analysts or Indentured Servants? Indian High-Tech Migrants in America's Information Economy." *Knowledge, Technology, and Policy* 19 (3): 27–43.

Chorev, Schaul, and Alistair R. Anderson. 2006. "Success in Israeli High-Tech Start-Ups: Critical Factors and Process." *Technovation* 26 (2): 162–74.

Cicurel-Inbal, Esther, and Tal Litvak Hirsch. 2009. "Druze Adolescents between Identity and Loyalty" [in Hebrew]. *Panim* 46: 30–16.

Ci-Rong Li, Liu Yan-Yan, Ma Hong-Jia, and Lin Chen-Ju. 2016. "Top Management Team Diversity, Ambidextrous Innovation and the Mediating Effect of Top Team Decision-Making Processes." *Industry and Innovation* 23 (3): 260–75.

Cohen, Erez, 2015. "Development of Information Technology Industries in Israel and Ireland, 2000–2010." *Israel Affairs* 21 (4): 516–40.

Cohen-Goldner, Sarit. 2006. "Immigrants in the Israeli Hi-Tech Industry: Comparison to Natives and the Effect of Training." In *The Economics of Immigration and Social Diversity*, edited by Solomon W. Polachek, Carmel Chiswick, and Hillel Rapoport, 265–92. London: Emerald Group Publishing.

Cox, Taylor, Jr. 1991. "The Multicultural Organization." *Academy of Management Executive* 5 (2): 34–47.

Cox, Taylor, Jr., and Stacy Blake. 1991. "Managing Cultural Diversity: Implications for Organizational Competitiveness." *Academy of Management Executive* 5 (3): 45–56.

Cramtom, Catherine Durnell, and Pamela J. Hinds. 2007. "Intercultural Interaction in Distributed Teams: Salience of and Adaptations to Cultural Differences." *Academy of Management Proceedings* 2007 (1): 1–6.

DiTomaso, Nancy, and George F. Farris. 1992. "Diversity in the High-Tech Workplace: Diversity and Performance in R&D." *IEEE Spectrum* 29 (6): 21–24.

Dover, Yael. 2004. "Organizational Discourse at This Time" [in Hebrew]. *Organizational Analysis* 7: 84–74.

Drori, Israel. 2000. *The Seam Line: Arab Workers and Jewish Managers in the Israeli Textile Industry*. Stanford, CA: Stanford University Press.

Elliott, S. Margaret, and Walt Scacchi. 2003. "Free Software Developers as an Occupational Community: Resolving Conflicts and Fostering Collaboration." *GROUP'03 Conference* 3: 9–12.

Enosh, Guy, and Adital Ben-Ari. 2013. "Perceiving the Other: Hostile and Danger Attributions among Jewish and Arab Social Work Students in Israel." *European Journal of Social Work* 16 (3): 427–42.

Estlund, Cynthia. 2003. *Working Together: How Workplace Bonds Strengthen a Diverse Democracy*. Oxford: Oxford University Press.

Florida, Richard. 2002. *The Rise of the Creative Class*. New York: Basic Books.

Ford, David L., Jr., and George L. Whaley. 2003. "The Digital Divide and Managing Workforce Diversity: A Commentary." *Applied Psychology* 52 (3): 476–85.

Garnero, Andrea, Stephan Kampelmann, and François Rycx. 2014. "The Heterogeneous Effects of Workforce Diversity on Productivity, Wages, and Profits." *Industrial Relations* 53 (3): 430–77.

Gates, Gary, and Richard Florida. 2001. *Technology and Tolerance: The Importance of Diversity to High-Technology Growth*. Washington, DC: Brookings Institution Center on Urban and Metropolitan Policy.

Gerlitz, Ron, Maha Abu-Salih, Michal Belikoff, and Ruth Weinschenk-Vennor. 2010. *From Barriers to Opportunities: Mapping the Barriers and Policy Recommendations for Achieving Equality between the Arab and Jewish Citizens of Israel* [in Hebrew]. Policy Paper 1. Jerusalem-Haifa: Sikkuy Association.

Gonzalez, Carlos. 2015. "The Future of Engineers and STEM Lies in Diversity." *Machine Design* 87 (10): 7–11.

Goren, Tamir. 2004. "'Joint Work between Jews and Arabs in Developing the Country—Is It Possible?' Cooperation between Jews and Arabs in the Haifa Municipality during the British Mandate" [in Hebrew]. *Jama'a* 12: 93–133.

Gornostiev, Sergei. 2005. "Family Values in a Tiny Fishing Economy in Acre" [in Hebrew]. MA thesis, University of Haifa.

Grinberg, Lev. 1995. "The Jewish-Arab Drivers Organization Strike: A Contribution to the Critique of the Sociology of the National Conflict in Palestine" [in Hebrew]. In *Arabs and Jews in Mandate Palestine: Reexamining Historical Research*, edited by Ilan Pappé, 157–78. Givat Haviva: Givat Haviva Publications.

Halabi, Rabah. 2000. *Dialogue between Identities: Arab and Jewish Meetings in Neve Shalom* [in Hebrew]. Tel Aviv: Hakibbutz Hameuchad.

Halamish, Aviva, 2005. "Mandatory Palestine: A Dual Society or a Colonial Reality?" [in Hebrew] *Zmanim* 92: 25–16.

Hall, Richard H. 1968. "Professionalization and Bureaucratization." *American Sociological Review* 33 (1): 92–104.

Hargie, Owen, David Dickson, and Seanenne Nelson. 2005. "Relational Communication between Catholics and Protestants in the Northern Ireland Workplace: A Study of Policies, Practices, and Procedures." *Australian Journal of Communication* 32 (1): 89–107.

Harley, Johansen, and Michele O'Neill. 2012. "Ethnicity vs. Citizenship in the Workplace Context: A Case Study of Macedonia." *Journal of Balkan and Near Eastern Studies* 14 (1): 93–111.

Hart, David M., and Zoltan J. Acs. 2010. "High-Tech Immigrant Entrepreneurship in the United States." *Economic Development Quarterly* 25 (2): 116–29.

Hermann, Tamar, Ella Heller, Chanan Cohen, and Dana Bublil. 2015. *The Israeli Democracy Index 2015* [in Hebrew]. Jerusalem: Israel Democracy Institute.

Hochschild, Arkie R. 1983. *The Managed Heart: The Commercialization of Human Feelings*. Berkeley: University of California Press.

Hoffman, John, and Kamil Najjar. 1986. "Readiness for Proper Social Relations between Jewish and Arab High School Students" [in Hebrew]. *Studies in Education* 43–44: 103–18.

Hsieh, Chang-Tai, Erik Hurst, Charles I. Jones, and Peter J. Klenow. 2013. *The Allocation of Talent and US Economic Growth*. Cambridge, MA: National Bureau of Economic Research.

Huber, Peter, Michael Landesmann, Catherine Robinson, and Robert Stehrer. 2010. "Migrants' Skills and Productivity: A European Perspective." *National Institute Economic Review* 213 (1): 20–34.

Hunt, Jennifer. 2011. "Which Immigrants Are Most Innovative and Entrepreneurial? Distinctions by Entry Visa." *Journal of Labor Economics* 29 (3): 417–57.

Jabareen, Yosef. 2010. *Arab Employment in Israel, the Challenge of the Israeli Economy* [in Hebrew]. Jerusalem: Israel Democracy Institute.

Kapur, Devesh, and John McHale. 2005. "Mobile Human Capital and High-Tech Industry Development in India, Ireland, and Israel." In *From Underdogs to Tigers: The Rise and Growth of the Software Industry in Some Emerging Economies*, edited by Ashish Arora and Alfonso Gambardella, 1–44. Oxford: Oxford University Press.

Katz, Y., M. Halabi, G. Naiman, G. Aasakla, Y. Feurko, R. Rosen, K. Shtiglitz, M. Shterenberg, and S. Shalbi. 2005. "On the Dialogue between Palestinians and Jews in the Israeli Organizational Arena" [in Hebrew]. *Organizational Analysis* 11: 46–59.

Kerr, William R., 2013. *US High-Skilled Immigration, Innovation, and Entrepreneurship: Empirical Approaches and Evidence*. Cambridge, MA: National Bureau of Economic Research.

Keshet, Yael, and Ariela Popper-Giveon. 2016. "Work Experiences of Ethnic Minority Nurses: A Qualitative Study." *Israel Journal of Health Policy Research* 5 (18): 1–10.

Klein, Menachem. 2014. *Lives in Common: Arabs and Jews in Jerusalem, Jaffa, and Hebron*. London: Hurst & Company.

Kokkonen, Andrej, Peter Esaiasson, and Mikael Gilljam. 2015. "Diverse Workplaces and Interethnic Friendship Formation: A Multilevel Comparison across 21 OECD Countries." *Journal of Ethnic and Migration Studies* 41 (2): 284–305.

Kunda, Gideon, 1992. *Engineering Culture, Control, and Commitment in a High-Tech Corporation*. Philadelphia, PA: Temple University.

Lawler, Andrew. 2000. "Asian-American Scientists: Silent No Longer: 'Model Minority' Mobilizes." *Science* 290 (5494): 1072–77.

Lis-Ginsburg, Gali. 2013. *Employment of Arab Academics in Israel: Dedicated Survey, Characteristics of Transport Arrangements between the Residence of Arab Academics in Israel and Their Workplaces* [in Hebrew]. Jerusalem: Ministry of Economy.

Lissak, Moshe. 2003. "A Late Look at Society and the Economy in the Mandatory Land of Israel." In *Economy and Society in Mandatory Palestine, 1918–1948* [in Hebrew], edited by Avi Bareli and Nahum Karlinsky, 617–26. Sde Boker: Ben-Gurion Research Institute Press.

Malach-Pines, Ayala, Dov Dvir, and Arik Sadeh. 2004. "The Making of Israeli High-Technology Entrepreneurs: An Exploratory Study." *Journal of Entrepreneurship* 13 (1): 29–52.

Malach-Pines, Ayala, and Nurit Zaidman. 2014. "Stress and Burnout in Bicultural Teams in Hi-Tech Industry." *British Journal of Management* 25 (4): 819–32.

Maoz, Ifat. 2011. "Does Contact Work in Protracted Asymmetrical Conflict? Appraising 20 Years of Reconciliation-Aimed Encounters between Israeli Jews and Palestinians." *Journal of Peace Research* 48 (1): 115–25.

Margalit, Lila, and Ron Oded. 2019. *Effective Voice: Integration of Arab Society into Decision-Making Processes in the Public Sector*. Jerusalem: Israel Democracy Institute.

Mohammadi, Ali, Anders Broström, and Chiara Franzoni. 2015. "Work Force Composition and Innovation: How Diversity in Employees' Ethnical and Disciplinary Backgrounds Facilitates Knowledge Re-combination." No. 413. London: Royal Institute of Technology, CESIS-Centre of Excellence for Science and Innovation Studies.

Montagna, Paul D. 1968. "Professionalization and Bureaucratization in Large Professional Organizations." *American Journal of Sociology* 74 (2): 138–45.

Nathan, Max. 2014. "Same Difference? Minority Ethnic Inventors, Diversity, and Innovation in the UK." *Journal of Economic Geography* 15 (1): 129–68.

O'Leary, Brendan, and John McGarry. 2016. *The Politics of Antagonism: Understanding Northern Ireland*. London: Bloomsbury Academic.

Or, Theodore, Hashem Khateeb, and Shimon Shamir. 2003. *Or Commission Report: Commission of Inquiry into the Clashes between Security Forces and Israeli Citizens in October 2000* [in Hebrew]. Jerusalem: Sha'ar Rishon.

Ozacky-Lazar, Sarah. 2000. "From a Hebrew Histadrut to an Israeli One, 1948–1966 [in Hebrew]." *Iyunim Bitkumat Israel* 10 (2000): 381–419.

Page, Scott E. 2007. "Making the Difference: Applying a Logic of Diversity." *Academy of Management Perspectives* 21 (4): 6–20.

Parrotta, Pierpaulo, Dario Pozzoli, and Mariola Pytlikova. 2014. "The Nexus between Labor Diversity and Firm's Innovation." *Journal of Population Economics* 27 (2): 303–64.

Paserman, Daniele M. 2013. "Do High-Skill Immigrants Raise Productivity? Evidence from Israeli Manufacturing Firms, 1990–1999." *IZA Journal of Migration* 2 (1): 1–31.

Peres, Yochanan, and Eliezer Ben-Rafael. 2006. *Closeness and Conflicts: Cleavages in Israeli Society* [in Hebrew]. Tel Aviv: Am Oved and Sapir Academic College.

Portugali, Juval. 1986. "The Urban Employment Field for the Arab Workers of Tel Aviv" [in Hebrew]. *Horizons in Geography* 17–18: 25–48.

Prat, Andrea. 2002. "Should a Team Be Homogeneous?" *European Economic Review* 46 (7): 187–207.

Ramon, Shulamit. 2004. The Impact of the 2nd Intifada on Israeli Arab and Jewish Social Workers." *European Journal of Social Work* 7: 285–303.

Ramon, Shulamit, Jim Campbell, Jane Lindsay, Patrick McCrystal, and Naimeh Baidoun. 2006. "The Impact of Political Conflict on Social Work: Experiences from Northern Ireland, Israel, and Palestine." *British Journal of Social Work* 36 (3): 435–50.

Ranganathan, C., and Ivan Alfaro, 2011. "Project Performance in Global Software Development Teams: Do Prior Work Ties and Nationality Diversity Matter?" *ECIS 2011 Proceedings* 72.

Richards, Stephen. 1992. "Diversity in the High-Tech Workplace: Making Engineers Feel at Home." *IEEE Spectrum* 29 (6): 29–30.

Roberts, Keith A., and Karen Donahue. 2000. Professing Professionalism: Bureaucratization and Deprofessionalization in the Academy. *Sociological Focus* 33 (4): 365–83.

Rosenfeld, Henry. 1978. "The Class Situation of the Arab National Minority in Israel." *Comparative Studies in Society and History* 20 (3): 374–407.

Saxenian, Annalee. 1999. *Silicon Valley's New Immigrant Entrepreneurs.* San Francisco: Public Policy Institute of California.

Schwartz, S. H. 1994." Beyond Individualism/Collectivism: New Cultural Dimensions of Values." In *Individualism and Collectivism: Theory, Method, and Applications,* edited by Uichol Kim, Harry C. Triandis, Cigdem Kagitcibasi, Sang-Chin Choi, and Gene Yoon, 85–122. Thousand Oaks, CA: Sage.

Shalev, Michael 1992. *Labour and the Political Economy in Israel.* Oxford: Oxford University Press.

Shor, Eran, and Yuval Yonay. 2011. "'Play and Shut Up': The Silencing of Palestinian Athletes in Israeli Media." *Ethnic and Racial Studies* 34 (2): 229–47.

Soen, Dan. 2005. *Israel: From Welfare State to Social Darwinism: The Stratified Cleavage in Israel* [in Hebrew]. Tel Aviv: Cherikover.

———. 2012. "Descent and Exclusion: Israeli Arabs at the Bottom of the Social Pyramid" [in Hebrew]. *Social Issues in Israel* 13: 6–31.

Taylor, Phil, and Peter Bain. 2005. "India Calling to the Far Away Towns: The Call Centre Labour Process and Globalization." *Work, Employment, and Society* 19 (2): 261–82.

Todaro, Mauro, Enrique Carozzo, and Luigi Stirpe. 2017. "Teams in Small Technology-Based Firms: The Roles of Diversity and Conflict Management." *Journal of Technology Management and Innovation* 12 (2): 11–17.

Trajtenberg, Manuel. 1999. *Innovation in Israel, 1968–97: A Comparative Analysis Using Patent Data.* Cambridge, MA: National Bureau of Economic Research.

Tzafroni, Gabriel. 1994. "Arab-Jewish Journalistic Cooperation" [in Hebrew]. *Kesher* 16: 119–26.

Varma, Roli, 2002. "High-Tech Coolies: Asian Immigrants in the US Science and Engineering Workforce." *Science as Culture* 11 (3): 337–61.

Wolkinson, Benjamin W., and Edilberto Montemayor F. 1998. "Inter-Ethnic Coexistence in Israeli Plants: The Job Experiences and Attitudes of Arab and Jewish Workers." *Ethnic and Racial Studies* 21 (3): 529–44.

Yashiv, Eran, and Nitza Kasir. 2013. *The Labor Market of Arab Israelis: A Review of Characteristics and Policy Alternatives* [in Hebrew]. Tel Aviv: Tel Aviv University, Department of Public Policy.

Zaidman, Nurit. 2001. "Cultural Codes and Languages Strategies in Business Communication: Interactions between Israeli and Indian Businesspeople." *Management Communication Quarterly* 14 (3): 408–41.

Zaidman, Nurit, and David M. Brock. 2009. "Knowledge Transfer within Multinationals and Their Foreign Subsidiaries: A Culture-Context Approach." *Group and Organization Management* 34 (3): 297–329.

Zaidman, Nurit, and Ayala Malach-Pines. 2014. "Stereotypes in Bicultural Global Teams." *International Journal of Intercultural Relations* 40: 99–112.

Zelekha, Yaron. 2009. "The Arab Population and the Israeli High-Tech Industry." In *The Economic Benefit of Integrating and Equalizing Arabs and Jews in Israel* [in Hebrew], edited by Uri Gopher, 106–11. Neve Ilan: Abraham Fund Initiatives.

Index

administrative vs. occupational roles, 19–20, 61, 72, 78–81

Advanced Training Fund, 54

Afghanistan, 3, 151

Aftema, Fadwa, 145

Ailon, Galit, 10, 123

Ali, Nohad, 113

Amara, Muhammad, 90

amicable social ties: British Mandate and, 132–33; categories of, 135; cross-sector comparisons of, 134–35, 138, 141, 148–49, 164–65; in health sector, 35, 47–49, 138–45, 148; ideal of apolitical work environment and, 47, 49, 51–52; patients' racism, support against, 35, 37, 39–42; private sphere spillover of, 135, 148–49; in production sector, 135–38, 148–49; in professional communities, 135, 160–61; religious beliefs and, 127, 130, 131; social change and, 164–65; split ascription and, 61–62; in tech sector, 135, 145–48, 164–65; violent events and, 150, 151. *See also* interdependency

apolitical work environment, ideal of, 47, 49, 51–53

Arabic. *See* language use; Palestinian Arabs

"Arab work," 9–10

Arnesen, Eric, 5

benefits. *See* pay and benefits

Bible, 112, 129, 155

British Mandate administration, 8–9, 16, 114, 132–33

Butler, John Sibley, 15

career trajectories and opportunities: administrative vs. occupational, 19–20, 61, 72, 78–81, 159–60; context for, 64–65, 67; cross-sector comparisons of, 80, 85, 87–88, 153–54; ethnonational identities and, 19, 57, 64–65, 73, 82, 87–88; in health sector, 19, 58, 65, 80–85; military service and, 15, 57–58; nurses' perceptions of, 55–56, 65, 80–85, 154; physicians' perceptions of, 19, 65, 80, 85–87, 154; in production sector, 19,

42, 54–55, 65–69, 153; relocation and, 76, 85, 88; in tech sector, 14–15, 19–20, 59–61, 63, 65, 69–80, 152–53

Cave of the Patriarchs, 112

Christians: in health sector, 11, 12, 19, 58, 84, 127–29; holidays of, 113–14, 122–25, 127, 155, 156; immigration and, 3; Israeli population of, 17; Muslims' status compared to, 30; in production sector, 13, 115, 120–22; religious beliefs and, 113–15, 120–22, 155–56; structural discrimination and, 56–59; workplace segregation of, 28, 155–56

Circassians, 13, 28

class consciousness, 121, 130, 156

collegiality. *See* amicable social ties

color blindness and color-blind policies, 122, 130, 145–46, 149, 163–65

Commando Disaster (1997 Israeli military operation), 29–30

conflict. *See* interethnic tensions; Palestinian–Jewish conflict; religion and religious identities

contact theory: claims of, 45–46; reassessment of, 4, 45, 162–64; split ascription compared to, 19, 44–46, 57, 61–62, 162–64

coping strategies, 4–5; apolitical work environments, 51–53; avoidance and redirection, 38; contact and diversity management theories overlooking, 162–63; literature on war-torn regions and, 7–8, 150–51; occupational vs. administrative career choices, 80; reports to management as, 31, 33, 39; sensitivity to, 165; silence/refraining from political and moral discourse, 7, 10, 23–25, 31, 41, 154–55; structural elements of employing organizations and, 157–60. *See also* language use; split ascription

Cunnison, Sheila, 5

Darr, Asaf, 10

Department of the Chief Economist (Israeli Ministry of Science), 14

CPSIA information can be obtained
at www.ICGtesting.com
Printed in the USA
LVHW040431040623
748748LV00004B/225